D0194684

WITHDRAWN

# Two Homes,
# One Childhood

# Two Homes, One Childhood

## A PARENTING PLAN
## TO LAST A LIFETIME

# Robert E. Emery, PhD

AVERY

an imprint of Penguin Random House

New York

AVERY

an imprint of Penguin Random House LLC
375 Hudson Street
New York, New York 10014

Copyright © 2016 by Robert E. Emery, PhD
Penguin supports copyright. Copyright fuels creativity, encourages diverse voices,
promotes free speech, and creates a vibrant culture. Thank you for buying an authorized
edition of this book and for complying with copyright laws by not reproducing, scanning,
or distributing any part of it in any form without permission. You are supporting writers
and allowing Penguin to continue to publish books for every reader.

Most Avery books are available at special quantity discounts for bulk purchase
for sales promotions, premiums, fund-raising, and educational needs. Special books or
book excerpts also can be created to fit specific needs. For details,
write SpecialMarkets@penguinrandomhouse.com.

ISBN 9781594634154

Printed in the United States of America

1  3  5  7  9  10  8  6  4  2

Book design by Gretchen Achilles

PUBLISHER'S NOTE

Nothing in this book is intended as an express or implied warranty of the suitability or fitness of any
product, service, or design. The reader wishing to use a product, service, or design discussed in this
book should first consult a specialist or professional to ensure suitability and fitness for the reader's
particular lifestyle and environmental needs.

All names and identifying characteristics have been changed to protect the privacy of the individuals
involved.

AUTHOR'S NOTE

All of the cases described in this book are composites. Essential details have been changed to protect
the confidentiality and privacy of my clients and research participants. The cases in this book are real
emotionally, but no case corresponds to any actual person, living or dead.

*To family, in its many forms*

# Contents

**PREFACE**

Two Homes, One Childhood     1


**PART 1**
_____

## Parenting Across Two Homes


**CHAPTER 1**

A Parenting Plan to Last a Lifetime     7


**CHAPTER 2**

A Hierarchy of Children's Needs in Two Homes     25


**CHAPTER 3**

Sharing Decisions and Time in Joint Custody:
Beyond 50/50     53

## PART 2

# A Developmental Approach
# to Parenting Plans

CHAPTER 4

## Infants: Attachment Security   89

CHAPTER 5

## Toddlers: Testing the Limits   125

CHAPTER 6

## Preschoolers: Play Is a Child's Work   155

CHAPTER 7

## School Age: Reading, Writing—Right and Wrong   192

CHAPTER 8

## Adolescence: Autonomy and Relatedness   227

CHAPTER 9

## Emerging Adults: College Years and Beyond   265

CHAPTER 10

## A Lifetime Is (Not) a Long Time   295

*Acknowledgments*   311

*Notes*   313

*Index*   319

# Two Homes,
# One Childhood

# Two Homes, One Childhood

If you have picked up this book, you or someone close to you must be raising a child in two homes. You may be in the middle of a divorce. Or maybe you already have been divorced, perhaps long ago. Maybe you never were married, but you live apart from the father or mother of your children, someone you may have lived with for quite some time—or not. Maybe you were in a same-sex relationship, and share a child you and your partner planned and birthed together, or perhaps adopted. (All of these experiences are "divorce" in my book, and in this book, so keep reading no matter how your child ended up with two homes.) Or you may have a friend, or perhaps a child, who is going through divorce. You are looking for a way to help him or her. If so, this book is for you too.

Whatever your situation, let's be clear about one thing from the very beginning:

Divorce stinks.

Divorce stinks if you got dumped by someone you thought you could trust forever. Divorce stinks even if, deep down, you think you may actually be better off living apart. Divorce stinks if you initiated the breakup and thought this was what you wanted, or needed, or had to do. Divorce stinks even if your decision to live separately was mutual, and you both are doing your best to do things right. Divorce stinks even if it's your friends, or your relatives, who are splitting up, not you.

Most of all, divorce stinks for children.

Whether you are eager to move on or so emotionally devastated that you think you never can, my goal is to help you make living in two homes less of a burden for your children. I don't want your children, or anyone's children, to be "children of divorce" or "children from broken homes." I hate those labels. Children do not have to be defined by their parents' romantic relationship. Children shouldn't be defined by divorce (in its many forms). And you can make sure that doesn't happen. You can make sure that your children get to be just kids. That is my goal for you and for them.

Children have only one childhood. Childhood can be, should be, a time of innocence, trust, wonder, joy, exploration, learning, making strong, worthy efforts—and making lots of mistakes too. Childhood is a time when forgiveness, fresh starts, and repeated mistakes all should be expected and accepted. Childhood is a time when nothing, even the sternest reprimand, should shake a child's sense of being loved, of feeling safe and secure. Childhood is about learning lessons of independence and responsibility, while venturing forth from the safe base of parental love. Childhood means being protected from deep wounds that refuse to heal, but not from life's bumps and bruises, from pain that teaches essential, if sometimes difficult, lessons.

Your children have two homes but only one childhood.

You, and I, want to protect and preserve your children's childhood.

You can do this, together with your ex. You can still share in your children's joys and fret about their frustrations. You can find a way to still be parents, even though you are no longer husband and wife (or whatever). And if you can still be parents, separately and together, your kids can still be kids, despite growing up in two homes.

Of course, being a parent is never easy. Parenting in two homes can be especially hard. To protect your children's childhood, you are going to need to put in extra effort, emotionally, practically, and financially.

You may think your ex is a narcissist—or maybe just a jerk. You may wish he or she were not your children's father or mother. If so, I understand that feeling. But you need to understand that your children probably do not feel the same way. And if they do, that may be a problem. Children shouldn't have to choose sides, picking one parent over the other. Even if your ex *is* a jerk, he is still your children's father. That isn't going to change. So you and your children are going to need to find some way to deal with him.

Right now, you may feel so devastated that you think you just cannot go on. You can't do this all on your own. You may be beyond exhausted, beyond depressed. You may have a great deal of emotional work to do. If so, I urge you to get started—for your children's sake, and for yourself. I can help you begin.

Or maybe you have a more friendly relationship. If so, good for you, and your ex too. That will make things easier, but not easy.

There are different styles of coparenting relationships—angry, friendly, and distant. What is distant coparenting? Distant coparenting is when you have little negative connection, or communication, with your ex. But you also have little positive engagement. Some people in distant relationships still feel a lot of tension or anger or pain. They find that keeping their distance is the best way to avoid explosions. For many people who have had an angry divorce, distance is the most, or the only, realistic goal.

If this is you, you can make distance work. You do not need to feel friendly toward your ex. But you do need to find ways to communicate and cooperate with her about the basics of rearing children in two homes. You also need to make sure that your distance is not some form of the "silent treatment"—filled with tension and ultimately a contest over your children.

Whatever your coparenting style, I have advice for you. Part of that advice is that being a parent is hard work, no matter what.

Parenting in two homes is going to cost you. You are going to lose time and money. You are going to lose patience and perspective. You are going to lose time with your children and the support of the people who helped you parent, including but not limited to your ex.

Eventually, you are going to need to let go of all of these losses. You are going to need to focus on your present and the future, not your past. You are going to need to focus on what is and how you can make it better, not on what might have been.

I won't sugarcoat what you face, or what you have fought through. I will urge you to keep fighting—not with your ex but for your children.

I expect you and your ex to disagree. Of course you will after all you have been through. And what parents don't disagree? But I also urge you and your ex to make your own decisions, as much as possible. And I urge you to make decisions together, as much as possible. Working through differences is what parents do, right?

This may be a good time to repeat your new mantra: We have to be parents so our kids can be kids.

I can help you to give your children the childhood they deserve. I can offer you a little perspective. And, based on decades of research and experience, I can act as your guide. I can help you understand and shape your children's life in two homes—now and as they grow through different developmental stages, even into young-adult life.

You and your ex can develop a parenting plan to last a lifetime. In order to do so, you need to begin to realize, right now, that the only parenting plan that will last a lifetime is one that grows and changes right along with your children's changing needs.

*Two Homes, One Childhood* is a guide to those changing needs. *Two Homes, One Childhood* is a guide to how you and your ex can keep your focus on your children's needs, despite all that you have been and are going through.

## PART 1

# Parenting Across Two Homes

## CHAPTER 1

# A Parenting Plan to
# Last a Lifetime

W hy are you such a control freak?" Justin screamed. It was not a question. His wife, Nicole, had sunk into her side of the couch in my office, on the verge of tears. Now she bolted upright, ready to counterattack. Justin beat her to the punch. "This is why I want a divorce!" he raged on. "You have to pull my strings, everyone's strings. I'm not going to let you do that anymore—not when it comes to my children!"

"*I'm* a control freak?" Nicole blasted back. "Who took all the money from our joint savings account and put it in *your* name? Who has over fifty thousand dollars in their account? And I have . . . what? Whatever is left from my paycheck last week!" With barely a pause, she stormed on. "You're such a hypocrite! If you cared so much about your children, we wouldn't be here. We'd be seeing a marriage counselor, not a mediator!"

I am a mediator.

I help separated, divorced, formerly cohabiting, and never-married couples—straight and gay—to work out agreements. (Throughout this book, I use *divorce* as shorthand to refer to all of these family types.) I focus especially on devising parenting plans for children, but like many mediators, I sometimes help people work out financial settlements too. With the guidance of a neutral third party, parents can create their own plans in mediation.

Most parents also want some legal advice, which I encourage. Even if they do not want to, I insist that my clients consult a lawyer before signing a final agreement. But mediation is different from the traditional legal process. Going to court typically widens a divorce divide that already is deep and dangerous for parents, and especially for children. Mediation encourages healthy, businesslike communication during divorce negotiations and beyond.

I was an early advocate for divorce mediation, which I have practiced and studied for thirty-five years. I also am a clinical psychologist, psychological scientist, and university professor. I urge parents to avoid expensive, divisive legal battles and to make decisions themselves in mediation, on their own, or perhaps using *collaborative lawyers*, attorneys who contract to negotiate for you but will not represent you if you go to court.

Saving money is one great reason for finding an alternative to a court battle. But my bigger goal is to help parents to protect their children and, ultimately, promote children's resilience, despite divorce. If no one helps parents navigate the emotional minefield of divorce, children can be left wandering—too often into an explosion.

"Are you saying I don't love my children?" Justin thundered back. Glaring at Nicole, he snorted, "You're crazy. I'm a good father. A great father! And I am just as entitled to time with my children as you are! Ask him!"

I didn't respond to Justin's assertion. That wasn't the issue, at least not yet.

Actually, I didn't do much of anything at this point. Neither Justin nor Nicole was ready to listen. Not to each other, not to me.

But I learned a lot from watching their interaction. I could see that Justin and Nicole had two big problems: their emotions and their children.

## What Fuels Anger

Justin and Nicole were angry, obviously. That was a problem we needed to address. If they were to have any hope of moving forward in their discussions, I had to help them get their anger under control. As you may imagine, doing so is no easy task. I had to do more than simply ask them to "be nice" or to "act rationally."

Instead, slowly and often indirectly, I explored the emotions that lay *beneath* their anger. I helped Nicole and Justin manage their anger by becoming more aware of what fueled it.

I always encourage parents to recognize feelings buried beneath the surface of their anger. Consider this: When we are hurt—and you know you are hurting in divorce—our natural, hardwired, evolved response is to want to hurt back. You stub your toe on a chair, hard. What do you do? You kick the chair again!

That's pretty stupid if you think about it.

But you don't think about it. You react. You react in the way evolution has wired you to react. If a predator attacks you, you are more likely to survive if you fight back rather than negotiate!

And for many parents in the middle of divorce, it feels like your very survival is at stake. You feel like you are under constant attack.

You are hurt by your divorce. You want to hurt back. Yes, you *are* furious. You are beyond angry. But underneath your anger is pain, just as with your sore toe. And also as with your bruised toe, the way to really fix your pain is to tend to it. If you keep kicking, you (and, of course, your children) end up with more and more wounds.

I want parents and children to heal.

As I discussed in my first book for parents, *The Truth about Children and Divorce*, pain is only one of several deeper, more honest emotions that lie beneath anger. Others include fear, longing, guilt, and grief. Just as with pain, you have to deal with these underlying feelings, not cover them up, if you are ever going to move forward instead of being stuck in your anger.

This basic insight has helped countless warring parents to become less angry—or at least to create a demilitarized zone around their children. I know this from the results of my research, not just based on hopeful experience.

Fear, mainly fear of losing his children, drove Justin's anger. Nicole's anger stemmed more from her longing to save her marriage—and from the painful fact that Justin didn't seem at all interested in that possibility.

You may or may not recognize these deeper feelings in Justin and Nicole. Doing so can be tricky. Operating in survival mode, the emotional parts of our brain convert fear or pain into anger. Our emotions also short-circuit the rational parts of our brain and make us ignorant about the motivations behind our own behavior. So the real trick is to learn to recognize these complex, often hidden feelings in yourself, not just in other people.

## Parents Are Never Completely Divorced

Justin and Nicole faced emotional challenges. They also confronted a real and hugely important practical problem. They had two children.

Intimate partners who have children cannot break up the emotionally natural way. Without the tie of children, Justin and Nicole could have done what we all have done during breakups in our younger days. They could have shouted, "I never want to see you again!" and perhaps followed through on that promise. But Nicole and Justin would be forever linked through their children. They might not have realized this yet, but because of their children, they could never completely divorce.

And their children presented a special complication. Justin and

Nicole had a two-and-a-half-year-old girl and a seven-month-old boy. How do you parent such young children in different households? This has always been a huge question for parents, of course. But now this is also the subject of a giant battle between various experts and advocates.

What is the best parenting plan for very young children, or children of any age? If you are constructing a parenting plan or have been living with one, how can the plan meet your children's ever-changing developmental needs? Once you get the emotions out of it, what should parents do?

## The Truth about Children and Divorce

I wrote *The Truth about Children and Divorce* in 2004 as an evidence-based guide through the turmoil of the divorce crisis. (I have also authored several books on divorce for professionals plus over 150 scientific papers.) Most divorcing parents and their families experience a crisis during the time shortly before and not long after they separate. Usually, the emotional upheaval goes on for a year, more likely two, sometimes three years or longer. During this same time, parents also face making monumental decisions about their children. And given the apparent demise of their family, children need their parents to be "all hands on deck" smack in the middle of their marital crisis.

I signaled a solution to parents' dilemma with the subtitle of *The Truth*. My goal for parents was *Dealing with the Emotions So You and Your Children Can Thrive.*

Dealing with the emotions is huge. As I said, it means looking at what fuels your anger rather than acting on it. Instead of trying to kill their ex, I asked parents to look beneath and beyond their rage. In doing so, I urged parents to remember this: The cause of your devastating pain is also your children's other parent. You may want to kill your former husband or wife, but you don't want to kill your children's mother or father.

As you read this, you may be saying to yourself, "*You want me to get along with my ex? We're getting divorced! Duh!*"

In one way or another, many parents have said this to me.

Giving advice is always easier than following it.

But yes, I do want you to find a way to work together with your ex.

I want you both to do your job, which is to raise your children as best as you possibly can.

You and your ex have a job to do, not a relationship to resolve. If you are having a hard time, the best way I know for you to do your job is to treat each other as business partners. Work to become partners in the business of parenting your children. Treat each other with the same respect, politeness, and emotional distance that you use with your boss. You do not scream at your boss, even when you are angry. You do not send long, emotional rants to your boss via text or e-mail. You do not call your boss late on a Saturday night to complain about work. You do not stop by your boss's home unexpectedly for any reason.

I don't want you to do these kinds of things with your ex either.

In this book, I do *not* assume that you have dealt, past tense, with all of your emotions. But I do assume that you are dealing with them. I assume—and hope—that you know where you need to go and are working on getting there. If you don't, please detour back and read *The Truth about Children and Divorce*.

## A Parenting Plan

Of course, divorce disputes are not just about emotions. We are talking about children too, your children. And uncertainties and conflicts about how to best raise children arise anew in the years long after the immediate crisis of divorce. Parents need concrete guidance about how to raise healthy, happy children in two homes at the time of divorce—and over time. Is shared custody best, or does joint custody involve too much back and forth for children? Does joint physical custody have to be 50/50, week on/week off, or are there other options? What should parents do about negotiating a parenting plan for children of different ages? What about *siblings* of different ages? Exactly how can parents know what is best for their children, particularly when they get so much conflicting advice from friends, family members, and even professionals? What is your children's role in making these decisions? Do parents have to follow the same plan forever, or can they renegotiate? How can they do that?

These are the kinds of questions I answer for you in this book. More important, I help you answer the questions for yourself, in ways that are likely to work best for your own children.

## Children Don't Calculate Percentages

Consider this. Even though Justin was right—he was just as entitled to time with his children as Nicole was—he also was wrong. His children needed him, and Nicole. They needed their parents, not Justin's or Nicole's entitlements. They needed a close, involved, loving, and yes, somewhat strict relationship with both of their parents, not exactly 50/50 divided right down the middle, as Justin initially argued for. (We revisit Justin and Nicole and their evolving story in Chapters 4, 5, and 6.)

Of course, Justin did not invent the 50/50 argument. In fact, at least two U.S. state legislatures, Florida and Minnesota, recently passed custody laws dividing children's time with each parent exactly 50/50. The governors of both states vetoed the laws.[1]

I don't want children to be a political football, or a football in families.

Arguing about who gets the bigger piece of pie? One person cuts, the other chooses their slice.

This may be a great solution for siblings squabbling about dessert. But when a parent tells me, "I want fifty-fifty," I cringe. Fifty-fifty is a solution for parents, not children.

This book is about children, and what children need in two homes. Children do not calculate percentages. Love is not divisible. Children need parents who keep their life together, across two homes, not parents who divide their lives in precisely equal halves.

So if someone says, "I want fifty-fifty," or whatever initial split, I ask them, "Why?" The answers to that question usually make me smile, not cringe.

"I want to still be a real father to my child."

I get that. I want that too.

Being a real mother or father requires time, no doubt. But creating two homes and parenting across households involves much more than dividing time. We are talking about a *parenting plan*, not dividing a pie. We are talking about parental love, discipline, children's responsibilities, being a team, sharing joys, balance and equity in parenting.

I recall one angry father who had adamantly demanded 50/50 when I first met with him and his ex. They had two school-age children, a nine-year-old boy with (relatively mild) autism spectrum disorder and a six-year-old girl. After much discussion about the children's needs, especially their son's, as well as their own schedules, the dad reluctantly agreed to try an individualized, if more complicated, arrangement. The parents decided to experiment with a plan that gave Dad every Thursday overnight and every other weekend with his children, as well as an alternating one-on-one Wednesday overnight with each of them.

The plan is not as complicated as it may sound. One of the kids was with their father two overnights in a row one week and three the next. And the parents had a good rationale for trying this plan:

Dad had lots of work demands; Mom's work was flexible. They both thought the children would do better with a pretty consistent start to the school week, especially the son with special needs. But both parents wanted lots of time with their kids, who often fought with each other. The parents agreed it was a delight, and a relief, to have some time with them one on one.

Despite their well-thought-out rationale, the father informed me, and his ex, that while he would try it, the schedule was *not* 50/50. It was 32/68! Dad decided that the experiment was a success, however, when a few weeks later his six-year-old daughter told him, "I like the schedule, because we have the same amount of time with you and Mom." Unlike Dad, the little girl did not do a spreadsheet. What she really meant by "the same amount of time" was not "50/50" but something like: "This schedule gives me plenty of time with both you and Mom. I feel like you're both on my side. This is working."

And that was what the dad really wanted too.

What the dad (and mom) also wanted, but did not realize yet, was a living, breathing parenting plan as well. Their children were not going to remain six and nine forever. The parents' lives were going to change too. So they had to keep their focus on parenting, not on 50/50 or 32/68. As you will see in Chapters 7 and 8, they did, even as the percentages changed.

## Children and Parenting Plans Should Grow and Change

This book is all about getting to what kids *really* need and want when they have two homes. It's about preserving children's one childhood even though they live in two homes. What do children of different ages need as a result of divorce? How do these needs change over time? How can you create or adapt a parenting plan to accommodate your children's development and help them—and your relationship with them—thrive?

Time is part of the answer to these questions. But time is a means to an end, not the end itself.

And you need to think about time not just in days and weeks, but in years. This book is for parents in the middle of divorce, but it also is for parents whose babies are now in first grade, whose toddlers have become adolescents. This book is for all divorced parents, because parents can never completely divorce.

In *The Truth about Children and Divorce*, I urged parents to deal with their emotions first. I wanted parents to slow down and worry second about working out the details of a parenting plan. That hasn't changed. Dealing with your emotions still has to come first in the tasks ahead of you. In this book, I offer lots of reminders about emotions, but I focus on your second task first. The emphasis of this book is on how to devise a parenting plan for children of different ages and across childhood.

I couldn't address both the emotions and all of the details of developmentally based parenting plans in enough detail in one book. In *The Truth*, I laid out a skeleton of ideas about alternative plans for sharing time with children based on their ages. I emphasized the overriding importance of parents working together in a flexible, child-focused "business" (a key metaphor for working toward an emotionally even parenting partnership). And I also varied the suggested plans based on the nature of the parents' relationship—whether it was angry, distant, or cooperative.

I continue to emphasize the importance of your coparenting style here.

*Cooperative coparenting* does not mean you must be friends with your ex. You may be, but the key to this coparenting style is actively working together, as needed, to help your children, even though you are parenting apart.

*Angry coparenting* is just that. You engage in open hostility or an ongoing silent contest. Talking is difficult, even to share happy news about your children. Your children feel the tension, even when they are with just one of you, and especially at events when you both are there.

*Distant coparenting* involves little direct conflict but not a lot of communication or cooperation either. Often the distance is a way of avoiding conflict. This coparenting style sometimes is called "parallel parenting." Kids live and parents parent in two worlds.

Many parents and professionals *loved* the part of *The Truth* devoted to developmentally and relationship-based parenting plans. It was and is an innovative approach. Today, some states are beginning to create parenting-time guidelines for divorced and never-married parents based on children's age and developmental stage. I'm convinced this is the wave of the future.

I want to bring you the future now by putting flesh on the skeleton of my earlier suggestions about developmentally based parenting plans. Much has changed in ten years—in social expectations about parenting in two homes, in the law, and in the very nature of "family." Research has changed too. Here, I share my latest research, while distilling evidence from dozens of new, important studies that have been published since I wrote *The Truth*.

For example, let's explore the complicated problem that Justin and Nicole faced: How do you raise very young children in two households?

## Can a Child Be Too Young for Shared Custody?

"Can a child be too young for shared custody?" KJ Dell'Antonia's Motherlode column posed this exact question in the *New York Times* on August 16, 2013. A few days earlier, the *Journal of Marriage and Family* had published my academic article, "Overnight Custody Arrangements, Attachment, and Adjustment among Very Young

Children."[2] We were writing for different audiences, but Dell'Antonia and I addressed the same pressing issue. What is a healthy way for parents who live apart to raise an infant or a toddler?

How to share custody of infants is a hot topic. Too hot. Ever since I completed my research, I have gotten volumes of e-mails. Most of these unsolicited comments come either from angry "fathers' rights" advocates accusing me of being against fathers, or from concerned mothers worried that their exes' visits are undermining their infants' mental health—for life.

When I speak about very young children at professional meetings, which is often, I attract large crowds. Most of the judges, lawyers, and psychologists in the audience are more than eager for guidance. They are desperate.

Sure, some of these professionals think they know what is best—based on their preconceived beliefs. Not too long ago, I gave a long workshop to a group of about thirty judges. I reviewed all kinds of issues and evidence for them. After the talk, one judge lingered. He came up to me and said, "You're an entertaining speaker." I smiled at the compliment. Then he said, "But I'm a fifty-fifty guy."

He might as well have been Nicole or Justin, locked into a fixed position and unable to hear a different point of view.

This is who might be deciding your case—a "fifty-fifty guy" or maybe an "every other weekend guy" or a "no overnights guy."

## Your Baby

But your family isn't a case, is it? We're talking about your baby.

As I discuss in Chapter 4, expert opinion about the best schedule for babies is all over the map. Some suggest that parents should swap their babies across households. Frequently. There are experts who argue that babies benefit from swapping homes, and cribs, every day or two.

At the other extreme are experts who think it is fine for a very young child to have a daytime visit, or two, with the "other" parent every week, or two. Many experts on this side of the fence tell parents that infants and toddlers should sleep in the same bed every night, and have the same caregiver available to comfort them, if needed. Some want this pattern to continue until a child reaches age four or so.

And then there are the courts. Judges all over America, all over the world, are faced with warring parents, dueling experts, and the politics of "mothers' rights" versus "fathers' rights." In the face of controversy and uncertainty, some judges are ordering parents to raise their babies according to untenable, seemingly abusive schedules. Breastfeeding can be used as a reason to deny more than a few hours of visitation with the father—or condemned as a manipulative tactic of "visitation interference." Some judges allow parents to see their babies only for a few brief hours, every other weekend. Other judges order parents to transport their babies across long distances so they can swap their infant on a schedule where a week or more passes before the child sees the other parent again.

What does such a grand experiment in "fairness" do to an infant?

Over the course of decades of practice and research on child custody disputes, I have refused a great many invitations to appear in court as an expert witness, including "invitations" in the form of a subpoena. My reasoning was (and remains) simple. I want parents to work together, make their own coparenting decisions, and stay out of court.

After more than thirty years of work as a psychologist, family therapist, mediator, and researcher, I broke my rule. A few years ago, I was compelled by outrage to testify in court for the first and only time in my long career. My testimony, in essence, suggested that a judge had erred in awarding week on/week off custody to the parents of a one-year-old baby. The parents lived a six-hour drive apart from each other. They were so angry and uncooperative that when they met on the highway to swap their baby, they refused to share information—or blankets, cuddly toys, or even medicine.

To the judge, the plan seemed fair to everyone. It may have been, except to the most important one: the baby.

## Parenting Is Not a Number

What is the solution for surprisingly common and seemingly intractable problems like this? How should these parents have raised their baby while living hundreds of miles apart? How should millions of parents raise their children in two homes? What guidance can legal and psychological experts offer?

Too many experts try to answer these questions with numbers. Rotate overnights every day. Restrict overnights until age four. Babies are too young for shared custody. Fifty-fifty is the best arrangement for children of any age.

As I said, I recently published research on this issue in the highly regarded social science outlet *Journal of Marriage and Family*. As I discuss in detail in Chapter 4, my new investigation was only the fourth study on this issue ever done in the world, and the biggest and best effort to date. We found that the rate of *insecure attachments*, a disruption in the bond between an infant and his primary caregiver, jumped to 43 percent for one-year-olds who spent one overnight or more per week with a nonresident parent compared to 16 percent for babies with fewer overnights.

This is really important because insecure attachments increase the risk for all kinds of psychological problems later in childhood. Babies with insecure attachments are more likely to become anxious and depressed children. Insecurely attached infants are more disruptive and disobedient in school and elsewhere. And children often re-create insecure attachments in future relationships. They may show their insecurity by being overly anxious and clingy. Or they

2 views

may instead show marked ambivalence in relating to others. They desperately want to connect, but they approach new relationships with hostility, rejecting others before they can be rejected themselves.

Does this mean infants should never have an overnight with their nonresidential parent? I don't see how. Babies with occasional overnights had *low* rates of attachment insecurity. Would I ever recommend overnights of once a week or more for infants? As a rule, maybe not, but rules have exceptions, especially if parents have a cooperative coparenting relationship.

Numbers offer helpful guidelines, but numbers will never answer questions about how to best rear babies across households.

To raise healthy babies across households, you need to do the hard work of working together, in some way, with your coparent. You may be lucky enough to be working with someone with whom you have a cooperative relationship. Or you may have to learn to love your children more than you hate your ex.

The hard answer, the right answer, is that building a parenting plan that works for babies, or your baby of any age, is about much more than days and nights, weeks and months.

You want to build a parenting plan to last a lifetime.

A parenting plan that lasts a lifetime is one that grows and changes along with the developing needs of children, and changing family circumstances too.

## Expect Change

The idea of building a parenting plan to last a lifetime may seem crazy. But expecting your plan to change also relieves a lot of pressure. You do not need to make forever-after decisions *right now*. Your parenting plan can and should evolve. Your child will change. Your life will change. Your parenting plan should change too, to fit everyone's needs, as best as it can.

So answering questions about how to best care for babies across households involves also answering questions about toddlers, preschoolers, elementary and middle school children, adolescents—and even young adults. Attachments, the earliest expression of parental love, matter a great deal to children beyond infancy. A *secure attachment*—knowing, emotionally, that one parent and hopefully both will be there to protect and nurture you—allows toddlers to explore; it enables preschoolers to separate from their parents; it helps school-age children form new relationships with peers and adults; and, while it may be hard for you to believe, a secure attachment is what allows adolescents to rebel! Teenagers can challenge you, sometimes in obnoxious ways, because (hidden deep down and fervently denied) they know that, in the end, you will still love them.

Attachment is not everything. But it is the foundation. Some things your child will need to build on their emotional foundation include responding to discipline, learning to regulate emotions, learning to share, developing friendships, learning to work independently at school, coming to accept responsibilities, mastering sports, playing by the rules, increasing independence, and developing intimate relationships. All of these tasks present ever-changing challenges across the course of your child's development. They therefore require you and your ex to negotiate, or perhaps renegotiate, not as former partners but as your children's parents.

Your child's development is a moving picture, not a snapshot. Expecting a schedule you created at one age to work years later is like expecting your child to fit into their baby clothes forever. The best parenting plans are living agreements that grow and change along with your children's developing needs, their unique personalities, and your changing circumstances too.

I have been divorced for twenty-five years. My experience with this topic is personal as well as professional. Maggie, my daughter from my first marriage, was married in 2011. Her mother and I planned and paid for her wedding together. We celebrated that special day together—and together with friends and family, including my wife, Kimberly, and the four children we have together.

Maggie's wedding was about Maggie, not her parents' divorce.

I have spent thirty-five years studying, writing about, and working with parents. I have worked with parents to try to save their marriage, separate, divorce, or split up after cohabiting, and with a number of parents who never lived together at all. I have worked with same-sex couples. All of these different circumstances involve similar emotional and practical challenges.

I also have worked with parents who have been divorced for years. For many, I am their family doctor. They know I am there but come to see me only when they have problems. Other parents seek me out for the first time for help with parenting plans long after a divorce. New complications make their old plans less than ideal. Maybe one or both parents have remarried. This can create problems due to jealousy, the complications of stepparenting, or perhaps the need to coordinate schedules so they work for two (or more!) sets of children. Maybe one parent wants to move or is moving, perhaps far away. What parenting plan can work now? Sometimes an adolescent rebels against a schedule that has worked for a long time. Should parents accommodate a teenager's wishes? If so, how?

This book is for parents in all of these circumstances, and more. In the chapters that follow, I outline and review major tasks in children's social and emotional development at different ages ranging from infancy into young-adult life. Throughout, we explore how parents who live apart can adjust their parenting, and parenting plans, to foster children's healthy growth and development.

Before you move on, let me share a bit about how you can best use this book. Everyone should read Chapters 2 and 3. These chapters outline the psychological and legal foundations for the entire book. From there, I expect you may want to jump to chapters most relevant to your children's current age. That's fine. But you should know that all of the chapters are relevant, no matter how old your children are. You should read as much as you can, so you will better understand where your children have been and where they are going developmentally.

You also should know that I cover some key topics in detail in particular chapters. Yet these topics are relevant at every age. Parent-child attachments are a focus in the infancy chapter. Discipline is an emphasis in the toddler chapter. But love and discipline obviously are essential to parenting at all ages.

More practically, I give you tips for planning a holiday schedule in the chapter on preschoolers. Of course, holidays are always important. I consider negotiating and paying for extracurricular activities when discussing school-age children, but these issues are relevant throughout childhood. I offer ideas about paying for college in the adolescence chapter. But you need to begin to think about saving for college long before then. And I discuss reconciliation with a rarely seen parent when discussing emerging adulthood. Yet knowing what may be coming down the road is relevant to decisions you may be facing years earlier.

These are just a few examples. There are many more. So feel free to jump around, but make sure you look carefully through every chapter.

Let me offer one more note about this book: I repeat myself a bit at times. I do this for a few reasons. I know some readers will skip around, so I raise a few key issues repeatedly so no one will miss them. I also repeat myself some, because, well, some things bear repeating. Here's one:

You want to build a parenting plan to last a lifetime. You can, by working on a plan that will grow and change right along with your child.

## CHAPTER 2

# A Hierarchy of Children's Needs in Two Homes

How can you promote your children's resilience in coping with life in two homes? How can you do your job of being a parent, so your kids get to be just kids? In this chapter, I offer you an evidence-based overview of children's needs in two homes. I synthesize findings from dozens of studies, but my message is practical. Here is what your children need. Here is how you can help.

Experts agree about what promotes children's healthy adjustment to their parents' divorce:

- Low levels of conflict between parents. Or at least conflict that is contained, so children are protected from parental disputes, while parents cooperate as best they can in child-rearing.
- A good relationship with at least one *authoritative* parent, that is, a parent who is both loving and firm with discipline. Children need to be loved. Children also need to learn rules and, eventually, to regulate their own behavior.
- A good relationship with the other parent too, especially if that parent also is authoritative. And most children want a relationship with both of their parents, even if all they really need is one authoritative parent.

Experts agree about what matters to children. Where experts some-times disagree is about what matters most.

Deciding what matters most is really pretty important. If you and your ex are at war, for example, what is better for your chil-dren? Is it better for them to spend most of their time with only one of you (assuming that parent is authoritative)? That way, your kids will not be living in the middle of your disputes. But they will have only a limited relationship with one of you.

Or is it better for your children to spend a lot of time with both of you? That way, your kids can benefit from having a relationship with each of their parents, even though they will have to deal with a lot of fighting.

Before moving forward to answer these questions, let me first take you briefly back in time. You may remember Abraham Maslow's hierarchy of human needs from some long-ago psychology class. Maslow's pyramid is more than half a century old, but it is still widely used today. Maslow brilliantly ranked human needs accord-ing to the simple figure portrayed here.[1]

**MASLOW'S HIERARCHY OF HUMAN NEEDS**

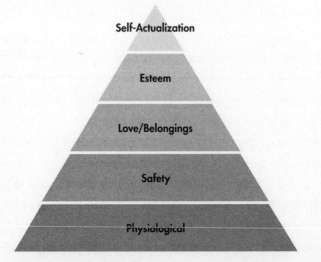

Maslow placed more basic, that is, more essential, human needs lower on his hierarchy. He put less basic needs higher up. A key principle in his ranking is that people will sacrifice less basic needs (for example, safety) in order to meet more basic ones (for example, food). People will do dangerous things—hunt fearsome animals or commit crimes—in order to meet their basic physiological needs.

The principle applies to psychological needs as well as to biological ones. For example, people will sacrifice self-esteem in order to obtain love.

That is pretty simple. And, I think, profound.

Children's needs in two homes can be portrayed as a pyramid much like Maslow's. Here is my unique, evidence-based Hierarchy of Children's Needs in Two Homes.

### HIERARCHY OF CHILDREN'S NEEDS IN TWO HOMES

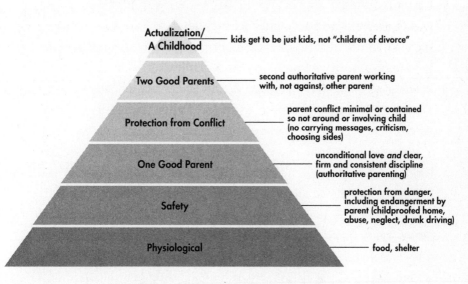

- **Actualization/ A Childhood** — kids get to be just kids, not "children of divorce"
- **Two Good Parents** — second authoritative parent working with, not against, other parent
- **Protection from Conflict** — parent conflict minimal or contained so not around or involving child (no carrying messages, criticism, choosing sides)
- **One Good Parent** — unconditional love *and* clear, firm and consistent discipline (authoritative parenting)
- **Safety** — protection from danger, including endangerment by parent (childproofed home, abuse, neglect, drunk driving)
- **Physiological** — food, shelter

Like Maslow's hierarchy, I have placed more basic or essential needs closer to the bottom of the pyramid. Less basic needs go higher up.

Physiological and safety needs remain at the base, more critical than any psychological needs. I *hope* that basic health and safety is not at issue for your children. If it is, protecting their safety must come first, ahead of any and all of their psychological needs. Because I focus on psychological needs here, you may need to put this book down if you are truly concerned about your children's health and safety. Sometimes you just cannot work with a deeply troubled partner. You have to turn to a court for protection. But if safety is not a concern, read on, even if you are dealing with a difficult ex.

Of course, all of children's psychological needs in two homes are important. But the hierarchy shows you in clear, broad strokes which needs are *more* basic. Thus, the hierarchy can guide you in circumstances when particular needs may be threatened or cannot be fulfilled. As with Maslow's scheme, children will be better off emotionally if their parents sacrifice less basic psychological needs for more basic ones. For example, protection from conflict *is* a more basic need than having involved relationships with both parents.

Let me be clear. I absolutely want children to have good relationships with *both* of their parents. All of children's needs in two homes are important. But based on research—and for reasons I discuss in detail in this chapter—living in the middle of a war zone between two parents is more harmful to children than having a really involved relationship with only one of them.

Does this thought make you sad or angry? It certainly evokes those feelings in me. If I am describing your circumstances, if you are in the middle of an angry divorce, the best solution—the only solution—is for you and your ex to get it together. Keep your child out of your stuff. Otherwise, one of you is going to end up making a big sacrifice, and so are your children.

But if you can keep your focus on your children, you can fulfill all of their needs. Your child can reach my equivalent of Maslow's self-actualization. Your kid can be just a kid, not forever a child of divorce.

In the following sections, I explain the reasoning and the research, the what and the why, behind my Hierarchy of Children's Needs in Two Homes.

## A Good Parent: Authoritative Parenting

Every parent, married or alone, should aspire to be authoritative. *Authoritative parenting* combines the bedrock of parental love with discipline that is clear, firm, fair, and well reasoned.[2] Authoritative parenting embraces Maslow's two most essential psychological needs, love and esteem. (Esteem is built on effective functioning in the world, a product of parental love *and* parental guidance.) Decades of research show that authoritative parenting is the best approach for raising children who are self-confident, independent, and well behaved.

Authoritative parenting contrasts with *authoritarian parenting*, where discipline is strict, perhaps harsh, and parental love is lacking or hard to come by. Children of authoritarian parents obey. They may cower. And, as they grow older, they may rebel.

Authoritative parenting also is different from *indulgent parenting*, where love is unconditional but there are no conditions on children's behavior. The indulgent parent's love gives children a sense of security. But the parent's lack of discipline means that children fail to learn their limits—or to respect other people's limits.

*Neglectful parenting* offers children neither love nor the guidance of discipline. Children of neglectful parents are the ones who need a parent substitute to give them the love and direction they need.

Children need someone, hopefully a parent, who is authoritative, who both loves them and guides them.

## Parental Love

Love is number one on most anyone's list of what children need for healthy social and emotional development, as it is in Maslow's hierarchy and mine too. And there is no doubt, based on all kinds of research, that having at least one healthy, loving parent is the best predictor of children's successful coping with divorce.

The famous developmental psychologist Urie Bronfenbrenner (1917–2005) was one of many champions of parental love. When he gave lectures, Bronfenbrenner frequently and emphatically exclaimed, "Every kid needs at least one adult who is crazy about him!" More formally, Bronfenbrenner wrote, "In order to develop—intellectually, emotionally, socially, and morally—a child requires participation in progressively more complex reciprocal activity, on a regular basis over an extended period in the child's life, with one or more persons with whom the child develops a strong, mutual, irrational, emotional attachment and who is committed to the child's well-being and development, preferably for life."[3]

That sounds like a pretty important job. And it is.

Children need to be loved. Love, and all the good things that grow out of being loved, forms the foundation of healthy emotional development—a child who feels safe, secure, accepted, cared for, understood, supported, trusting, believed in, and valued.

Love does not "spoil" a child. Love does just the opposite. Love allows children to venture forth. Love offers a safe base that encourages children to explore their world. Secure in the knowledge that there is a safe place to return to for reassurance, children who are well loved can indulge their curiosity and face their fears. (We consider this process more formally in Chapter 4, where I discuss *attachment theory*, the psychological foundation of love.) Love also encourages children to be generous, to be loving, and not to be selfish.

Bronfenbrenner said that children need to be loved by at least one adult. He did not say "parent." An adoptive parent, grandparent, stepparent, other relative, foster parent, or even a special adult friend may be able to provide a child with the love he or she needs.

But for most children, a parent is in the best position to provide the sustenance of love. And evolution probably created a bias in human nature. Of course, you can love a child who is not your own biologically. But parents may find it easier, more natural, to love and care for their biological offspring. Proximity and biology—and social expectations about what is healthy or normal—combine to make a parent the number-one candidate to give children the love they need.

As Bronfenbrenner implied, children benefit from love from more than one adult. In my Hierarchy of Children's Needs in Two Homes, I am particularly concerned with the love a child may, and I hope will, receive from both of his or her divorced parents. But children in all kinds of families are fed and fueled by the love of other adults too: family, friends, and perhaps special professionals in their lives.

## Adult Love Is One-Sided

Siblings, peers, and romantic partners can love children too. Their love may be enriching and sometimes magical. But like Bronfenbrenner, psychologists emphasize children's need for an *adult's* love. A healthy adult's love is much more one-sided than a peer's love. A healthy adult shows love in giving, not in receiving; in nurturing, not in being nurtured.

Divorcing parents sometimes need to remind themselves that children need to receive nurture, not give it. Divorcing parents can fall into the trap of looking to their children to replace their own lost love. It may seem natural to draw on a child for support. Your seven-year-old may be begging to sleep with you anyway. It feels good to have him there with you. Or you may feel extra close to your fifteen-year-old when you confide in her about your own struggles.

Deriving a little support from your children surely is fine. But leaning on them too much reverses family roles. Parents are supposed to be children's secure base, not vice versa. If you depend on them, you will impede your children's ability to become independent. Where is *their* safe base?

On the outside, children who care for their parents may look strong and responsible. But they often become hyper-responsible. They are "parentified."[4] They come to believe that their job is to take care of other people's feelings. As a result, they often neglect their own feelings—in their families and in future intimate relationships.

Children need one-sided, I-am-here-to-protect-you, healthy adult love—what many people call *unconditional love*. That kind of adult love offers children a profound sense of safety, protection, and security.

"I am here for you" gives children of all ages a sense of reassurance. "You are here for me" throws the weight of responsibility for another's happiness onto a child who is too young to accept that tremendous obligation.

## Parental Love Never Ends

In divorce, children learn a painful lesson about love: Romantic love can end.

But they also need to learn this: Parental love never ends.

You may need to explain this difference to your children, maybe especially to younger ones. But children of all ages can wonder: How can you still love me when you no longer love each other? If your love for each other has ended, will you stop loving me too?

Parsing love can be a struggle. In later chapters, I suggest ways you can help your children of various ages distinguish parental and romantic love. Later in this chapter, I suggest ways that you can try to parse romantic and parental love for yourself.

# Discipline Is Loving

Love is the foundation, but children need parental discipline in order to build on that structure. Children test the limits. This means that parents need to set limits. Authoritative parenting, not indulgent parenting (love without discipline), is essential in my Hierarchy of Children's Needs in Two Homes. Remember, an authoritative parent is loving *and* firm but fair in discipline.

Actually, saying no is an act of love. Typically, it is harder to say no than to say yes. If that isn't putting kids first, I don't know what is.

Your kids will not thank you for disciplining them. (But they do reward you for giving in: They stop whining. So be careful not to fall into the "caving in" trap.) Still, in the end, children gain a sense of security from knowing there are limits. Discipline teaches children how to behave—and that you will guard, protect, and guide them.

And if you are fair in your discipline and explain the reasoning behind your rules, your children will eventually internalize the lesson. They will do a better job of regulating themselves and require less discipline from you.

Ignoring discipline is a mistake that divorced parents sometimes make. You may feel too tired to deal with discipline. Or maybe you just want to have fun with your children and not start a fight. Perhaps you feel guilty and wonder if your child's misbehavior is a sign of inner emotional struggles due to your divorce. (Maybe it is, but children still need to "use their words," to talk about being angry rather than taking their anger out on a sibling, or you.) And some kids are clever in pushing their divorced parents' "guilt buttons." They know how to manipulate you.

All of these possibilities lead to the same answer: Say no.

Saying no is more work in the short run, but it is less work in the long run. Discipline teaches children the right way to get along. Lack of discipline teaches them the wrong way. And remind yourself, because this really is true: Parental discipline *really is* a loving act. Avoiding discipline is avoiding responsibility.

Let me tell you about what I consider one of my finest moments in parenting. I vividly recall one blistering hot and humid Virginia July day from more than a decade ago. I was loading my middle three children—Julia, eleven; Bobby, ten; and Lucy, eight—into the car. We were heading to our swim club, Fry's Spring, to cool off. In unison, the kids protested for the millionth time, "Do we *have* to go to the pool? It's *boring.*"

I held my temper, looked into my yard at a dilapidated wooden fence I was repairing, and had an epiphany. "No," I said. "You're right. The pool *is* boring. You can help me build our fence instead."

I won't recount the protests. But I will say that the fence got built. And we all learned important lessons. My kids learned about physical labor. I learned that my young kids were old enough to be a big help in fence building. My kids learned a lesson in responsibility. I learned how much better I felt about them, and myself, when I demanded responsibility from them. And we all learned just how good the pool felt after sweating through some honest labor.

You want to be an authoritative parent, but don't get me wrong. No one is perfect. You should not expect perfection from yourself in parenting or any other way. Actually, a perfect parent would be a *horrible* parent. If you were perfect, your children would never learn essential lessons. Your children would never learn that life is full of challenges. Your children would never learn that life is full of mistakes and disappointments. What better way to teach your children about the importance of saying "I'm sorry" and asking for forgiveness than to do so yourself, when you have messed up?

I hope your children can have not one but two authoritative parents. But your divorce does not need to be perfect either. If your ex is authoritative too, your children surely will benefit from his or her love and guidance. His or her good parenting will make it easier for you to be a good parent too. Yet studies consistently show that the most important predictor of children's successful coping with divorce is having *one* authoritative parent. That is why "One Good Parent" is the most basic psychological need in my Hierarchy of Children's Needs in Two Homes.

## Protection from Conflict

Children need parental love and guidance from one and hopefully both parents. Children do *not* need to be caught in the middle of their parents' war.

In fact, parental conflict can be toxic to children. I say "can be" because conflict happens. And conflict often is necessary to move forward, to resolve disagreements. But parents can manage their inevitable conflicts well or badly.

## Conflict before and after Divorce

Research has long supported the intuition that parental conflict harms children. In 1982, I published one of my most cited academic papers, "Interparental Conflict and the Children of Discord and Divorce."[5] Research then and now shows that children who live in high-conflict two-parent families have many more emotional problems than children who live in low-conflict two-parent families. Studies also show that if there was a lot of conflict in the two-parent home, children typically fare *better* after divorce. They escape from a life full of venomous parental disputes.

The flip side of this finding also is true. When parents in an unhappy marriage protect children from their disputes, kids actually do worse after divorce. That is, moving from a low-conflict marriage to a higher-conflict divorce also harms children.[6]

This raises a dilemma for good but unhappily married parents, those parents who keep their children out of their relationship disputes. One option for parents like this might be to stay together. Since you are reading this book, I assume that is no longer an option for you. So what do you do if you are one of those good parents, and you are headed for a separation or divorce?

First, let me tell you what not to do. You will *not* make divorce easier for your children by creating open warfare in your marriage so your kids will be relieved when you split.

Instead, I suggest you give your children some warning about what is or may be coming. Many young people have told me that they learned of their parents' marital problems for the first time when their parents sat them down for "the talk"—the day their parents told them they were separating. These kids were blindsided and devastated.

If you had a terminal illness, you would give your children some warning about what was coming. The same principle applies to divorce.

If conflict between *married* parents is unhealthy for children, would you be surprised to learn that conflict between *divorced* parents harms children too? Dozens of studies show that children who grow up in low-conflict divorced families have far fewer emotional problems than children in high-conflict divorces (or high-conflict marriages).

I doubt that this surprises you. But many people are pessimists about conflict in divorce. They give up on the possibility that divorced parents can get along, even just about parenting, even when parents' fights are wrecking their children.

Obviously, I'm not one of those people.

I am an eternal optimist. And I make no apologies for being ever hopeful. I urge you to join me in living in a glass-is-half-full world, even if your glass seems empty right now.

## Put Yourself in Your Children's Shoes

Why is conflict so destructive to children? I discuss research that answers this question shortly. But first, I want you to try to answer this question for yourself. Put yourself in your children's shoes. If you can better understand your children's perspective, you will learn a lot about how to handle your disputes better.

So let me ask you a few questions.

How do you feel if you are riding on a crowded subway, and two rough-looking guys start screaming and threatening each other right next to you?

Answer: scared. Or maybe angry. Or maybe both. Psychologists and biologists call this reaction the *fight-or-flight response*. It's a behavior pattern that is wired into our genes. Fight-or-flight reactions are observed across a wide spectrum of animal species. Think of how a cat responds to a barking dog. It either lashes out with its claws or runs up a tree. Fight or flight is an adaptive response to threat. Evolution made the response a part of our nature, because fight or flight increases our chances of survival.

Next question. How do you feel if you are out to dinner with a couple you really like, just the three of you, and they get in a nasty argument? And what do you do?

Answer to the first question: You feel uncomfortable, at best. Answer to the second question: You try to change the subject, or somehow distract your friends from their dispute. If that doesn't work, maybe you try to mediate: "Come on, you guys. Can't you hold off? Can't we just enjoy our meal?" Or if nothing else is working, you may yell at them, "I've had enough. Act like adults, will you?" Or maybe you leave in a huff. You think, "Let them make fools of themselves, but leave me out of it!" And afterward, you probably decide that it will be a *long* time before you have dinner with those people again.

However you react, here is what you are doing: You are trying to get rid of your own discomfort by somehow quieting or getting away from the fight. Psychologists call this process *emotion regulation*.

A related question: What if you cannot get away? What if you have to have dinner with this warring couple every day?

Answer: You keep working and working to stop their fights, so you can regulate your own emotions. Maybe your efforts at distraction work. Or maybe your mediation works. Or maybe your anger works. If so, you successfully regulate their fight, and your feelings. And in the process you learn to become the clown, the mediator, or the volcano.

If nothing you do works to stop the fighting, your only choice is to turn inward to regulate your emotions. You tell yourself how little you care for these people anymore. You grit your teeth and wait expectantly for the check.

A different question: How do you feel, and what do you do, if one of your bosses tells you to finish an assignment right now, but your other boss says not to worry about it—go home early?

Answer: confused or torn or maybe delighted that your other boss came along when she did. You probably like that second boss a lot more than the first, at least temporarily. And unless you really are the dedicated type, my bet is that you will not get your work done. But you may wonder, "Is this any way to run a business?"

One more question: How do you feel if you complain about your brother to a friend, and the friend tells you what a *horrible, terrible* person your brother is, and how she has always *hated* your brother and so has everyone else?

Answer: Well, either you really, really hate your brother's guts, or you feel protective and maybe under attack too. After all, he is your brother. Blood is thicker than water!

I hope I do not need to say this, but I will just in case. Your children feel all of these things when you and your ex fight: scared, angry, sad, uncomfortable, confused, torn, under attack, and maybe delighted when you are contradicting each other and allowing them to get their own way.

And they also feel like they need to fix your fights, partly to protect you and partly to regulate their own emotions. They try to distract you, to mediate. They yell. They leave. They feel caught in the middle, torn in their loyalties to each of you. They try to get along with you both. If they cannot, maybe they take sides, or pretend that they are on your side—and pretend to their dad that they are on his side too. They take advantage of your inconsistency and undermining of each other. They learn to play you against each other so they get to do pretty much whatever they want. They get sick of you both, diminish you both, and leave.

That's how your kids feel about your fights.

## Better Ways to Manage Conflict

As I said, a long tradition of research shows that children deal with conflict in precisely these sorts of ways. Mark Cummings, a developmental psychologist at the University of Notre Dame, has done the work I find most compelling.

A longtime friend and colleague, Cummings has been studying children's reactions to parental conflict for over thirty years. Much of Cummings's work involves elegant laboratory experiments.[7] For example, he sometimes asks parents to simulate a fight in front of their kids. Then Cummings studies children's reactions to this experiment. He and his students have asked children how they feel about the fight. They have used physiological recordings to monitor children's emotional reactions. They have observed children's behavior—for example, whether they intervene to try to stop the fight.

You know what the research finds. You just put yourself in your children's shoes.

Cummings also has cleverly demonstrated how children react to different kinds of conflict. For example, he has shown that kids are upset not just by open fighting but also by "the silent treatment." Children remain upset even when actors stop fighting but continue to behave coldly toward one another.

You can just *feel* the tension of the silent treatment. So can your children.

Your children feel it when you and your ex sit on opposite sides of the auditorium, scowl, and generally "bad vibe" each other. Your children feel the tension when you wait at opposite ends of the stage, in a silent contest to see which parent they will approach first after getting their award.

True, the silent treatment is better than yelling and screaming. But I want you to aim higher. So do your children. Sit together and talk about the weather. Or if that is too much, then sit apart but keep your ill will to yourself—even if your ex doesn't. You can be the bigger person.

Actually, what I find most compelling about Cummings's work is not what it reveals about where parents go wrong. His research also indicates how parents can better manage their conflicts. Children are less distressed by parental disputes if:

- The fights are not about the children
- The arguments do not occur in front of the children
- The expression of anger is less emotionally intense
- There is no physical fighting
- Children are not asked or expected to get in the middle or to take sides
- The conflict is resolved, even if parents only agree to disagree

These findings have practical implications for you.

- Much of your hurt and anger is not about your children. Don't make it about them. Yes, your kids tie you to your ex—forever. But don't use your children as a weapon, or an excuse, in battling over old issues that really are *your* issues, not your children's.

- You and your ex need to communicate, at least some. It may seem like a convenient time to talk when you are exchanging the children, but do *not* try to talk about anything important then. Unless you have a cooperative relationship, you will end up fighting right in front of your children. (In Chapter 3, I discuss parenting conferences as a much better plan for talking with your ex about your children.)

- Keep a rein on your emotions around the children. You can show a range of feelings around your children, including sadness, anger, and fear. But except for positive emotions like love or joy, set the "temperature" of your emotional expression to lukewarm or cooler. Rant to your best friend, not to or around your children. (And be careful about what your children may overhear when you are fuming to your best friend on the telephone or over a glass of wine on the deck.)

- Never get physical. Ever.

- Do not ask or expect your children to take sides. There are not two sides here, yours and your ex's. There is only one side: your children's. Be on that side.

- Do not ask or expect your children to get in the middle. Do not ask them to carry messages from you to your ex. This is your job. Do your work. Also, do not pump your kids for information about what's going on at their other house. If you have to ask, it is probably because your children sense the tension. If they feel free to share, that is awesome—and so are you.

- Work it out. If not today, tomorrow. If not tomorrow, the next day. Conflict is inevitable. And conflict is not necessarily bad. The key is to get somewhere, to come to some resolution. Even agreeing to disagree is a form of resolution. So is accepting the fact that you do not have the power to change things that are not within your control (even though you wish you could).

- Finally, do not criticize your ex to your children. Praise your ex, by all means. But remember. Your children are part you and part her. If you put her down, you are disparaging your children's DNA.

Let me expand on this last point just a little. As you learn about divorce and especially custody conflicts, you may encounter the word *alienation*. Proponents of the idea say that alienation occurs when one parent constantly puts the other parent down. Advocates of the alienation concept say that a parent who says horrible things about his or her ex to the children "alienates" them from the parent who gets put down.

At the moment, the idea of alienation is "hot" among many custody experts. I am not hot on the idea. I am sure alienation occurs, rarely. I am much more convinced that "what goes around, comes around." If you constantly put down your ex, your criticisms are going to boomerang. They will distance your children from *you* more than from *him*.

One of my recent graduate students, Jenna Rowen, completed her dissertation on this topic. To distinguish her research, Jenna coined the term *parental denigration*, to describe when one parent puts down the other to their children. She found no support for the idea that denigrating your ex alienates her from your children. In a study of almost one thousand young people, Jenna did find that you will distance your children from someone if you put down your ex.[8] That someone is you.

## Separating Marital and Parental Roles

How can you get over your anger at your ex, or at least get started?

Over and over again, I have been amazed and inspired by parents who succeed in protecting their children from their own disputes, from their own anger and pain. These people find a way to separate the emotions they feel toward their former partner as a parent from their potent, almost overwhelming, crushed feelings owing to lost romantic love. These people somehow maintain their loving feelings toward each other as parents. Or perhaps they just maintain their liking or mutual respect—I will take anything on the positive side of the ledger.

Some of these parents even manage to continue to celebrate holidays together. I especially like it when parents celebrate their children's birthdays together. Children do too.

I have seen perhaps a surprising number of divorced parents who treat each other like extended family, even after one or both of them remarry. And perhaps more realistically for many, I know of scores of divorced parents who bite their tongue, put a smile on their face, and chat idly with one another, so their children can see them standing or sitting together, on the sidelines or in the audience, sharing their love for their children, without words, maybe without ever acknowledging that sharing parental love is what they are doing.

It may take some time for you to get there. But it is a worthy destination.

## Jim and Juanita's "Conscious Uncoupling"

Even as I write this, I cannot help but think of Juanita and Jim, parents with whom I worked quite recently. Jim and Juanita came to me for guidance after multiple failed attempts at couple therapy. They had never married, but they had three wonderful children together: six, nine, and eleven years old.

Juanita was a free spirit, which had long been a source of excitement and agony for Jim. He was never bored in their relationship. But he was never secure either. He had asked Juanita to marry him multiple times during their fourteen years of living together. He even bought her three different engagement rings.

But Juanita never had wanted the ties of marriage. She had repeatedly told Jim, "Marriage is just a piece of paper." Juanita always told Jim their love for each other had to be bigger than marriage. She would not be betrothed. If their love died, she did not want to be tied to Jim by some legal anachronism; she did not want Jim to stay with her if he no longer loved her either.

Sadly and ironically, by the time Juanita's philosophy changed, so had Jim's feelings. As he described it, Jim taught himself to hold back from allowing himself to truly feel his love for Juanita. Reining in his love was Jim's way of protecting himself from his constant fear of losing her. Each time he proposed, and was rejected, he pulled back a bit further.

When Juanita turned the tables and proposed to *him* (about a year and a half before they came to see me), Jim had a horrible revelation. His love for Juanita was dead. He put off his answer to her proposal but eventually told Juanita the truth.

Juanita and Jim came to me, in part, for help in exploring and explaining their painful dance around love and commitment.

Much to her credit, Juanita continued to tell Jim that she still loved him. She still wanted to marry him. And at the same time, she still did not want him to stay with her if he did not love her.

Much to his credit, Jim was honest and clear too. He had tried and tried to recover his love. Yet his feelings were gone. He was more than willing to talk with Juanita about anything and everything, for as long as she wanted. But he was not willing to lie to her about how he felt.

All of this was incredibly painful, as I am sure you can imagine.

Jim did his best not to hurt Juanita unnecessarily. But he spoke the truth she did not want to hear: "I don't love you anymore."

Juanita was in agony. She could have tried to hurt Jim back. She certainly had the weapons. But she did not indulge her anger. Instead, she allowed herself to feel the stabbing pain of rejection. And although Juanita never denied her own love for Jim, she soon decided not to voice her feelings anymore. That became *way* too painful.

When I spoke with her alone, Juanita told me that she knew she would have to deal with her pain, loss, and longing on her own.

She was right.

When you love someone but he does not love you back, he cannot heal you, even with a gentle lie. Ultimately, you must grieve your loss alone.

After half a dozen excruciating yet still somehow tender meetings, Juanita and Jim agreed to accept the inevitable. They would separate.

In shifting their focus onto the children, Jim and Juanita vowed to preserve the best part of their relationship, the parent part. Of course, they also would do everything in their power to protect their children, the best things that had come from their years together.

Juanita was clear. She didn't want to see much of Jim for a while. Doing so would hurt too much. She would need time and space to get there, but her goal was to get to a place where she could work with Jim, even like him. She could say the words now, even though she could not yet act on them fully. Her goal was to remain his partner, to be on his side—as a parent.

Jim agreed that he very much wanted to be Juanita's parenting partner too. He wanted to share all aspects of raising their children with Juanita, not only time and decisions, but also joys and worries. And he still wanted to do special things together, as a family. Jim said he could respect Juanita's need for some time and distance. He could be patient in waiting for her to get to where she needed to be emotionally. When she was ready, he would be too.

Many divorcing parents do not part with the emotional integrity of Juanita and Jim. I hope I have conveyed a sense of how excruciating their "conscious uncoupling" was. (Yes, the term sounds glib. And I'm sure the actress Gwyneth Paltrow, who was skewered for using it, suffered through a painful parting.)

Honestly, I was not as well put together as Juanita and Jim when I went through my own divorce. But if you have children, aiming for a cooperative divorce is the right target, no matter what you may need to do to hit it.

## Two Good Parents

You do not need to be Juanita and Jim to have a cooperative coparenting relationship. But if you both are going to remain deeply involved in your children's lives, which I hope you will do, you need to keep your children out of your emotional "stuff." You need a decent, or at least a distant, working relationship. "Two Good Parents" is higher up than "Protection from Conflict" in my Hierarchy of Children's Needs in Two Homes, because research shows that the absence of conflict matters more to children's mental health than having a good relationship with both parents.

But I want you to meet *all* of your children's needs. Your children certainly do.

Even though you hear it all the time, your children do *not* live in a single-parent family. Children whose parents divorce have two parents. And unless something is terribly wrong with one of them, children want to have a relationship with both of their divorced parents. They want to have a two-parent, divorced family.

And let's be honest. We are mostly, although not exclusively, saying that we want fathers to remain involved in their children's lives after divorce. According to recent U.S. Census data, about 85 percent of children live primarily with their mothers when their parents live apart.[9] About 15 percent live mostly with their fathers. It is true. More children than in the past now live mostly with their fathers, but the percentage still is small relative to children living mainly with mothers. (The census does not track joint physical custody, where children split substantial time between Mom's house and Dad's house. We discuss this in the next chapter.)

Today's fathers also see their children more frequently, even when the children live primarily with their mothers. In a recent study, Paul Amato, Catherine Meyers, and I compared national samples of U.S. families from 1976, 1988, 1996, and 2002.[10] We showed that divorced fathers' contact with their children increased over time. In 1976, for example, 33 percent of divorced fathers had not seen their children in the past year; by 2002 that number declined to 18 percent. And on the positive side, the proportion of divorced fathers who saw their children at least weekly grew from 19 percent in 1976 to 37 percent in 2002. (Unlike in most of this book, *divorce* here refers only to formerly married fathers in these statistics. Never-married fathers maintained somewhat lower levels of contact with their children.)

## Love Matters

Why is a relationship with both parents so important to children? Honestly, research indicates that having *one* authoritative parent is what predicts outcomes like children's school success or positive mental health. Having a second authoritative parent does not boost children's chances of success in these areas very much.[11]

Is a good relationship with the second parent nice but redundant? Is the "other" parent a mere copilot in coparenting?

No. Frequent contact with both parents is essential to children feeling close to both Mom and Dad. And feeling loved by both parents is important in its own right, whether or not that wonderful sense of security predicts anything else.

Let me tell you about a study of children and divorce that I conducted over a decade ago with my former graduate student Lisa Laumann-Billings.[12] Our focus was on what we called emotional pain, children's hurt feelings and ongoing worries about their relationships with their parents. We believed then, and now, that emotional pain is a critically important part of emotional experience, whether or not pain is related to psychologists' traditional measures of children's success in school or tests of their mental health.

This study included 100 successful college students from divorced families. We included only resilient students. They had bounced back from any struggles owing to their parents' divorce, a divorce that occurred at least three years in the past, another criterion for participation in this study.

Here is a startling thing we discovered about these highly resilient young people, who, like most kids from divorced families, lived mostly with their moms. Nearly one third of them endorsed the item "I sometimes wonder if my father really loves me."

I think that's a pretty important, and sad, outcome.

My number one goal as a father is to make sure my children feel loved.

Another important finding was that young adults from divorced families reported the greatest feelings of loss due to divorce if they saw their dad only once or twice a month while growing up. This is equivalent to the common "every other weekend" schedule. If the college students saw their dad at least once a week, their pain was less. Interestingly, the young people who saw their father infrequently or not at all also reported fewer current feelings of loss.

What do these findings mean? We interpreted our results this way: If you did not see your father much after your parents divorced, you grieved the loss. But eventually your mourning ended. If you saw your father a lot, you discovered you really did not have much to grieve after all. Both your parents remained front and center in your life. But seeing your dad every few weeks was just enough to keep your hopes alive—and to have them constantly dashed.

Honestly, I cannot be certain whether our interpretation is right. But the study does suggest that there are some important, hard-to-measure benefits of having a good, involved relationship with both of your divorced parents. Avoiding grief is a pretty big benefit in my view. So is feeling loved by *both* of your parents.

## Putting the Cart (Coparenting) before the Horse (Shared Time)

How can we increase the number of kids who see their dads (and moms) a lot, and decrease the number who see them rarely? This topic is the focus of the next chapter (on joint custody). But let me give you a little taste of what is to come, so you can truly understand why "Protection from Conflict" is a more basic need than "Two Good Parents" in my Hierarchy of Children's Needs in Two Homes.

In the 1980s, I began what surely is the most important study I have ever done.[13] I studied 71 families. The parents had just filed a petition for a contested child custody hearing. (The custody contest places these parents among the top 10 percent of most angry divorces. That is some distinction.)

I assigned these parents, at random, either to participate in an evaluation of the court (the litigation group) or to try mediation (a new idea at the time). Random assignment was a key to my study, or any study. This scientific procedure allows researchers to determine causation, not just correlation.

In random-assignment studies, there is no guesswork. You know what caused what.

I found that mediation caused almost *90 percent* of families to settle their custody dispute without ever arguing their case before a judge. In contrast, a judge had to decide the custody plan for 70 percent of the court evaluation group. About 30 percent in this group settled their case through attorney negotiations prior to trial.

More important, I followed these families for twelve years.[14] The more cooperative approach of mediation caused both parents to be much more involved in their children's lives twelve years later. For example, if they went to mediation instead of litigating, *three times* as many parents whose children did not live with them primarily still saw their kids every week. *Five times* as many parents who mediated spoke with their adolescent children on the telephone every week.

An average of six hours of mediation twelve years prior *caused* these huge differences. Mediation also caused parents to get along with each other better and to rate each other as being better parents twelve years into the future.

For the parents in my study, the horse of trying to work with their ex in mediation pulled the cart of parenting time, parenting quality, and coparenting quality twelve years into the future—and probably beyond that too.

The second study that I want to mention was completed recently by an outstanding group of researchers at Arizona State University.[15] These investigators, who also studied families over time, wanted to know how father involvement versus coparenting conflict predicted the adjustment of children years into the future.

When the children in the study were adolescents, the investigators used statistics to identify different patterns of dads' involvement with their kids. The computer procedure uncovered three groups: (1) fathers who were very involved with their children but had a lot of conflict with their co-parent; (2) fathers who were moderately involved with their kids and had low conflict with their co-parent; and (3) fathers with low involvement with their children and moderate conflict with their co-parent.

The psychologists followed the adolescents for nine years. They then asked the question: What pattern predicts better psychological adjustment during young-adult life? The answer? Moderate involvement combined with low conflict. High involvement combined with high conflict offered no more benefits to children than low involvement combined with moderate conflict.

Conflict is more damaging to children in divorce than having only a limited relationship with your other parent. Now you know some more reasons why protection from conflict is a more basic need than a good relationship with both of your parents in my Hierarchy of Children's Needs in Two Homes.

## When Divorced Parents Meet Children's Needs

Will your children be harmed by your divorce—maybe forever? Can you protect them?

You certainly can do a great deal to protect your children from the negative fallout of divorce. I hope this chapter and the Hierarchy of Children's Needs in Two Homes gives you a clear sense of where you want to head in order to do so. Later chapters offer more specific directions, tell you what signs to look for, and suggest how you can steer through all kinds of twists and turns. Divorce is a long and winding road.

But I have to be honest. No parent can completely protect children when their family unravels. You face many challenges and all kinds of stress. So do your children.

Children are often devastated to learn that their parents are splitting up. And living through your separation is scary. Your children will find it lonely when they are not able to see you both, whenever they want. They will worry about you. Both of you. Moving from their house will be hard, if they have to move. So will changing schools, losing old friends, and making new ones, if that has to happen. Like you, they may worry about money. They may resent not having enough money to have and do things like they used to.

Yet if you take your children's hierarchy of needs to heart, you can expect your kids to be just as normal, and just as unique, as they would have turned out to be anyway. Most children from divorced families are no different psychologically from children whose parents remain married. Most are resilient. They bounce back from the challenges and the changes and get on with the business of living their life.

I hope this will be your kid. You can make that happen.

One more thing: In the short run and in the long run too, divorce is likely to be painful for your children. Pain is not a psychological disorder. But pain hurts. For the rest of their lives, your kids may remember the day when you told them you were separating. They may recall the time of day, the room, the mood, and the words they did not want to hear. As adults, some children from divorced families write songs and stories about this moment.

Your children can reach self-actualization in my Hierarchy of Children's Needs in Two Homes. Your children can be just kids, not forever children of divorce. Yet your children will be kids who have experienced real pain in their life. But in the long run, living through the pain of divorce may make your children emotionally deeper, richer, and more sensitive. No one would intentionally inflict pain on children in order to achieve these goals. Yet perhaps there is some solace in knowing that your children—and you—can grow through pain.

## CHAPTER 3

# Sharing Decisions and Time in Joint Custody: Beyond 50/50

Everyone shares joint custody today, or so it seems. But what exactly does joint custody mean?

If you have joint custody, does this mean that you and your ex have to agree about *everything*? Cloth diapers only? Bedtime at 8:30 for your nine-year-old son, no ifs, ands, or buts (for him or for you)?

And how do you share time with your children in joint custody? One week on, one week off? Mondays and Tuesdays with one parent, Wednesdays and Thursdays with the other, and alternate weekends Friday afternoon through Monday morning? Does time *have* to be shared 50/50? Is Saturday to Wednesday with one parent and Wednesday to Saturday with the other joint custody? How about weekdays with one parent and weekends with the other? Or the school year on the East Coast and summers on the West Coast?

And do all of your children have to be on precisely the same schedule? What about the different needs of babies, preschoolers, and school-age children? How about teenagers' own busy schedules? What do you do if different children say they want different schedules? And what if your children have some pretty serious sibling conflicts? Should your children, and you, have some separate "alone" time?

Before addressing these questions and more, I need to warn you. You are going to find a wide range of opinions and "facts" (that are not facts) about joint custody. To simulate what information a typical parent may hear, I did what everyone does: a Google search. Websites vary widely about what joint custody is, whether it works, and when it works (or doesn't). Opinions differ about strategies for negotiating or resisting joint custody, as do various assertions about what judges, lawyers, psychologists, parents, and children think.

You can expect the people you consult to hold different opinions about joint custody too. So don't be surprised if your lawyer and your ex's lawyer offer conflicting recommendations. Or maybe your own lawyer will disagree with your therapist, who may disagree with your children's therapist . . . Then there's your best friend (who is great friends with her ex and loves joint custody), your dad (who believes children belong with their mother), your ex's mom (who wants joint custody so she can keep seeing her grandchildren regularly), and your ex's best friend (who is in the middle of a bitter divorce and is suing for sole custody).

You get the picture.

And here is my opinion, based on more than three decades of working with divorcing families in therapy and mediation, plus conducting my own research, reviewing scores of studies, and, yes, personal experience. I'm an advocate for joint custody—under the right circumstances. From my Hierarchy of Children's Needs in Two Homes, you already know one key to making joint custody work: keeping children out of parents' conflicts.

But now it's time to get into the details. My goal is to help you make your circumstances the best they can possibly be, so you can make joint custody work for your children.

## Joint Custody Defined

Let's start with some indisputable facts about joint custody. Then we can deal with some murkier but important questions.

In the law, joint custody involves sharing two broad and sometimes complicated essentials of parenting: making decisions about your children and dividing their time between you and your ex. Decision making is often called *joint* legal *custody*. Time is typically called *joint* physical *custody*.

I am much more concerned about time and decisions—about parenting—than I am about what you call your arrangement. More and more state laws reflect that same view. Many states have dropped loaded terms like *custody* and *visitation* altogether. These laws instead describe your goal as negotiating a *parenting plan*. (Yes, custody laws vary from state to state, sometimes quite a lot. So there's another source of disagreement about joint custody.)

Actually, I love the term *parenting plan*. It puts the focus on what you have to do—parent—not on some legal abstraction. Deciding between, or fighting over, joint or sole custody can feel like you face the prospect of winning or losing your children, or perhaps of carving them in two. Negotiating a parenting plan isn't easy, but it at least *sounds* like something you can manage. And it is.

Joint legal and physical custody both are relatively new ideas, dating mostly to the 1970s and 1980s, when divorce rates increased dramatically in the United States. Both arrangements have become more common over recent decades.

In fact, today most divorced and never-married parents share joint *legal* custody, that is, formal decision making. Attitudes have changed so much that many professionals and state laws automatically assume that parents will share joint legal custody.

For many experts, including me, joint legal custody is a no-brainer, the default arrangement. The only exception to this rule occurs when there is a really good reason *not* to share decision making. One good reason for not sharing legal custody can be when parents disagree so vehemently that they repeatedly end up in court litigating parenting disputes, even minor ones.

What about sharing time in addition to decisions? More and more parents are sharing joint physical custody too. Today's fathers definitely are more involved with their children in divorced families, in never-married families, and in married families too. Still, unlike legal custody, most parents do not share joint physical custody.

In the United States, perhaps one in five families share physical custody.[1] I have to say "perhaps," because we have no good national data on joint physical custody in the United States. Some states have higher rates of joint physical custody, while other states have lower rates. Surprisingly though, no one has reliable numbers for the entire United States—or good numbers from most states either. But one in five is a reasonable estimate for the United States based on what we know from similar countries like Australia and Canada, as well as from information available from various states.

Do joint legal and physical custody always go together? No. It is common for parents to share joint legal custody, but for one parent to have sole physical custody—or just more time, whatever the label. It also is common for parents to share both joint legal and physical custody. Sometimes that's just a label too. Actual time can be shared pretty unevenly, despite the joint physical custody label. What is uncommon is for one parent to have sole legal custody, but for the two parents to still share joint physical custody. How can you share time if you fight so much that you cannot share decisions?

Now that you have a basic understanding of what joint custody is, let's drill down into the details. We'll start with joint legal custody. Later in this chapter, we'll discuss joint physical custody.

# Sharing Decisions in Joint Legal Custody: Theory and Reality

As a parent, you make dozens of judgments every day. Some of these choices are small. Others can be pretty important. Does joint legal custody mean that everything is a 50/50 decision? Do you each get a vote on every one of your parenting choices?

Some parents initially treat joint legal custody this way. But soon they are as deadlocked as the U.S. Senate, tied at 50/50 over and over again.

How about if you take turns? Mom decides bedtime one week. Dad decides the next.

I don't think that's going to work.

So you know what you don't want to do. How *do* you want to manage parenting decisions across two homes? That's a good question. Let's consider it in detail.

# The Law's View of Joint Legal Custody

Even though some people initially think otherwise, the law does not expect divorced parents to share every childrearing decision equally in joint legal custody. In fact, most state laws define joint legal custody as requiring parents to share only three major kinds of childrearing decisions:

- Elective medical care
- Religious training
- Education

This means that you both must consent if your child is going to get braces or go to a therapist. (And, of course, you need to figure out how to pay for these expenses.) These are elective medical decisions. But if your child ends up in the emergency room—scary but something that is likely to happen once or twice in eighteen years—you do *not* need to frantically search for your ex to get his or her permission for stitches, or worse.

Joint legal custody also means that both parents must agree about whether a child goes to a church, synagogue, mosque, or some other place of worship. The same goes for deciding about public versus private school (and how to pay for the latter).

(Parents with joint legal custody also share authority over a handful of less-routine decisions, like getting a passport for a minor, or permitting a child to join the military or get married before age eighteen. If you have joint legal custody, both parents' consent is needed in these circumstances.)

You may be wondering—you *should* be wondering: Aren't parenting decisions more complicated than that?

Yes, parenting is far more complicated than that. And when it comes to making routine parenting decisions, the law is silent in principle—and confused in practice.

I will be neither silent nor, I hope, confusing.

To get a better idea of how joint legal custody gets confused in the law, let's look at educational decisions more closely. In theory, shared educational decisions involve only the biggest choices, like whether your son will go to public or private school. Joint legal custody does *not* mean that you and your ex need to agree about how and when your son completes his homework. You do not need to agree about how much he reads instead of playing video games.

This example solves one problem for you. With joint legal custody, you and your ex only need to make a few big decisions together. But the law does not say *how* parents should make these decisions together.

And what about intermediate decisions? What about decisions

that are a pretty big deal to parents, and to kids, but are not on the law's list? What about things like piano lessons versus soccer for your daughter? What about whether your son should join the football team? And for that matter, what about how much your son reads versus wasting time playing video games? For many parents, that's a pretty big deal too. Count me as one of them.

The law does not say that divorced parents must share these intermediate decisions in joint legal custody. And if parents decide that they want to or should share some important, intermediate-sized decisions, the law does not guide them in how they should do that either.

But divorced (and never-married) parents can always litigate. The law allows judges to hear cases not only about parents' disputes regarding major disagreements about religion, schooling, and elective medical care, but also about soccer versus piano, football or no football.

And judges must render a verdict. I know of some judges who try to divide custody into specifics: Dad gets sports custody. Mom gets school custody.

Really? Really.

As I said earlier, sharing joint legal custody makes sense as the default for most parents—until parents show that they cannot share decisions.

Giving one parent sole legal custody is one solution. I want to suggest what I think is a better solution, or rather, a series of better solutions.

## Parents, Not Judges, Should Decide

Let me share the logic behind my better solution. In my all-time favorite ruling about coparenting litigation, a New York State judge summarized the reasoning far more eloquently than I can:

*Dispute between parents when it does not involve anything im-*
*moral or harmful to the welfare of the child is beyond the reach*
*of the law. The vast majority of matters concerning the up-*
*bringing of children must be left to the conscience, patience,*
*and self-restraint of father and mother. No end of difficulties*
*would arise should judges try to tell parents how to bring up*
*their children.*[2]

In this case, a New York state court *refused* to make a decision for
parents who disagreed about their child's schooling. The court said
to the parents, "You work it out." The wise judge knew that opening
the door to litigation between parents would produce "no end of
difficulties."

In this case, *People ex rel. Sisson v. Sisson*, litigated in 1936, the
parents were *married*. In fact, American courts routinely refuse to
hear disputes between married parents. Our courts know that if
they get in the middle of disputes between married parents, it's only
going to make things worse, not better.

I don't think parenting is so different in married and divorced
families.

In married families, and in divorced families too, both parents
are likely to remain involved in rearing their children. The involvement of both parents means that cooperative coparenting is of huge
importance to the well-being of children, whether you are married
or divorced. Whether you are married or divorced, your children are
still better off if you present a "united front," even when you disagree privately.

And you are less likely to work out important parenting decisions on your own if you know that you have the option of appeal-
ing to a higher authority. This is true whether you are married or
divorced.

## Divorced Parents Cannot Make Agreements

The fact that judges get involved in disputes between divorced (and never-married) parents creates another huge problem. Once a custody case comes before a court, a judge, and only a judge, has ultimate authority to make decisions about the children involved. Why? When a matter involving child custody is brought before an American court, legal theory holds that the state becomes the parent.

This means that in theory and in practice, judges can and often do contradict *agreements* between divorced (and never-married) parents. Even though our courts know enough not to get anywhere near *disagreements* between married parents, judges can and do overturn *agreements* between divorced parents.[3]

I'm not making this up.

Even if divorced parents *agree*, their agreement technically is invalid. Only a judge, not the parents, can make final decisions about matters that affect the children of divorced parents.

I don't want to exaggerate or scare you unnecessarily. We are mostly past the days when judges would overrule an agreement between parents to share joint custody of their children. Mostly. But it was not so long ago that some judges exercised their authority to throw out joint custody agreements. These judges disagreed with the parents' agreed-upon plans. So they ordered divorced parents to follow a custody arrangement that the judge liked better.

Today, judges routinely rubber-stamp parents' custody agreements. But judges can and do intervene in parents' agreements in other, problematic ways. For example, in 2013 the Commonwealth of Pennsylvania banned the use of *parenting coordination*, an innovative dispute resolution procedure increasingly used by divorced parents.[4] A parenting coordinator first acts as a mediator, trying to help parents resolve disagreements on their own. According to a contract the parents sign, if the parents cannot agree, the parenting coordinator becomes an arbiter who makes pressing decisions for the parents. For example, if parents are in dispute about who gets the kids during the week of July 4, and it's June 25, a parenting coordinator may make that decision for them.

You can guess what the Commonwealth of Pennsylvania ruled. Only judges, not parenting coordinators, can make these decisions. And besides, divorced parents do not have the authority to ask someone else to make parenting decisions for them. How could they? Divorced parents don't have ultimate authority over their own children. Judges do.

In Chapter 4, I introduce you to another huge problem this legal paradox creates. Divorced parents cannot make enforceable agreements about how their parenting plan will evolve over time, no matter how logical and reasonable their plan may be. For example, an agreement between parents is unenforceable if it indicates that Dad will have more overnights when his infant becomes a toddler. A plan like this makes all kinds of sense for a baby's welfare, for reasons we discuss in detail in Chapters 4 and 5. But divorced parents do not have the authority to make such a plan. As you will see, this circumstance discourages parents from making creative, child-focused parenting plans. It also encourages conflict and litigation.

## Aiming Higher: Effective Coparenting

I want you to aim higher. A key premise of this book is that the best parenting plan is a living agreement, an arrangement that grows and changes along with your child's changing needs. You can do this. You can be a bit of a rebel, even if the law currently does not support your commitment to change. After all, I wrote scores of successful, lasting joint custody agreements in the 1980s before Virginia law even recognized the existence of joint custody!

Besides, a court would overturn your agreement only if one of you changes your mind. So go ahead and make plans. But you should understand how the law does work, even if you choose to work around it. You or your ex *may* change your mind. If this happens, you are likely to find that the agreement you thought you made is invalid.

I still want you to take a chance on working together, but I do want you to know about the chances you are taking.

Parents constantly make important decisions about children's appropriate clothing, diet, bedtime, chores, rules, discipline, friends, use of electronics, schoolwork, and extracurricular activities. The list goes on and on. Sharing these kinds of decisions is *not* required in joint legal custody. But good parenting involves at least some degree of cooperation in all of these matters. After all, your seven-year-old will suffer if her bedtime is eight p.m. in one home and eleven p.m. in another. Your teenager will suffer if you ground him for three weeks for a horrible report card, but your ex tells him, "No problem. Have fun with your friends. You aren't grounded at my house!"

Parenting with your ex, *coparenting*, is more complicated than dividing up decisions. Effective coparenting is about *making* decisions, often together.

When I say I want you to aim higher, I want you to aim at being the best parent and coparent that you can be.

## Don't Sweat the Small Stuff: Accepting Limited Control

How can divorced parents share those smaller decisions that really are not so small? First, you need to accept your limited control over your children's other parent. Your ex is going to need to make a lot of little everyday decisions about what your children wear, eat, and do. So are you.

You may not like some of your ex's parenting decisions. She may be more lenient or more strict than you are. But you just cannot control most of her choices. You will only make things worse if you try. Your kids will see you fighting. You will undermine each other's authority. You will drive each other crazy. And when you try to control what you cannot, you always end up back at square one, feeling frustrated and powerless.

Effective parenting and coparenting is not about control. It is not a competition either. Sure, we all love allies. But pulling your children in your direction really means pulling them in *opposite* directions. You are yanking on the left arm, and your ex is yanking on the right.

You have to let go of a lot of small stuff, but at the same time, it really is important to try to be on the same page as parents and coparents. Your children do need bedtimes that are pretty similar, if not identical. The same is true of rules about appropriate dress, diet, and activities. You surely know kids who play their parents against each other. Do you want to teach your children that lesson?

And then there are some parenting issues that are really important to you. You just cannot let go. You *have* to second-guess your ex. What about that?

Actually, the ideas of giving up control *and* cooperating, of accepting your ex's autonomy *and* raising differences of opinion, are not as contradictory as they may sound. Often, the best step toward coparenting together actually is to accept the limits of your control, to respect your coparent's independence.

No one likes to be micromanaged, at work and especially at home—especially across two homes. So you really do need to pick your battles. Don't sweat the small stuff.

Let stuff go. But if you are going to cooperate, at least to a degree—and sometimes second-guess—you and your ex do need to do one thing: communicate.

## Parenting Conferences

One of my favorite communication strategies is scheduling parenting conferences. You and your ex should plan a regular time to talk about your children. Use your conference to share the ups and downs you experienced during your kids' time with you. Voice your worries. Our concerns are eased when we share them, and there is no one better to share them with than your kids' other parent. Talk about your children's health, schoolwork, friends, activities, and emotional well-being. Make sure to share points of pride—and details about upcoming events. If you have a disagreement to discuss, this is the time to raise that too.

Knowing that you have a time to talk will help you let go on a day-to-day basis. Hold that thought until Thursday when you have a scheduled parenting conference. And who knows? What seemed like a huge deal on Monday may not be a big deal by Thursday.

Knowing that you have a time to talk also will help you not to intrude into each other's lives. When your phone rings, you won't be wondering if it's your ex. You talk on Sunday evenings, so the call on Saturday afternoon is probably from someone else. You don't need to tense up.

Pick a time that is convenient for both of you to talk. Make sure it's a time when the kids are occupied and out of earshot. Maybe the best time is Sunday at nine p.m., when the kids are usually in bed, doing homework, or enjoying a little downtime—and you are planning the week. Or maybe Thursday at noon is better, when you are both at the office and you need to finalize weekend plans. You get the idea.

One warning: Having a parenting conference just before or after a transition may not be a great time to talk. You are handing the kids off, and it sure helps to know what is what. But as I said in Chapter 2, unless you have a *very* cooperative relationship, don't try to have your parenting conference during transitions. Transitions often are busy and sometimes difficult. The kids are right there. And if you get into an argument, they are going to see. So schedule your parenting conference for the night before or the morning after.

A few more rules will increase the likelihood that your parenting conferences will be successful. First, keep the focus on the children. This is the time to discuss their stuff, not your stuff. Second, keep it brief. Unless you have something really important to discuss, fifteen minutes, maybe less, should be plenty of time. Third, be polite. You are talking with your business partner, so stick to the issues, not the emotions, and focus on the future, not the past. Fourth, focus on the positive, not just the negative. We all like to hear good things, especially about our children—or ourselves. Fifth, if you have a bigger concern, expect to identify the problem in your parenting conference, but do not expect to solve it. You should anticipate that solving the problem is going to take longer and perhaps require you to speak in a different forum.

## Other Means of Communication

What about other means of communication? Texts and e-mails are great—for little things. Tennis lessons are at 5:30 this week. The school play is scheduled for December 15. Texts and e-mails are *horrible* for bigger issues about your kids, and especially about your relationship. You may type something into your computer that you would never say in person. Or your ex may read way too much into your ambiguous, hurried note. Then she dashes off an impulsive reply that escalates things further. You both read and reread the chain of texts. You each brood. You show all of the e-mails to a friend, who agrees that you are great and your ex is a jerk. Your lawyer advises you to keep your texts as a record. They may end up as evidence in court.

You *know* how e-mails and texts can explode, so follow my rules. Keep them short—no more than two or three sentences—and to the point. If you need to talk, text to set up a time. You will be better off exploding over the phone or in person. Why? First, you are likely to behave better in person or over the telephone than you may be typing into a computer. Second, you have a chance to correct misinterpretations during an actual conversation. Third, you won't find yourself rereading some stupid remark over and over again. And fourth, you, or your ex, won't have a written record.

Meeting in person occasionally can be a great idea anyway. You may have lunch once in a while to supplement your parenting conferences. Lunch can be a great way to share your parenting joys and concerns, particularly if you have a cooperative divorce.

Even if your relationship is strained, but you have some important difficulty to work out, an in-person meeting still may be a great idea. Meet some place that is quiet but still public. That way, you both will be better behaved. Other people will be watching.

If you cannot work out an important difference on your own, you and your ex can go together to see a mediator, perhaps a therapist or a collaborative lawyer. You will probably need only one meeting, or a few. Many of my clients come back to see me when they hit a tough spot. They also find it helpful just to know they have somewhere to go. So you may want to cultivate a professional relationship with someone, just in case you need it.

Some parents use *parenting logs*, diaries about the children, as a substitute for parenting conferences. That's fine if you have an angry or a distant relationship. But unless hearing your ex's voice really grates on you, I recommend trying telephone calls. Over time, you and your ex hopefully can discover a newfound connection, perhaps even trust, in continuing to share in the best thing to come from your union.

In the end, it comes down to this: I want joint legal custody— parenting decisions—to be something more than a 50/50 division between you and your ex. I want you to make big parenting decisions together, small parenting decisions on your own, and intermediate ones like married parents do—with some discussion, plenty of give-and-take, and ultimately by presenting a (mostly) united front to your children.

## Joint Physical Custody: What Works, What Doesn't

What about joint physical custody? Does joint physical custody mean that you and your ex must share time with your children 50/50?

I don't think so. I want your time with your children to be beyond 50/50 too.

Sure, some people, especially some fathers' rights organizations, argue that 50/50 is the only "true" joint physical custody. They want divorced fathers and mothers to get equal time with their children.

I have some sympathy with this position. After all, I am in the club. I am a divorced father myself.

But 50/50 is not my position, or how most experts define joint physical custody. Parenting across two homes is not about 50/50, dividing time with your children, and responsibility for them, right down the middle.

Many experts and research studies define joint physical custody as being at least 25 percent time with each parent. That means that weekdays with one parent and weekends with the other *is* joint physical custody. So is the less-than-ideal but sometimes-necessary arrangement where a child goes to school on the East Coast and spends summers on the West Coast.

I hope you weren't expecting your children to spend one week in New York and the next in Los Angeles. Sadly, I have seen some parents try, literally flying their children across long distances to maintain a 50/50 schedule. It is obvious to me, and I hope to you, that these parents were focused on getting their share, not on their children's needs and happiness.

You may recall the Old Testament story in which King Solomon threatened to cut a baby in half, so two disputing mothers could each get her share of a child they both claimed was her own. The false mother thought Solomon's proposal was fair. She would get her fifty percent. The true mother was horrified. She offered to give up her baby in order to spare it. In his wisdom, Solomon knew that someone who loves her baby wants to protect it, not divide it in two.

Here's how I see it. Your children don't count minutes, and neither should you. Fifty-fifty *may* be a great schedule, but it is not necessarily *the best or the only* schedule.

And because I want you to think about a parenting plan to last a lifetime, consider this: You may end up with 50/50, or something close to it. But you may get there by letting the years divide themselves, not by always dividing your children's overnights and weeks exactly equally.

You may decide (for reasons we will explore) that living mostly in one home works best for your baby. But babies grow, and so can your schedule.

And even if your daughter currently is going to middle school in Florida and living there with your ex, who knows? She may decide that she wants to go to high school in Oregon and live with you. Or maybe *you* will get transferred back to Florida and resume that week-to-week schedule that you had before you moved.

I want children to spend a *significant* amount of time with both of their divorced parents. Yet in my view, a significant amount of time may mean equal time with Dad, it may mean more time with him, or it may just mean a lot of time.

I have four big problems with the 50/50 position.

- As you already know, the focus on "equal" time makes me ready to jump out of my skin. Equal is all about getting your share. "I want my half of the pie!" Equal is *not* all about the children. And I hope you know that I am all about children. Craft a plan that will work for your children.

- I am more concerned with quality than quantity. So are children. Kids don't count overnights. Kids *experience* parenting. I want children from divorced families—your children—to feel well loved and to be well directed by both of their parents. So I want divorced fathers, and mothers, to have enough time with their children. Enough means enough time for you to establish an involved, authoritative relationship with your children.

- Research does not support a focus on time.[5] In fact, the amount of time children spend with their divorced dads actually is tied only weakly, or not at all, to measures of children's psychological well-being. What does matter to children's emotional well-being is having an authoritative father. (I am sure the same is true for mothers, but there is little research on the effects of divorced moms' time with their children.)

- The equal-time position puts the cart before the horse, as I said in the last chapter. What makes (more) equal time successful is having a cooperative or at least a distant, businesslike relationship with your ex.

## How Do Children Adjust in Joint Physical Custody?

But don't children do better in living in joint physical custody? Some claim they do, and as you will see, there is some truth to the claim. And there are problems with the claim, as you will also learn. In fact, different answers to this question form the basis of many arguments for, and against, joint physical custody. So let's have a look at the arguments and the evidence.

Opponents of joint physical custody typically claim that the back-and-forth is too disruptive for children. They note that children need stability and predictability in their life. Opponents often ask: If switching homes is so easy, why don't the parents go back and forth, while the children stay in one place? In fact, children sometimes do stay home, while parents move in and out. This arrangement is called *birdnesting*, but it is pretty rare. So the question about parents moving instead of children seems to raise a good point.

Proponents of joint physical custody recognize that moving between homes can be challenging. However, they argue that maintaining close ties with both parents is more important to children than living without disruption in your life. They suggest that children are better adjusted when they live in joint versus sole physical custody. And when given a choice, proponents say, children want equal time with their parents.

Not surprisingly, the truth is somewhere in between these two extremes, as it usually is. There is not a lot of good research on how children fare in joint versus sole physical custody. But there is at least a small body of reasonable studies. As a group, these studies indicate that in comparison to sole physical custody, children who live in joint physical custody generally are better adjusted emotionally.[6] They also have somewhat better relationships with their parents, particularly their fathers. Parents who share physical custody generally get along better too.

But wait a minute. You may remember the phrase from some long-ago psychology class: Correlation does not mean causation. This logical warning certainly applies to evidence on children living with joint physical custody. We know that parents who choose joint physical custody got along better *before they divorced*.[7] Parents who choose joint physical custody also were more involved with their children before the divorce, particularly fathers. Parents who share physical custody also are better educated and more financially secure than parents with sole custody.

Given all of this, I would be really surprised if children living in joint physical custody were *not* better adjusted. The same children probably had better emotional health before their parents split up too.

So the observed "benefits" of joint physical custody may *not* be caused by the arrangement. We need better research to document this conclusively. But even without conclusive research on correlation versus causation, we do know this: The well-being of children living in joint physical custody is better than that of kids living in sole physical custody—but only a little bit better. The difference in well-being is equivalent to only about 20 points on an SAT.[8] I definitely prefer higher SAT scores, but I am not sure how much money I would pay for an SAT prep class that only raised my son's score from 500 to 520.

On the other hand, there really is no evidence that, as a rule, joint physical custody is too disruptive for children. But rules have exceptions.

## What Makes Joint Physical Custody Work?

Joint physical custody can be the best arrangement for children— and the worst one too. Joint physical custody is the best when parents cooperate, circumstances allow for it, and children are the right age and personality. In other circumstances, joint physical custody can be the worst.

Because I want you to make joint physical custody the best it can possibly be for you and your children, let's take a careful look at what makes the arrangement better or worse.

## Practicalities

There are a number of practical considerations to take into account when considering joint physical custody. In order to maintain more equal time with their children, parents need to live reasonably close to one another. Both parents also need readily available transportation to get their children between homes, as well as to school or childcare. Of course, parents must have space for their children to live in each of their homes too, and they need the money to pay for it.

The added costs surely are one reason why joint physical custody is more common in families with higher incomes. But if you and your ex live pretty close to one another, and you have the space so your children can feel at home in both your homes, joint physical custody is a practical option, and hopefully more than that.

## Cooperative, Distant, or Angry Coparenting

Some advocates (not me) argue that parents should *always* have joint physical custody—even in an angry divorce. They assert that joint physical custody is best, even when parents do not agree to it. These people want judges to order joint physical custody in contested cases. Some even say that even when it puts children in the middle of their parents' conflict, joint physical custody is better. A few of these advocates claim, hopefully, that joint physical custody will force angry parents to resolve their disputes.

But many professionals, including me, are worried that children can be harmed by joint physical custody when parents cannot contain their disputes in an angry divorce. As my Hierarchy of Children's Needs in Two Homes shows, parents need to be able to work together reasonably well to make joint physical custody work for their children. In fact, some excellent research done in Australia provides clear evidence of widespread skepticism about joint physical custody in an angry divorce.[9]

Unlike in the United States, family law is the same across the entire country of Australia (over twenty million people). And since 2006, Australian national law has favored divorced parents sharing equal time with their children. If forced to make a custody decision for parents, Australian judges must first consider equal time. If they decide against equal time, Australian law says that judges must next consider "substantial and significant" shared time.

Despite the law, only about one in five parents share joint physical custody in Australia. But the really interesting finding is how the frequency of shared care (the term Aussies use for joint physical custody) differs based on coparenting style. A major study found that in 2009, 59 percent of parents shared joint physical custody when they had a cooperative relationship. Among parents with a distant relationship, only 21 percent did. And for parents with an angry relationship, the percentage declined to 19 percent.

What about cases where judges need to decide custody?

In my view, one good definition of an angry divorce is when you have to ask a judge to make that vital parenting decision for you. Well, in 2012, Australian judges ordered shared care in only 3 percent of these contested cases. That isn't a typo: three percent. And this percentage represented a *decrease* compared to previous years under the 2006 Australian law. Even though Australian law required them to first consider equal and then substantial and significant shared parenting time, the judges still decided against shared care 97 percent of the time.

Clearly, a great many judges, and parents, see an angry divorce as creating problems for children living with joint physical custody. Some direct research on children also shows the same thing. Increased conflict between parents predicts more problems among children living in joint physical custody.

The importance of cooperative coparenting to making joint

physical custody work leads me to want to repeat my goal for you: I want you to make your family circumstances the best they can possibly be, so you can make joint custody work for your children. If you have an angry or even a distant divorce, the work you face involves improving your coparenting partnership. You don't need to "be friends" with your ex. You do need to try to find ways to work together in the business of parenting your children in two homes.

## Children's Age and Personality

Children's age and personality are two more factors to consider in deciding on whether to try joint physical custody. For reasons I elaborate on in Chapters 4 and 5, joint physical custody does not work well for very young children, who benefit from having a stable, secure base early in life. At the other end of childhood, adolescents sometimes rebel against dividing their time between their parents' homes. A teenager's own schedule can be complicated enough without the transitions introduced by joint physical custody (see Chapter 8). But joint physical custody can be a great arrangement for preschoolers and school-age children (and often for adolescents) if you and your ex can find a way to make it work for them.

Right now, I hope all of this reminds you of one of my main points: A parenting plan that lasts a lifetime grows and changes along with your children. Sharing a lot of time with your children may not work for them or for you right now. But this can change. Change can be good for your children, and, of course, for you too.

In addition to age, you should know that some children just have a hard time with joint physical custody for their own reasons. A child's personality, special needs, or emotional problems can make switching homes feel chaotic. Some kids *really* need sameness, routine, and predictability. They get way out of sorts when their "stuff" is a mess—or at their other house.

Unfortunately, there is little research predicting which kids will do better or worse based on their personality or mental health needs. One fascinating study (from Belgium) found that teenagers who were more conscientious did less well in joint physical custody than in the mother's sole custody.[10] The opposite was true for less conscientious children, who did better in a shared time arrangement than living primarily with just one parent. The researchers speculated that the disruptions of living in two homes are stressful for conscientious children, who gravitate toward plans and predictability. For less-conscientious children, the benefits of having a close relationship with both parents outweighed the costs of going back and forth—and their personality may have made back-and-forth not such a big deal anyway.

Research predicting which kids will struggle in joint physical custody, and which ones will thrive, is sparse and tentative. I would never recommend for or against joint physical custody based on your child's conscientiousness. But the research makes an important point. Some kids flourish in shared physical custody, and some don't, for reasons that have more to do with them than their parents.

## Finding a Schedule That Works

Fortunately, I have a solution to the dilemma of trying to predict whether your child will adapt well to joint physical custody. Experiment. You don't need to guess whether shared physical custody will work—and then be stuck with it if you're wrong. You can *see* if joint physical custody works for your children. If it does, that's awesome. But if joint physical custody or whatever schedule isn't working, you can and should try Plan B. Come up with another arrangement. You and your ex can both remain deeply involved in your child's life, while addressing what wasn't working about the plan you tried.

For example, maybe you and your ex think that a week on/week off arrangement will work best for your six-year-old daughter. You try the schedule for six weeks, but your daughter, an only child, seems to struggle with being away from both of you for a whole week.

If so, you may try dividing each week for her instead. She spends Wednesday afternoon through Saturday afternoon with one parent, and Saturday afternoon through Wednesday morning with the other.

Or you may try the much-discussed 2-2-5-5 schedule. She spends Mondays and Tuesdays with one parent, and Wednesdays and Thursdays with the other parent. You take turns alternating three-day weekends from Friday until Monday morning. (The schedule is called 2-2-5-5 because these are the number of days a child spends consecutively in one house during any two-week period.)

Or perhaps your ten-year-old son's schoolwork suffers as a result of midweek transitions or a week-to-week rotation. If so, he may do better with having one "headquarters" for the school week and the school year. You can accommodate this schedule, yet still ensure that he spends lots of time with both of you. How? You can think creatively about weekends, school vacations, and summers. He can spend school time mostly with one parent, and vacation time more with the other (or equally between both).

Or you could come up with ways where he can spend lots of time, but not a lot of overnights, with one of you.

And don't forget that the new schedule is subject to change too. Maybe his schoolwork will improve with maturity. Or after some time passes, maybe he will get more used to your divorce and to living in two homes. Or maybe the "headquarters" idea really is the best plan, but your house becomes the new headquarters when your son starts high school.

Another possibility to consider is that the problem is not the schedule. It's the transitions. If so, see if you can craft a plan with fewer transitions. Or you may change the way transitions work.

Consider changing the timing, location, and nature of the transition, including basics (like who does the drop-off) and the emotional climate of the exchange (like tension between you and your ex—or the intrusion of your own anxieties about separating from your children). Maybe *you* are making transitions hard on your child. If so, you can change that, even if you have to pretend to feel different than you really feel.

Let me give you a detailed example of how all of this can work.

## Bethany, Roger, and Clan Change the Plan

When I first met Bethany and Roger, I had experimentation in the back of my mind, along with other principles to encourage child-focused creativity, which I summarize shortly.

Roger and Bethany had been married for sixteen years. They had been separated for almost two years but were legally divorced only recently. They also had a "problem" I could appreciate: Four children, ages thirteen, twelve, nine, and three. Yikes! As a father of five children, I could sympathize, and I told them so.

Within minutes, it was clear to me that Bethany and Roger were both high-energy, intelligent, and successful businesspeople and parents. Roger had built a business from scratch. It was now worth several million dollars. He was semiretired, managing his company from a distance, and devoting himself to his family and his athletic pursuits.

Bethany had limited herself to twenty-five flexible hours of work per week during her marriage, so she would be available for the children. (Roger had worked sixty-plus hours a week when building his company.) Despite her limited schedule, Bethany still worked her way up the corporate ladder. But she had made a recent change too. She quit her job to become executive director of a small nonprofit organization. The change was not for the children, though. It was for her. She now worked thirty-five flexible hours per week. But unlike her previous position, her new job fulfilled and engaged her.

I never know whether new mediation clients will be cooperative, distant, or angry. I always prepare for World War III, just in case. But after fifteen minutes, I knew that Bethany and Roger fit squarely into the cooperative category. They glowed when speaking about their children. They were mostly respectful of each other too, despite their strong personalities. Watching them, I could still sense some lingering pain over their failed marriage. But Bethany and Roger focused their high energy and strong emotions on the future, not their past. As parents, they respected and were grateful for one another. As individuals, they were moving forward.

But they talked openly about the complications of trying to parent four children in two homes. Parenting four children *is* complicated, especially when parenting apart.

The problem that brought them to see me was this: With the help of their lawyers, Roger and Bethany had negotiated a week-to-week schedule for sharing time with their children. The one exception was Bella, their youngest. They separated when Bella was two. The parents agreed that, until she was three and a half years old, Bella would stay mostly with her mother. The parents didn't want to disrupt Bella's clear attachment to and preference for her mother while she was very young. So during Roger's week with the other three kids, Bella had spent only the weekend plus Wednesday overnight with her dad.

About two months earlier, Bella had turned three and a half, and her planned week-to-week schedule kicked in. Both Roger and Bethany worried that Bella was struggling with it.

Bethany said that Bella often asked her anxiously, "When do I go to Daddy's?" During transitions to Roger's house, Bethany had to tear Bella out of a desperate grasp onto her.

Roger said that Bella seemed fine at his house as long as she was engaged with her siblings or engrossed in some activity. But most evenings around bedtime, Bella cried for her mom. Getting her to sleep had become a struggle.

None of this had been much of a problem under the earlier schedule. And both parents agreed that things had not gotten better after close to two months with the new plan.

Bethany and Roger knew they did not have a legal problem. Neither of them had even called their lawyers. They came to me partly for help in negotiating a new plan, but also for some expert advice and guidance.

When meeting with Roger and Bethany, I worked through my mental checklist of possible problems. I asked them questions like these: How did Roger spend time with Bella at his house? How did Bethany spend time with Bella at her house? How did they manage transitions between homes? How did Bella act in all of these circumstances? Did the parents have any worries about Bella's emotional adjustment, health, and well-being? How did Bella get along with her siblings? How did the parents balance the time with all of their children's competing demands? How had the other children adjusted to the week-to-week schedule? How did they react to Bella's worries?

I also silently worked through another mental checklist of possible problems. Did Roger and Bethany *really* have a cooperative relationship? Could these competitive people be competing over Bella's affections? Was Roger genuinely attuned to the needs of a young child? Was Bethany having trouble letting go of her baby? Were other people contributing to Bella's struggles? Was Roger delegating too much parenting responsibility to his girlfriend, for example? Or perhaps was Bethany afraid that he did? Did either parent have an ulterior motive that may be undermining the schedule, for example, concern about a change in child support?

Luckily, I was able to cross off most of the items from my lists. Roger really had reset his priorities. He was doing lots of hands-on parenting. Bethany loved all of her children, but she was ready to let go. Neither of them had a "hidden agenda," where they were fighting about children but the real problem was money, a new relationship, or unresolved issues from the collapse of their marriage. Bella was a happy, healthy three-year-old in school, with her siblings, and mostly at home. The parents had honestly tried to make the new schedule work, and would stick with it if that was what we decided was best. But they wanted to make sure they were being sensitive to Bella's needs.

In the end, we all agreed that Bella still wasn't quite ready for a whole week away from her mother, despite the continuity provided by three older siblings. Three and a half is still young. The problem, it seemed, was that the parents were implementing a good plan a little too soon.

During our discussions, we also unearthed two other issues. One small problem was that Roger always picked up the children and dropped them off at Bethany's house. He was trying to make up for all the years when Bethany did most of the driving.

I appreciated Roger's good intentions, but I suggested that Bethany might try dropping the children off at Roger's, while he continued to drop them at Bethany's. Children usually transition away from a parent more easily when that parent drops them off. I asked Bethany to imagine how Bella might react if her preschool teacher came to pick her up. She might dawdle, protest, and cling to Mom in that situation too. But when Bethany dropped her off at preschool, Bella was prepared to say good-bye—and caught up in the excitement. Maybe they should try the same approach going from Bethany's house to Roger's house?

A second, bigger issue was the boys. The boys, who were twelve and thirteen, frequently complained to Roger, and increasingly to Bethany, that they never got to "do things" with Dad. Bella, or her eight-year-old sister, was "always in the way." And both of the parents felt that the boys' unhappiness was taking a toll on the girls.

Their brothers picked on them, and they could get quite mean when angry about the girls' interference with Dad.

After a few meetings, some head scratching, and plenty of time to mull over options, we came up with a new schedule to try. Bella would spend every other Wednesday through Sunday at Dad's, during his week, of course. Looking at the world through Bella's eyes, four days away from Mom seemed much more manageable than a whole week. Plus, adding the Thursday overnight to the earlier schedule would mean one less transition for Bella. And this compromise also seemed more like a step forward toward week-to-week, rather than a step back to their previous plan.

After five months, when summer vacation started, they would attempt the week-to-week schedule again. Everything was much more fluid in the summer. We all hoped that Bella, who turned four in July, would adjust more easily to week-to-week during the fun and freedom of summer. Her siblings would be around a lot more, and that should help too. If all went well, Bella might ease into a new school year with the week-to-week schedule working just fine. If we were wrong, well, we would meet again and come up with a different plan.

Roger and Bethany also agreed to try to accommodate the boys and all of their children. Roger would start dropping the girls off at Bethany's on Sunday mornings of his week, keeping the boys into the early evening. He also would pick up the boys on Bethany's Sundays, as long as that worked for her. This would give the three boys sports time on Sundays. Roger had already named it: "Sunday soccer." Plus, the change would shorten Bella's separation from Mom a little, and create some "girl time" too.

Roger also used mediation to tell Bethany that he and his girlfriend were planning to marry next year. He wanted her to hear the news from him, not from the children, whom he was planning to tell soon. Even though they had moved on, the news clearly was not easy for Roger to deliver, or for Bethany to hear.

But they managed their unease the way they usually did. They turned Roger's plans to remarry into a discussion of the children. Roger agreed that he would text Bethany once he had spoken to the children, so she would know that they knew. After that, Bethany would tell the children that she knew too, so the kids did not feel like they had a secret to keep. And Roger also made it clear that he would tell the kids that Krystal would remain their "adult friend," nothing more, nothing less. They already had a wonderful mother.

## Make "Share" a Verb, Not a Noun

Bethany and Roger weren't stuck on 50/50. Even though they were aiming for equal time, their focus was on their kids. Roger didn't lose time with Bella. Bethany didn't lose time with the boys. They both won when their children were happier.

Roger and Bethany *shared* parenting. For them, *share* was a verb. They shared parenting time, parenting responsibilities, and parenting joys and frustrations.

I worry that too many parents treat *share* as a noun. "I want my share. Fifty percent. Exactly. Right down to the penny."

I want you to approach sharing time with your children using creative, long-term, and child-focused principles like Roger and Bethany did. I want you to think beyond dividing your children like you divide a pie or a bank account.

In subsequent chapters, you will find specific alternative schedules to consider for children of different ages and as your children grow older. I hope you can approach this menu of alternatives and developmentally based concerns like Roger and Bethany did. Before you turn to this task, let me offer you some principles to keep in mind as you do.

# Parenting Time Principles

You may find it agonizing to think about dividing weeks, summers, and holidays with and without your children. Your task is complicated further, because no one—not me, your lawyer, whoever—can tell you what schedule is best for your children or you. You and your ex have to figure this out, like Bethany and Roger did.

No one has a one-size-fits-all solution. Your children are unique. But I can suggest some key principles to guide your decision making.

*Make child-focused decisions.* As I have said, and will repeat again, your parenting plan is about your children, not your divorce. If your focus is truly on your children, please accept my congratulations and admiration. You have mastered a difficult, emotional task by putting your love of your children ahead of your own "stuff."

*Be fair.* You want to be fair to your children. You want to be fair to yourself. And you want to be fair to your children's other parent. If being fair seems like a crazy, impossible idea, you need to revisit the child-focused principle.

*Be creative.* Roger and Bethany came up with a plan that was child-focused, fair, and creative. No judge would have ordered "boys' time" and "girls' time" on Sundays. No psychologist would know enough about the family to recommend that either. Bethany and Roger created their own plan for their own family. To help you think creatively, I will suggest all kinds of schedules for your consideration. But only you can create the best, custom-made schedule for your children and your family.

*Individualize.* As you think creatively, you want to consider off-the-rack parenting plans like week on/week off. But you may want to go further and individualize your schedule not only for your family but also for each of your children. Bethany and Roger did this. And if you do agree upon a somewhat different schedule for different children, you will have created *extra* time for each of you to be with your children. That's nice. Plus, your extra time now includes treasured one-on-one times. That's *really* nice.

*Experiment.* Once you have come up with a plan you think will work, try it for a while. A fair trial usually lasts between one and three months. You may have created a schedule that seems to fit your children's needs and yours too. But you cannot know if the plan is *really* going to work until you try it. Trying, evaluating, and maybe changing a parenting plan together with your ex can be challenging. But experimenting makes infinite sense. You shift your focus from what you *think* will work to, simply, what works.

*Plan long-term and be open to change.* Long-term planning means you view time with your children in terms of months and years, not just days of the week. You can come up with a schedule that works well for you and your child now. But you and your ex should also plan to make changes as your child develops and your lives develop too. You can anticipate changes when your baby becomes a toddler, your preschooler starts kindergarten, or your preteen starts high school.

You also can expect changes if you start a new job, maybe have to move, or as always happens, life pulls you in some unexpected direction. When confronting possible but unplanned changes like relocation, it often makes more sense to decide *how* you will rearrange the schedule instead of what you will do. But, like Roger and Bethany, you may want to make specific plans for things that clearly will change, like your children's developmental transitions. Some people find a specific plan reassuring. Either way, if you plan long-term, you can expect—and hopefully welcome—the inevitability of change. And if you also agree that your current plan does not have to last forever, you will find it easier to reach an agreement now.

*Make your own decisions.* I want to give you lots of ideas. So will your friends and the professionals you may work with. But in the end, I want you to make your own decisions about your own children. Honestly, I thought Bethany and Roger were a bit too ambitious in trying to move Bella to the week-to-week schedule. But in the end, I always defer to parents. You are the ultimate expert on your children and your family.

Together, these principles are the keys to creating a parenting plan to last a lifetime. Whatever schedule you create, it is unlikely to remain exactly the same from birth onward. What can stay the same through those years, and beyond, is your plan to work flexibly with your ex in raising your children in two homes.

## PART 2

# A Developmental Approach to Parenting Plans

## CHAPTER 4

# Infants: Attachment Security

No matter how old your child may be, you worry that divorce will mean losing time with your child and influence in his or her life. But if you are the mother or father of an infant (birth to eighteen months), the anxiety can feel overwhelming. How can you be apart from the perfect baby that you just brought into this world? How can you do this to your infant? How can your ex do this to you both?

There may be other stomach-turning ingredients in your bubbling cauldron of fear. You have not had much time with your infant. You may not have had much with your partner either. Nicole and Justin, the couple I introduced in Chapter 1, were lucky in this regard—if you can call anything about splitting up when your children are so tiny "lucky." They had been married for several years, and parented their two-and-a-half-year-old daughter together.

Some parents of infants are splitting up when they have been married only briefly or not at all. Some have never lived together. Some barely know one another.

You may be one of those parents.

Then add this to your stew. You may be facing the prospect of coparenting across two homes when this is your first time parenting at all. How are you supposed to know what schedule is best for your baby? You may be still trying to master the art of getting your baby to eat and sleep! You may be juggling changing diapers, running your household, trying to keep your job, staying awake, and just managing all that baby stuff. You may be constantly trying to figure out the best ways to get your baby to stop crying. Is he . . . hungry? Tired? In need of a diaper change? Scared? Lonely? Just being fussy? What?

These kinds of questions can seem hard enough. They are.

On top of all of this, maybe you have never been apart from your baby. You don't want to leave her alone. You don't trust a sitter—or your ex—to take care of her as well as you do. Or maybe you are away from him for eight hours a day, while he is in childcare. You feel guilty enough about leaving him already. Now, you are supposed to see him even less, so he can be with his dad or mom?

Just how much can you handle?

Take a deep breath. In this chapter, I offer you detailed guidance about raising babies in two homes. I discuss a few controversies and give you advice about finding the best middle ground for your baby.

So you don't need to panic. You are going to get through this.

Your anxieties will not dissolve. And they shouldn't. Your worries motivate you, keep you focused, and get you to ask good questions. You are going to take wonderful care of your baby, despite your divorce.

In fact, it won't be long before you are reading the chapters on toddlers, preschoolers, and school-age children. If you have older children, you're reading about them now. Even if you don't have older children, you still may want to read ahead. Doing so will give you a good idea about what's coming next for your baby and for you—coming before you know it.

## Parenting Infants in Two Homes

Deciding how to parent an infant in two homes may seem like something that affects only a small number of parents, but that's wrong. About 20 percent of divorces occur within the first five years of marriage, when children are still very young.[1] *Forty-one percent* of babies in the United States today are born outside marriage, only about half to cohabiting couples.[2] And cohabiting relationships break up faster and more frequently than marriages.[3]

So we are talking about big, important numbers of parents. You are not alone, even though you may feel like you are.

Parenting an infant is enchanting. No words can describe the warm glow of holding your baby close, breathing her smell, and feeling her mold herself into your body. What's the meaning of life? Your newborn is your answer, at least for now and for as much of the future as you can foresee.

Parenting an infant also is challenging. Developing patterns around basic activities like eating and sleeping is anything but simple. If only he would sleep through the night—or for four hours straight. Little things like running to the store now require planning and effort. Diapers need to be carried everywhere and changed, well, wherever.

You have so much to anticipate, and so much to worry about. You carefully mark your baby's physical growth, emerging cognitive skills, and social development. You do this for fun and for reassurance. He's on time. She's ahead of schedule! Why isn't he crawling? Your friend's baby is a month younger, and she started crawling six weeks ago.

How can you do all of this across two homes?

You start by focusing on what's most important: love. Love is the most basic psychological need in Maslow's hierarchy, and the most essential element of authoritative parenting in my Hierarchy of Children's Needs in Two Homes. Love also comes first in importance in your baby's—or any baby's—social and emotional development.

## Attachment Security

The central emotional task for infants is forming a secure *attachment*, the selective bond that develops between a baby and her caregiver(s).[4] A *secure* attachment is one where a baby "knows"—emotionally, not intellectually—that a familiar, reliable adult is available and will respond with sensitivity to her signals. A securely attached baby knows that she will be loved, supported, and protected. She knows, emotionally, that her attachment figure will respond to her distress, reassure her when she is anxious, and keep her safe if danger approaches.

Knowing he can trust someone special, a baby's sense of security allows him to trust others too (once they become familiar to him). A secure attachment also gives babies and toddlers a safe base from which to explore their ever-expanding world. And it gives them a place to return to seek reassurance when frightened.

Not any adult will do. Attachments are selective. Parents and other caregivers promote secure attachments by being consistently available, sensitive, and responsive to their baby's needs. And attachments develop over time. The central attachment figure, usually a mother, or perhaps a father, "proves" herself or himself to the very young child by being consistently sensitive and consistently responsive. The caregiver's actions make the attachment secure—or not.

## The Evolutionary Logic of Attachments

Attachments are basic. Attachments are about biology, not psychology. A rudimentary form of attachment called *imprinting* explains why ducklings swim in a line behind their mothers on a pond in the springtime. Ducklings' desire keeps them close to their mothers or, if necessary, to a substitute caregiver.

Ducklings and infants form attachments to whomever they interact with. I have a photo from a British newspaper showing a duckling following a hen around a barnyard. This special bond developed when a duck egg got mixed together and hatched with chicken eggs. You may recall this happening to a baby swan in the children's story "The Ugly Duckling."

In fact, the Austrian biologist Konrad Lorenz, who studied geese, not ducks, won a Nobel Prize in 1973 for his work documenting the process of imprinting. In one of his studies, Lorenz acted as the substitute caregiver for his goslings. Sure enough, they imprinted on him. Search the Internet and you will find videos of Lorenz's baby geese following him around like Mother Goose.

For fathers, the point is this: Children form attachments based on interaction, not gender. Your baby will become attached to you, perhaps strongly, if you care for her frequently—and are sensitive and responsive in doing so.

In humans, we have a word for the desire that motivates the formation of attachments: love. Love motivates attachment behavior in babies, but love and attachment are not the same thing. As children grow, eventually into adults, love becomes bigger, more complex, and involves much more than just attachment.

Yet the evolutionary logic of attachment is about survival, not love. Helpless babies, and ducklings, are more likely to survive if they remain close to their mothers (or substitute caregivers). The infant's motivation to form an attachment has been bred by evolution. In other words, babies are born to love, selectively.

The logic of evolution, maintaining proximity to the caregiver, helps us understand when and how babies form attachments. Ducks and geese imprint on their caregivers almost immediately. Evolution dictates that they must, because ducklings and goslings can wander away into danger almost from birth.

In humans, attachments become notably strong during the second six months of life. Separation anxiety emerges around eight or nine months, and stranger fears follow soon thereafter. Why then and not earlier? Babies begin to crawl around the same time. Soon, babies can walk away from the safety of their caregiver. The security of love and the anxiety of separation keep growing babies and their caregivers close together. The evolution of infant-caregiver love is profoundly logical.

## Multiple Attachments and Attachment Hierarchies

Babies typically form attachments to more than one adult. A baby may be attached to Mom, Dad, Grandma, and perhaps a child-care provider. Yet attachments are hierarchical.[5] They play favorites. Children know who they want to go to *first*, when they are frightened or hurt. Stereotypically, you can envision a mildly injured toddler screaming, "Not you! *I want Mommy!*" even as a loving father desperately tries to comfort his child in an effort to assist his harried mate.

It is adaptive for infants and toddlers to form multiple attachments and to have a hierarchy of attachment figures. Multiple attachments give babies options. If one attachment figure is unavailable, well, fortunately there is another adult to protect you. Whew! The hierarchy of attachments makes for fast decisions. If danger appears, an infant needs to seek protection *now*, not decide which attachment figure to run to. With a hierarchy of attachment, that critical decision is made in advance.

Psychologists call the collection of an infant's or child's attachment figures the *circle of security*. The circle of security works wonderfully—as long as the loop is closed to protect a child, not pulled apart to divide her. Conflict and division between attachment figures promotes insecurity, not a sense of security.

## Building Secure or Insecure Attachments

The formation of at least one secure attachment early in life is important psychologically. About two thirds of all babies are securely attached to their primary caregiver. One third are insecurely attached.[6]

An *insecure attachment*, caused by parenting that is not consistently sensitive and responsive, fails to teach love's lessons. Insecurely attached children cannot trust their caregiver unconditionally. As a result, they may have trouble trusting others, or ultimately themselves. Having an insecure attachment forecasts a variety of future difficulties. Insecurely attached babies often grow into children who have trouble regulating their emotions and their relationships. They also may experience a variety of psychological problems.

Unfortunately, you cannot assess your infant's attachment security with some easy, ten-item checklist. The best assessments involve complex procedures. And these techniques are available only for use as research tools, not as clinical instruments. So you cannot even go to your pediatrician or local psychologist to get your infant tested for attachment security. But an introduction to the original gold-standard measure of attachment security can help you understand what a secure attachment looks like.

The measure is called "the strange situation."[7] It was developed by Mary Ainsworth, a famous Canadian American psychologist and giant in the field of attachment theory. (I was lucky enough to work closely with Ainsworth in developing the clinical psychology program in my early years at the University of Virginia.)

Briefly, the strange situation involves the observation of a baby, typically about one year old, playing in a room with a parent, most commonly the mother. According to a standardized procedure, a stranger then enters the room. After a while, the mother leaves. But soon the mother returns. Both adults eventually leave the baby alone. Then the stranger returns. The mother returns next. Finally, the stranger leaves. Throughout these procedures, observers note several key aspects of the baby's behavior in relation to the attachment figure.

Securely attached babies explore away from the attachment figure, using her as a safe base. When the attachment figure is present, these babies engage the stranger. But securely attached children also show distress when the attachment figure leaves. In turn, these babies are pleased and seek physical comfort from the attachment figure when she returns. Soon, securely attached babies are exploring away from their attachment figure again.

In contrast to secure attachments, psychological scientists have identified three types of insecurely attached babies. *Anxious-avoidant* babies explore little, generally ignore the attachment figure, and show little emotion upon separation or reunion. *Anxious-resistant* babies, sometimes called *anxious-ambivalent*, are distressed even before separation and clingy and difficult to soothe afterward. *Disorganized* babies do not seek or use proximity in a well-developed fashion. Generally considered to have the most troubling form of insecure attachment, disorganized babies may act fearfully at different times throughout the strange situation but not clearly in response to separation. They also exhibit contradictory emotions and actions, such as approaching and then avoiding the attachment figure.

These observations from the laboratory may help you better gauge your baby's reactions to both you and your ex, as well as to transitions between you. You do not want to be overly analytical in diagnosing attachment problems in your baby's relationship with you—or with your ex. But you do want to respond to her signals. You want her to be able to use you both the way nature designed the attachment system. You want to be a source of security, comforting your baby when she is distressed. You also want to be confident in her independence, encouraging exploration when she feels safe.

Doing so will help you to maintain or build her secure attachment to you.

Attachment security is a foundation of psychological health. Benefits reverberate throughout emotional, cognitive, and physical development. But insecurely attached babies are not doomed. With time—and especially with the support, protection, and love found in new or newly improved relationships, many children can and do develop a fresh sense of security.

## Attachment Insecurity and Divorce

Several studies have found that infants are more likely to have an insecure attachment to their mothers when their parents are divorced rather than married. The increased risk for insecurity likely is attributable to two factors. First, because of their own emotional preoccupations, divorced parents often are less sensitive and responsive to their children than are married parents. Second, attachment security may be disrupted by the repeated and sometimes prolonged separations involved in the plans some parents craft for sharing time with their babies.

The goal in addressing the first problem is clear-cut and uncontroversial. Divorced parents need to work to be sensitive and responsive to their infant's cues, despite their own struggles. But again, don't panic. You do not need to become a helicopter parent, constantly hovering over your baby. In fact, studies show that parents of securely attached infants are only sensitive and responsive to their infants about half the time!

All parents get tired, distracted, and irritated, including you. The key to rearing a securely attached infant is how you manage those inevitable ruptures. Your baby may become distraught when you suddenly leave him to go turn off an overflowing pot on the stove.

Eventually, you need to soothe him. That is being sensitive and responsive. But by all means, prevent a fire (or just a mess) even if your sudden departure causes (temporary) separation distress in your nine-month-old son!

There is much more controversy[8] about the second potential contribution to attachment insecurity. Parents—and professionals—are debating questions like these: What schedules ensure that babies develop a secure attachment to at least one of their parents, and hopefully both? Should babies spend few, if any, overnights away from the primary caregiver, usually their mother, in order to protect attachment security? Or should babies spend lots of overnights with both of their parents, so they can develop secure attachments to both?

So be prepared to find conflicting opinions about what to do, even among professionals. You also should know that only a handful of studies have directly investigated this topic. (We will have a look at them shortly.)

And beware. Gender politics have entered the nursery. "Mothers' rights" advocates tend to claim that attachment relationships are fragile. "Fathers' rights" advocates tend to claim that attachment is flexible—or overrated. Since most infants form primary attachment relationships with their mothers, the self-serving nature of each of these positions is transparent.

The gender politics are fueled by genuine theoretical differences about the nature of attachment security and what experiences threaten it. Unfortunately, like the political positions, these theoretical views also tend to be polarized.

One extreme thinks of attachments as bonded with superglue. Those who hold this perspective fear that attachments can be irreparably broken by virtually *any* prolonged separation from a primary caregiver. Some advocates of "attachment parenting" strenuously argue that parents must be almost constantly available to a baby, or the attachment bond will be broken. In reality, though, parenting with superglue is more likely to create insecurity than supersecurity. Whether divorced or married, parents who are fearful about virtually any separation from their infant often are responding to their own anxieties, not their baby's needs. Remember, attachment is all about security *and* independence.

The other extreme sees attachments as superelastic. Those who offer this argument say that infants whose parents are divorced can have *two* primary attachment figures, as long as they spend a lot of time, including lots of overnights, with both parents. But this claim is mathematically impossible. Two firsts? It also ignores the evolutionary logic of attachment. As we discussed, multiple attachments make sense. They give you options. But if you believe babies can have two *primary* attachment figures, answer this question: Whom should ducklings follow on a pond if Mom and Dad swim in opposite directions? If the duckling doesn't have a preference, that is, a hierarchy of attachment figures, it's going to be stuck in the middle—and in danger.

Very young children, like children of all ages, need a circle of security that supports rather than divides their emotional life. Multiple attachment figures need to work together, or they undermine each other and their infant's feeling safe, secure, and loved. In fact, research shows that conflict between parents contributes to insecure attachment in divorced and married families.

## Schedules for Infants

In thinking about creating a schedule for your infant, you need to understand both the importance of attachment security and the limits of arguments about it. Ideally, you and your ex will work together to build your infant's secure attachment to you both.

So what is the best schedule for infants to spend time with both of their parents? Honestly, no one can answer this question with scientific certainty. But you want and need guidance, so let me suggest what range of schedules appears to be best—and how and why I reach this conclusion.

## A Wide Gulf of Opinion

As I said, opinions vary widely. On the bonding-with-superglue side of the debate, some experts recommend *no* overnights away from the primary caregiver (usually Mom) until a child is three or even four years old.[9] On the superelastic side, some experts say that babies should rotate overnights with Mom and Dad every day or two, avoiding long separations from either parent.[10]

Yes. That's a huge difference.

My response to the no-overnights argument is this: Are divorced (or married) parents undermining attachment security when they leave their babies with Grandma for a night or two? My response to the back-and-forth argument is this: What grandmother would approve of a baby swapping parents, homes, cribs, and routines every day?

Just to be clear, I desperately looked forward to an occasional night or two alone with my wife when my children were babies. Thanks, Grandma (and Grandpa)! And my grandmother, if she were still alive, would vehemently disapprove of a back-and-forth schedule. I can hear my nana saying, "The poor baby. Be sensible!"

## Middle Ground?

So where is the sensible middle ground?

Recently, my graduate students and I completed the largest direct study ever done on infant overnights and attachment security in babies.[11] The study included 1,023 one-year-olds drawn from a sample (called Fragile Families) that represents the population of twenty U.S. cities with over 200,000 people. This research linked frequent overnights away from the mother during the first year of life to a significantly increased risk for attachment insecurity. In this study, we defined "frequent" as an average of one or more overnights per week. The rate of insecurity was 43 percent for infants with frequent overnights away from their mother during their first year of life, compared to 16 percent for those with fewer overnights.

To get a sense of where you stand in comparison to others, you may be interested to know that only 7 percent of this sample shared overnights with their babies as often as once a week or more. Another 6 percent had an occasional overnight, less than once a week but more than once a month. A quarter of fathers had at least one overnight with their baby, but that happened less often than once a month. A little over half of dads just saw their babies during the day. Ten percent of fathers had no contact with their infant.

As you think of these numbers, keep the population of large cities in mind. The Fragile Families sample has many more unmarried, low-income minorities than the entire U.S. population. No one knows the numbers for all of the United States, although a study of a nationally representative sample of Australian families found comparable percentages.

Only three other studies in the entire world have examined the relationship between overnights away from mothers and the well-being of infants in divorce.[12] Two of the three studies found reasons for caution. So, including my work, three of four studies raise concerns about babies spending too many overnights away from the primary caregiver in the first year to eighteen months of life.

Four studies, all with flaws of one sort or another, do not provide scientific certainty, as I said earlier. But that's all we have right now.

And you should still wonder: How many is too many? Once a week? That's the definition I used in my research. An Australian study used the same definition and also found some problems among infants with frequent versus fewer overnights. So right now, less than once a week is the best evidence-based guideline.

So, as a rule, you probably want to think about having less than one overnight per week away from the primary caregiver during your baby's first year of life. But rules have exceptions. In my study, not every baby with frequent overnights had an insecure attachment. And, of course, I have no way of knowing what will work for your baby. You certainly cannot know for sure either. The research can give you some guidelines, but let's go back to some of the principles we discussed in Chapter 3: Experiment and be open to change over time.

## Cooperative, Distant, and Angry Coparents

If you and your ex have a cooperative relationship and create a strong circle of security, I think you can be comfortable experimenting with occasional overnights, maybe one every two or three weeks, perhaps beginning around age six months or even sooner. If all goes well, you may move slowly to more regular overnights, perhaps one per week by age twelve or eighteen months.

As long as your baby seemed to be doing well, I think my nana would accept that plan. (Her approval was hard to win.) Of course, your baby's reactions are the key to evaluating your experiment. If she becomes overly distressed, clingy, or difficult to soothe (remember how attachment security and insecurity are assessed in the strange situation), you want to pull back. You also may pull back if her sleeping schedule is disrupted by the overnights. You can try to increase the frequency again in a month or two, or whenever you think she seems ready for another try.

Highly cooperative parents may try experimenting with a schedule that includes even more overnights at a younger age. In particular, I am a lot less worried about frequent overnights if your relationship is so good that your baby can stay in familiar surroundings while you and your ex exchange sleeping quarters for at least some overnights. A familiar crib, toys, and even smells promote a sense of security. This can make changing parents a lot less stressful. Some married parents take turns putting their baby to bed. If you and your ex are working together really well, you may try some variation on that plan.

You have far fewer options if your coparenting relationship is distant or especially if it's angry. If so, I recommend limiting the frequency of overnights during the first year or eighteen months. You may consider one every two weeks, or once a month, or maybe none at all—yet. In this case, the parent who has few overnights should have the opportunity to spend time alone with the infant during relatively brief but frequent daytime contacts. (Frequent daytime contacts are a good idea even if you have regular overnights.) A common guideline is one to three such visits per week, each lasting perhaps three to six hours.

If your baby is in childcare, this is an ideal time for a visit (assuming that fits with work schedules). The childcare facility is a neutral place for pickups, so you and your ex don't need to interact. And everyone gains, since your baby loses no time with the parent who is doing most of his care.

I realize that accepting limited contact is incredibly difficult if you are the parent who is getting few or no overnights. If that's you, let me remind me of a few things. First, this is not about you, or your ex. This is about your baby. Second, as always, you can create options for yourself—and create a far better family environment for your children—if you can find ways to improve your coparenting. Work on that, even if it feels like you are the only one putting in the effort. Third, we are not talking about forever. Even if you have an angry divorce, I'm comfortable with parents trying overnights (starting with fewer and moving up to one per week) around age twelve months and certainly by eighteen months (see Chapter 5).

## A Yellow Light of Caution

Let me offer a few last thoughts about the reasons behind my recommendations. I advocate for a somewhat cautious middle ground. Why?

Here is how I see it. Research is inconclusive. Evidence is not like a red light: No overnights ever! Evidence also is not a green light: As many overnights as you want! What little evidence there is suggests caution—a yellow light.

I know some people speed up to get through a yellow light; others slam on the brakes. I'm usually in the first category when driving my car. But when it comes to babies and attachment security, I am braking. Why? I am much more worried about infants having zero secure attachments than I am about them having a secure attachment to only one parent (for the time being). That second relationship—your relationship—can and should grow. He'll be a toddler soon, and a preschooler in another blink of your eyes.

I'm taking the long view to try to protect your baby. I hope you will too.

You also may want to know that while there are controversies, I am far from alone in suggesting that you step on the brake when it comes to protecting your baby's attachment security. My suggestions are broadly consistent with (if a bit more liberal than) those made by some attachment specialists. For example, expert attachment researcher Alan Sroufe of the University of Minnesota, who does *not* conduct divorce or custody research, said this about preferred schedules:

> *My opinion, informed by our research is this: for babies prior to 18 months of age, overnights away from the primary carer should be quite rare. It is not that you couldn't do something like one every two weeks. But I would not start with that. The*

*situation needs to grow and change over time. So you say for the first 3 months there are no overnights, but in fact, maybe even more frequent day contacts than we'll have later. After the first 3 months, we can do an overnight every few weeks, but we'll back down a little bit on the frequent day contact. You would get to more overnights at the right pace. Why can't court orders be written like that?*[13]

Similarly, in their analysis of infants and overnights, child custody experts Jennifer McIntosh, Marsha Kline Pruett, and Joan Kelly outlined a set of concerns that fit nicely with my Hierarchy of Children's Needs in Two Homes.[14] They worried about an infant's safety first, followed by a baby's trust and security with each parent, the parents' mental health, the baby's health, development and behavioral adjustment, coparenting quality, and practical factors like the distance between parents' homes. The number of overnights these experts recommended for infants and toddlers ranged from none, when there are many problems on their list; one to four per month, when there are a few; and five or more overnights per month, when most problems are absent.

That's a long way from rotating homes daily. It is also a long way from no overnights until age four. And it's pretty consistent with what I've outlined here.

Maybe experts are finding some common ground in the middle of this vehement debate.

## Divorcing in Infancy versus Moving into Infancy When Divorced

A parenting plan to last a lifetime is one that grows and changes along with children's changing needs. To help you anticipate and make changes in your parenting plan, in every chapter I discuss differences between divorcing when your child is a given age versus moving into that developmental stage when you are already divorced.

This is a basic distinction. For example, the experience of teenagers is much different if you split during their adolescence than if you separated when they were young but they have now entered their teen years. Obviously, you and your ex are parenting teenagers in both cases. But you, your ex, and your teenage children will have a different outlook on a divorce that occurred long ago compared to a divorce that is happening right now.

If you are the parent of an infant, this obvious difference in experience is not so obvious. Parents who separate when their children are babies cannot have much of a history of living apart.

## Your History with Your Ex

Still, parents of infants can have different experiences of being together themselves. Perhaps you and your ex have been married or cohabited for some time. Maybe you raised other children together. You may have lived together for a substantial part of your baby's young life. If so, like Nicole and Justin, you and your ex have a real relationship. You have a complicated relationship, to be sure, but you do have a history.

If this is you, each of your relationships with your baby is likely to be better developed too. During his critical early development, you and your ex may have interacted regularly with your infant for several months or more. Hopefully, you each supported your baby's relationship with each other during this time too. These kinds of experiences can promote your baby's secure attachment to you both. Together with your more extensive history together, this can create more options for how you can share time with your baby now.

These same kinds of advantages do not extend to parents who split early in infancy or perhaps who never lived together at all. If this is you, you need to expect your infant to take longer to develop a secure attachment to both of you. You may be sharing little or no time with your baby right now. This means that she may be developing a secure attachment to one of you. But she may not have much of a relationship with the other one.

You cannot change this circumstance overnight, and you should not try to do so. For the time being, your options for sharing time are going to be more limited. If you want to protect your baby's budding mental health, you are going to have to move slowly in developing his relationship with both of you. You probably are also going to have to move slowly in developing your relationship with each other.

These are some general considerations. Let me be more concrete.

## Nicole and Justin's Parenting Plan

Nicole and Justin separated two months after I first met them, when their baby, Nathan, was now nine months old. Once they began to get their emotions under control, they became very child focused. Both parents worked full time, but they agreed that Nicole had done most of the hands-on childcare. Nathan probably was securely attached to both of them. Yet he clearly preferred Mom. Justin could comfort Nathan when he had him alone. But Nathan typically "demanded" to be held by Nicole as soon as he saw her.

Justin and Nicole wanted to ensure that Nathan would adjust well to their separation. They believed that at this critical stage in his development, his attachment to Nicole needed special protection. They also knew that long separations from either of them would undermine Nathan's attachment to both of them. And as you may recall from Chapter 1, Justin wanted to remain *very* involved in parenting. Nicole wanted this too, as long as her relationship with Nathan was protected.

It won't surprise you to learn that I agreed with their concerns.

Nicole and Justin developed a complex parenting plan—an initial experiment—in an effort to address their concerns and goals. Nathan would spend every weekend with Dad from 3 p.m. on Saturday until 3 p.m. on Sunday. Justin would take time off from work on Tuesday afternoons, pick up Nathan at daycare at 12 or 1, give him dinner, and return him to Nicole's house at 7 in the evening. On Thursdays, Justin would go to Nicole's home around 5:30 for a "family dinner." He then would put Nathan to bed at Nicole's house, while she went out to run errands.

They decided to follow the same schedule for their two-and-a-half-year-old daughter, Madeline. The one exception was that Madeline would spend every Tuesday overnight with Dad. He would drop her off at her daycare on Wednesday mornings.

Justin and Nicole's parenting plan is an example of the exception, not the rule, of what I typically recommend. The schedule involved several transitions, and a lot of contact between Nicole and Justin. But the arrangement also ensured lots of contact between the children and both parents, while allowing Nicole to remain available as a consistent attachment figure.

Nicole and Justin expected both of their children to experience some distress around transitions, just as they had with daycare at first. They also expected the children's distress to resolve quickly, because both children were attached to both parents. Perhaps most important, they promised to be honest in sharing information about the children's reactions, even if that meant revising their plan.

All of this would be way too complicated for many parents. But Nicole and Justin made it work.

## What If Nicole Barely Knew Justin?

What if Justin and Nicole barely knew each other? What if they only had seven-month-old Nathan, had not raised an older child together, were unmarried, and had, in fact, never lived together? What if they actually had only known each other for a few months before Nicole got pregnant? What if Nicole had done almost all the childrearing up to this point, and Justin had only seen Nathan alone a few times?

I hope it is obvious that I would never recommend a similarly complicated schedule under these circumstances. Before even considering overnights, I would want Nathan to build a relationship with Justin. The attachment that Nathan hopefully would develop to his dad would need to grow slowly.

I also would be even more concerned with protecting Nathan's secure attachment to his mom. And I would want to see if Justin and Nicole could build a relationship with each other too, before even considering anything complicated.

Still, I would encourage the parents to work on a plan that would evolve over time. For example, I might suggest that Nicole and Justin try an initial arrangement that involved something like this: Dad would be with Nathan every Saturday from 10 a.m. to 2 p.m., assuming this worked around Nathan's nap schedule. Dad also could see Nathan and play with him, remaining at his childcare center, on Tuesdays from noon until 2 or 3 p.m.

If Justin followed this schedule consistently for several weeks, and Nathan was becoming attached to him, we might expand the Saturday hours to include a nap. We also might lengthen Tuesdays by a couple of hours. Now, Dad probably would take Nathan away from the childcare center. Perhaps Justin would have Nathan all afternoon, eliminating the need for childcare and saving everyone some money. We would consider the experiment a success if Nathan managed transitions well and began using Justin as an attachment figure, as part of his circle of security.

We would take further steps in the coming months as Nathan developed a secure attachment to his dad. For example, we might add dinner with Dad on Thursday evenings. Or instead of another transition, we might lengthen Saturdays with Dad to include most of the day. And somewhere in this progression, we probably would try an overnight and see how that worked.

In short, we would work in the same direction as the real Justin and Nicole, but the pace would be slower. Future plans would be more tentative too. And we would need to evaluate the success of each change carefully, especially until Nicole and Justin developed a better coparenting relationship.

## A Leap of Faith: The Law and Divorced Parents' Evolving Agreements

The real Justin and Nicole wanted their schedule to evolve over time too. They tentatively planned that when Nathan was around two years old, Dad would start having two consecutive overnights with him and Madeline. Without putting the details in writing, they discussed how, in about a year or so, both kids would spend every Thursday and Friday overnight with Dad. Dad also would keep having dinner with the kids on Tuesdays. Maybe he would alternate overnights with each child after the Tuesday dinner, instead of just having Madeline. Eventually, perhaps when Nathan was three, Justin and Nicole wanted to follow a schedule that was 50/50, or something close to it.

All of this sounded (and sounds) reasonable to me. I hope it does to you too. But you should know that Justin took a leap of faith in agreeing to this plan. As we discussed in Chapter 3, judges, not divorced parents, have the ultimate legal authority to make these kinds of decisions. Because of this legal technicality, the agreement that Justin and Nicole made about their future parenting was not legally binding. Their agreement would not be legally binding even if Justin and Nicole spelled out future schedules in detail, included precise dates for making changes, and signed a carefully crafted contract. As I noted in Chapter 3, our laws do not give divorced parents the authority to enter into binding contracts like this.

Until the law changes, you need to know this: You too will be taking a leap of faith in making an agreement about how your parenting plan will evolve in the future.

Consider this. A clever attorney may encourage a duplicitous mother in Nicole's position to agree to make changes—with no intention of ever doing so. In a year, the lawyer could argue that the parents' agreement didn't matter to the children. Time did. And the children had lived mainly with Mom for a year. They should stay with her.

Of course, a clever attorney for Justin should foresee this potential tactic. The lawyer would then warn Justin that he needed to protect himself. The best way to do so would be to insist on getting more time with the children *now*. Even if Justin thought making changes over time was best for the children, his lawyer may encourage him to safeguard himself against Nicole's possible manipulations.

As you can easily foresee, this kind of maneuvering increases the likelihood of custody battles—and discourages sensitive, child-focused evolving agreements.

I still strongly recommend that you make a plan that evolves over time for your baby. But you need to be aware that a court may rule that any agreement you make is invalid.

Now you know another big reason why I want the law to treat divorced parents more like it treats married parents. Judges refuse to get involved in the *disagreements* between married parents. Our legal system understands that "No end of difficulties would arise should judges try to tell [married] parents how to bring up their children" (see Chapter 3).

I realize that when divorced parents disagree, judges sometimes need to make decisions for them. All I want is for our laws to respect divorced parents' *agreements*.

Until that happens, I want you to know about the legal risks you may be taking in agreeing to a parenting plan that will grow and change along with your infant. But I still hope that you put parenting first and legalities second.

## Talking to Children about Divorce

Unlike the parents of older children, you and your ex do not need to decide what and how to tell your infant about your divorce. In fact, you may be relieved to hear that children who were very young when their parents split often later say that they were not distressed by their parents' divorce. Why? They never knew a different kind of family life. Very young children are spared from a transition that older children typically find difficult, sometimes agonizing.

But another thing that changes as your children grow is how you explain your divorce to them. Eventually, you will want to talk to your child about what happened when she was a baby. So you should know that in the chapters to come, I discuss this topic. You will find suggestions about how to tell children of different ages that you are splitting up. And you will find ideas about providing a bit more explanation as your children grow and perhaps ask new questions about old issues.

## Parenting and Coparenting Infants

### MAJOR DECISIONS AND JOINT LEGAL CUSTODY CONCERNS

As the parents of an infant, you and your ex face only a few decisions that involve legal custody. (Recall from Chapter 3 that joint legal custody involves sharing decisions only about religion, schooling, and elective medical care.) You may or may not want to baptize your infant, for example. Or you may or may not choose to have your son circumcised, either as a part of a bris or for medical or cultural reasons.

If you and your ex share joint legal custody, you will need to make these kinds of decisions together.

If you have sole legal custody, you can make these choices on your own. Even so, it often is good practice at least to consult your coparent. You may also offer to include him in any important ceremonies. Put yourself in his shoes. Wouldn't you like to be asked? Your relationship may be strained now, but you have a long road of coparenting ahead of you. You are more likely to get to your destination if you start out together, even if the beginning is tense. And even if your ex rejects your offer, you have the solace of knowing that you made a generous gesture.

Of course, it's quite possible that you do not yet have an agreement about legal custody. What do you do then? Well, I advise you two to talk, maybe with the help of a third-party mediator, to see if you can find common ground. Married parents make these kinds of decisions all the time—without involving lawyers. If you two can agree, I don't see why you need a legal agreement yet.

If you don't have a legal custody order and you disagree, you are going to have to put things on hold. This is particularly true if your dispute is about something irreversible, like circumcising your son.

Even so, I urge you to first try to reach a decision together with the help of a mediator, a therapist, or collaborative lawyers.

Hire a trial lawyer only as a last resort. Why? It is much easier to become more adversarial than it is to de-escalate from legal warfare. Sure, sometimes you need to go to war. Sometimes your ex is seriously troubled, or worse. But for your baby's sake, before turning to legal weapons, give peace a chance.

## BREASTFEEDING

As you know, parenting a baby is a little more complicated than making a few big decisions. You constantly face new questions. When should we introduce solid food? And what foods do you want your baby to eat? Many parents today work hard to make sure their baby eats only organic. You may be one of them. Do you need to relax, or does your ex need to learn to make the effort to feed your baby right?

And here is an issue that almost certainly will arise. Should Dad's visits be limited based on the demands of breastfeeding? Or to facilitate an extended visit, should a nursing mother give a bottle of expressed milk to her ex? How long should a mother breastfeed her infant anyway?

Custody law does not even try to answer questions like these. Instead, the parents of infants—you and your ex—must try to develop ways to communicate and hopefully share decisions about these more routine parenting matters.

As an example of how to communicate and compromise, let's consider how you might handle important and often emotional questions about breastfeeding. (See Chapter 3 for tips on *how* to communicate about these kinds of issues.)

Your first step in making a decision should be to get information— objective information, not whatever you may have found on the web that supports your position. You can talk to your pediatrician—

together. (You may want to make it a habit to go to doctor appointments together. If you do, use this as a time to listen, not debate.) You are likely to hear that, noting its many health benefits, the American Academy of Pediatrics recommends *exclusive* breastfeeding for about the first six months of life. The academy then recommends introducing complementary foods together with continued breastfeeding until a baby is at least twelve months old.[15]

So breastfeeding is good for your baby's physical health. Breastfeeding probably has positive effects on your infant's emotional health too. Several studies have found that attachment security is not directly related to whether a baby is breastfed. But breastfeeding mothers are more sensitive and responsive to their infants.[16] As you know, maternal sensitivity and responsivity promote secure attachments.

Based on information like this, you may agree that breastfeeding is an important goal. If so, you are hardly alone. Roughly three quarters of American mothers currently breastfeed their babies, and that number is increasing.

So how can you negotiate a parenting plan that supports breastfeeding? The website of the La Leche League, an organization that promotes breastfeeding worldwide, has several articles discussing breastfeeding, divorce, and parenting alone. You may be relieved to know that their recommended schedule is pretty much the same as what we have already discussed in relation to attachment security. Dad can have briefer but more frequent visits with his baby than he might with older children, mostly during the day.

The La Leche League's online information also underscores this important point. While Dad is compromising in order to support breastfeeding, Mom should do everything she can to encourage her baby's relationship with his father. This could include expressing milk for Dad to give to the baby, or maybe being OK with it if Dad uses formula. Mom's support like this would help Dad have extended visits, perhaps including occasional overnights, with his baby. And, of course, Dad's contact can and should increase near his baby's first birthday, as we have discussed.

## VACCINATIONS, CHILDCARE, AND OTHER HOT TOPICS

Decisions about babies—and topics of potential dispute—extend well beyond eating, sleeping, breastfeeding, and schedules. Some parents hold strong feelings about organic cloth diapers as well as organic foods. Other parents are skeptical about medical care or giving too many medications to infants. Are you OK with using antibiotics to treat the ear infections your baby is sure to develop? If so, how quickly and how often do you opt for the antibiotic?

Some parents also hold strong negative opinions about vaccines. But I feel compelled to insert a little information on this sometimes controversial topic. Arguments about the link between vaccinations and autism spectrum disorder (which I discuss briefly in Chapter 5) have been widely discredited by scientific research—and by documentation of the unscrupulous behavior of some "experts" who advanced the theory. And vaccines prevent dangerous childhood illnesses. Outbreaks of illnesses like measles have increased in recent years as more parents have chosen not to vaccinate their babies. In the end, vaccination is your decision. But I urge you to base your choice on scientific evidence, not rumor.

There are many more topics of potential dispute. Do you and your ex hold the same feelings about childcare—or what makes a good childcare provider? Do you agree that better-quality care is worth the added expense? How do you feel about having one or both sets of grandparents caring for your baby? (More on these topics shortly.)

In addition to facing decisions big and small, you also will experience new joys: your baby's first smile, first steps, and first words. And new challenges: Think *teething*.

How will you and your ex make decisions and share the delights of raising your baby?

It all comes down to communication.

Communication is critical to successfully coparenting children at every age. But much like your schedule for sharing time with your baby, you and your ex probably will need to speak more frequently, if perhaps more briefly, about your infant. You may need to talk every few days if you are going to make basic parenting decisions together. If you don't, one of you will be left in the dark, while the other will be left to cope, or celebrate, alone.

## Troubled and Troubling Infants

All parents, but particularly divorced parents, worry about their baby's emotional health. Of course, you also wonder about your infant's emerging personality. Babies differ. Some babies are much easier than others. How should you adjust your parenting plan based on your baby's personality or developmental disability?

Unfortunately, most mental health difficulties cannot be reliably diagnosed in infants. For example, professionals hope to learn how to identify autism spectrum disorder early in life. Doing so may lead to the development of more effective treatments one day. But as of now, there is no way to detect autism accurately in a baby.

### DEVELOPMENTAL DISABILITIES

On the other hand, many developmental disabilities can be identified at birth if not in utero. Down syndrome, the most common cause of intellectual disability, is one example. How should your parenting plan differ if you have a baby with a developmental disability?

Sadly, there is no research on this important topic. But I can offer you a little advice based on conventional wisdom.

Babies with developmental disabilities require even more effort than normally developing babies. So it is especially important for you and your ex to work together if your baby has special needs. Yet one big concern is that infants (and older children) with special needs may have a harder time managing change. So your schedule for sharing time may need to accommodate your baby's difficulty with transitions. At the same time, the parent who is doing most of the care for a baby with disabilities needs a respite. So one option to consider is arranging visits with your baby at her usual residence. If your baby requires special equipment, this may be your only option.

But, as always, no one knows your child better than you. If your baby seems to happily accommodate change, then you can follow the plans for infants already outlined in this chapter.

## INFANT TEMPERAMENT

A baby's personality also can influence whether he adapts to change easily. Again, there is no direct research on how an infant's personality affects his adjustment to living in two homes, but I can offer some general suggestions based on research on infants' temperaments. Psychologists typically classify babies' *temperaments*—inborn personality styles—into three types.

*Easy babies* accommodate change, well, relatively easily. Easy babies generally are good-natured. They seem relaxed. When they become distraught, they usually are easy to soothe. Even easy babies can take a while to develop sleeping and eating routines. But easy babies fall into a pattern sooner than most. Easy babies often *like* new foods, even healthy ones. But don't get me wrong. Easy babies have normal needs. All of the concerns about attachment security apply to easy babies.

*Difficult babies* accommodate nothing. Difficult babies are fussy.

They often are colicky, crying for reasons that parents find difficult to discern. They definitely are not easy to soothe. Difficult babies often have trouble getting to sleep. It can take forever before a difficult baby develops any consistency in sleeping routines. Difficult babies can have limited food preferences too, or they just may be lousy eaters. Difficult babies sometimes handle transitions well and, more often, horribly. They may strongly demand the attention of one attachment figure and may only (and slowly) be calmed by elaborate routines.

*Slow-to-warm-up babies* are shy and anxious. They are wary of anything new. Slow-to-warm-up babies can be good sleepers and good eaters—as long as they are in a familiar setting. But they do not respond well to change. When their routines are disrupted, or they are distraught for whatever reason, slow-to-warm-up babies often look and sound frightened, even when crying. Their fearfulness contrasts with the angry protests of the difficult baby. Slow-to-warm-up babies may be easily soothed, but only by the right person. They are "good" babies in familiar settings. In unfamiliar settings, they are not so much "bad" as they are frightened.

Researchers have not directly studied how infants with different temperaments cope with living in two homes or with different overnight schedules. In later chapters, we discuss a few studies of older children. Unsurprisingly, research shows that children with difficult temperaments have a harder time with divorce than children with easy ones.

Even without clear guidance from research, you and your ex will want to consider your baby's temperament when constructing a parenting plan and evaluating its success. By definition, easy babies are more likely to accommodate change. Of course, you still want to limit separations and transitions according to your baby's developmental needs. But when you are ready to try an overnight or other, extended separation, the odds of success—for you and for your easy baby—are greater.

The opposite is true for difficult babies. In fact, if your baby is difficult to soothe, you may be reluctant to disrupt the routines that you are still working to establish. This is understandable. Instead of napping or spending an overnight in an unfamiliar bed, you may want to stick to the patterns you are developing. Perhaps you can share one parent's home for naps or an occasional night of birdnesting. Or you may have to wait longer to try something new, so you don't wreck the progress you've made getting your difficult baby on a schedule. Whatever you do, be prepared for a challenge. You both are going to need a break. In order to get one, you are going to have to work together more than other divorced parents might.

Transitions can work well for slow-to-warm-up babies. For them, your concern is less the timing and more the pace of change. A slow-to-warm-up baby may respond well to separations at the same age as an easy baby. But her first separation may need to be shorter or managed in a way to soothe her anxiety. For example, a six-month-old slow-to-warm-up baby may respond better to long stroller rides in a familiar stroller. An easy baby, in contrast, may be ready for more direct play during a visit. Similarly, a slow-to-warm-up nine-month-old may need more, longer, or more recent daytime visits before she is comfortable spending an overnight with her other parent.

All of this is a reminder that your baby's unique personality plays a role in what works in parenting across two homes. It isn't just you. Keep this in mind when you are down on yourself—or your ex.

## Other Relationships and Your Infant

Your infant's most significant relationships should be with you and his other parent. But other people may also play an important role in your baby's life. Other people also can affect your relationship with your baby, your coparenting, or both.

## SIBLINGS

What should you do if your baby has older brothers and sisters, perhaps full, half, or stepsiblings? Can you coordinate times so the children are always together? If so, does everyone have to fit into your infant's schedule? Or can your baby adapt to the other children's schedule?

There are some clear advantages to children traveling in a pack, including a simplified schedule and increased opportunities for sibling interaction. Older siblings also may be a source of familiarity for younger children. Older siblings can become a part of your baby's circle of security.

Because of this, many experts are more comfortable with an "older" schedule for younger children who travel in a pack with their siblings. By an "older" schedule, I mean a schedule involving longer separations from one or both parents, and fewer transitions between households than may be typical for a child of that age.

I agree with this position. But not for babies.

Attachment concerns are different for babies than for, say, preschoolers. Preschoolers have already developed secure attachments and have used multiple attachment figures as a safe base. Babies either have not had these experiences or are only beginning to have them. Siblings are alternative sources of security, but siblings are not primary attachment figures.

So if you have multiple children, you and your ex will need to negotiate two sets of plans. You need one plan for your baby and another for your older children. Having two schedules is more complicated, of course. But it can be a good thing for all of your children. Maybe your older children would like their schedule to be individualized a bit for them too. As I have said before, everyone loves a little one-on-one time.

## GRANDPARENTS

Grandparents can play a huge role in caring for babies. Grandparents also can be tremendous practical, financial, and emotional supports for parents. Some grandparents provide an occasional and much-needed break. Others become part- or full-time childcare providers, substituting for professional childcare. A grandparent may even move in with a divorced child who is caring for an infant, or the adult child may move in with the grandparent. The living arrangement or direct financial assistance can make the difference between a decent lifestyle and financial hardship, perhaps poverty. According to U.S. Census data, over half of single mothers live near or below the poverty line.[17]

Despite many benefits, problems can arise between grandparents and children or their exes. One trouble spot is when grandparents act more like parents than like the parent's supporter. Sometimes a grandparent usurps a parent's role. This can create conflict with adult children who do not feel like they are being treated like adults. Other times young parents expect grandparents to act like parents, so they can act more like teenagers.

In some families, grandparents spend more time with their grandchildren than the other parent does with his or her own child. This may not be the grandparents' fault, but it can be an understandable source of hurt and frustration for a parent who wants more time.

Grandparents also can become overly protective of their children and grandchildren in relating to exes. I understand those protective feelings. But in the long run, I see little good and considerable potential harm from taking sides like this. A baby needs both of her parents.

A grandparent's role is to support the parents, not to get in the way of a baby's relationship with either parent. In the long run, a parent who is angry or hurt needs to find a way to work with her ex.

A grandparent should not stand in the way of that goal. In fact, a grandparent who takes sides with his own child against her ex may one day find himself at odds with his own daughter. She may change her mind and turn the tables—allying with her ex against her own overly protective parent.

So what can a grandparent do? Offer all the help she is willing and able to offer, practically, financially, and emotionally. But when it comes to emotional support, the best role a grandparent can play is sympathetic listener. A grandparent can act a little like a therapist, someone who can understand how one parent feels, maybe how both parents feel. But like a therapist, the most helpful grandparent does not meddle and does not take sides.

None of this is easy on the grandparent, not just listening, not staying out of the middle, not caring for a baby long after raising your own children, and not providing financial resources. All of which means that children, and hopefully the exes of children, should show their appreciation for grandparents who offer a lot and ask little in return.

## CHILDCARE PROVIDERS

If grandparents help most when they love babies, support parents, and keep out of the middle of disputes, the same is true of paid childcare providers—in spades. As a parent, do not put a childcare worker in the middle. Doing so is not fair to the worker, to your ex, or to your baby. The same goes for pediatricians or anyone who has regular contract with your baby.

You especially do not want to put childcare providers in the middle if you and your ex use a childcare setting for brief visits or for your baby's transitions between you. Making exchanges or visits where your baby receives childcare can be really helpful practically and emotionally. Doing so cuts down on contact between you and your ex. But if your childcare provider is willing to help you in this way, make her job easier, not harder. Help the childcare worker facilitate transitions. Don't turn her into a spy, policeman, or judge about your ex.

If you are lucky enough to have a live-in nanny or au pair, this can be a tremendous source of support to you, your baby, and transitions between homes. It is the exception, for sure, but I have worked with a number of families where nannies traveled with children between their two homes. In this unusual circumstance, the nanny's consistent availability may open up creative possibilities for schedules for sharing time with a baby.

As I said, your infant's most significant relationships should be with you and his other parent. Unfortunately, sometimes one parent is pretty uninvolved with her baby. What should the involved parent do to encourage an infant's relationship with his father or mother? Do everything you can to encourage the relationship. But you cannot make that relationship happen. In the end, that's up to your ex. All you can do is try—and know that you did.

## CHAPTER 5

# Toddlers: Testing the Limits

As infants become toddlers (eighteen to thirty-six months), your sweet baby can transform into a willful monster. The "terrible twos" usually begin not with your baby's second birthday but closer to a year and a half.

As locomotion improves from awkward first steps to serious toddling and beyond, a toddler's curiosity can propel him into discovery and danger. Toddlers test all kinds of limits as their universe expands. Wrecking an organized house is one thing. Yet much to their frustration, two-year-olds encounter "No!" as they reach for a hot stove, grab the tail of a not-so-tame dog or cat, or veer toward a moving swing or a busy street.

And much to their parents' frustration, toddlers soon learn to turn the tables. "Eat your peas." "No!" "Pick up your toys." "No!" "Come here." "No!"

How can behavior so wrong be right? In a pattern to be repeated, especially in the early teenage years, toddlers are learning an essential lesson in independence. As they test the boundaries of their autonomy, toddlers try to control far more than they possibly can. But toddlers also begin to learn to control what they should. This includes, to a degree, their behavior, their own emotions, and you.

With luck, your toddler's rebellion will be quelled by the time she turns three. For some children, though, the revolt continues until closer to four. And for other babies, the twos are not so terrible. Maybe you are one of the fortunate parents whose two-year-old is *not* throwing regular temper tantrums. If so, lucky you. But your toddler still faces the same developmental challenges. Your slow-to-warm-up child actually may need your encouragement to test her limits. Or perhaps your temperamentally easy toddler's quest for independence is a quiet revolution instead of an uprising!

For all parents, married or single, a toddler's adventures and assertions mean that parenting must take on a new dimension. Love is no longer enough. You need to guide and sometimes discipline your toddler as well as love him.

And here is something essential to recognize from the outset. You may be able to love your children separately. But you have to direct and correct them together. This means that with toddlers and older children, coparenting takes on a new dimension too.

If you have older children, you already know about discipline. Your parenting experience probably taught you how to set limits. But if you do not have older children, or if you relied on your ex to discipline your older kids, you now confront a whole new challenge in parenting. You have to learn how to say no.

And you and your ex need to learn how to say no separately, while still operating together as a united front. Alone yet together, you two need to find the most effective ways to offer direction and set limits. You need to do this so you can teach your toddler how to navigate her world effectively, safely, and sensitively.

Don't get me wrong. Loving your toddler still is the most important ingredient in authoritative parenting, by far. All of the concerns about babies and secure attachments I discussed in Chapter 4 apply to toddlers. Yes, your schedule can be a little more flexible, as we discuss shortly. Separations can be somewhat longer, in part because your toddler can understand a little better, but more because his circle of security hopefully now includes both you and your ex.

So if you skipped Chapter 4, make sure you read it, preferably before this chapter. Maintaining at least one secure attachment is still your toddler's number one need. Disciplining your child is an add-on to loving her like crazy, to being sensitive and responsive, not a replacement for your unconditional affection. You want to be big and strong in guiding your toddler. You also want to be kind, wise, and most of all, loving. In fact, you and your ex will need to correct your toddler less the more secure she feels in your love.

## Testing the Limits

There is no testing-the-limits equivalent to an insecure attachment as a risk factor for predicting psychological problems among toddlers. But research shows that toddlerhood is a critical training time, both for toddlers and for their parents. If you fail to learn your lessons now, you may be able to learn them later. But if you wait, both you and your toddler will find everything much harder to master.

Toddlers are propelled by twin desires: to explore and to control their world. You may not have recognized it at the time, but you witnessed the emergence of these motivations when your toddler was still a baby. Remember how she played with her food instead of eating it? She was exploring her new motor skills—and what blueberries look like when you smash them. Remember how she delighted in repeatedly throwing blueberries off her high chair and onto the floor? She was learning to control the blueberries, her eating, and you. You groaned. She giggled!

Now that she can toddle—or run—there is so much more to discover. She can explore tabletops and far beyond. She can engage adults and other children. She can communicate some of her basic wishes. And more and more, she can—and should—get her way, but only when it comes to things she can and should control.

## SELF-CONFIDENCE AND SELF-CONTROL

Why should your toddler get his way much of the time? As toddlers wrest autonomy away from their parents, they develop the rudiments of self-confidence. Toddlers exult in their newfound freedoms. "No, no, no! Not that one. This one!" And toddlers' growing competence builds confidence. They are *proud* of their achievements, whether mastering the art of walking up stairs (good-bye baby gate) or picking their own clothes (even though the colors may clash horribly).

Yet toddlers must also learn that there are limits. Your toddler needs to gain a sense of self-control as well as self-confidence. She should get her way much of the time. But she certainly should not get her way all of the time.

Think of how a toddler learns *not* to touch a hot stove. His first lesson may be, "Noooo!" as that curious little hand reaches toward a hot oven, and you grab his arm in the nick of time. Lesson number two may involve you holding his hand gently but firmly, so he can feel the heat. You say, "Hot! No touch! Hurt you. Ouch!" Your toddler practices his third lesson on his own. He approaches the stove, but stops short and repeats your words inquiringly, "Hot? No touch?" Lesson number four is a mere confirmation that nothing has changed. He no longer reaches toward a hot oven. But he may occasionally remind you, and himself, "Stove. Hot!" "Yes," you say. "The stove *is* hot. Ouch!"

Psychologists say that your toddler now has *internalized* the rule. He has developed self-control.

Your toddler needs to internalize all kinds of little and big lessons in self-control. She must be taught how (and how not) to touch her baby brother. She needs to learn that bedtime really means turning out the lights and going to sleep. You need to teach her how to use the toilet, one of toddlerhood's biggest lessons in confidence and control (which we discuss later in this chapter).

As she reaches her third birthday, your toddler even should have learned this big lesson: No means no. When you say no, you are not trying to thwart her. You are trying to teach and protect her. You are helping her to learn what she can and cannot control, including how to begin to control her own emotions. Her experience with your sensitive instruction, responsive understanding, and successful limit setting prepares her for the new lessons that she must absorb as a preschooler. Soon she will gain confidence and master self-control in the complex and exciting world of peer relationships.

## SETTING LIMITS

As I said, you need to learn too. You may need to learn to say no repeatedly and patiently, perhaps dozens of times each day.

You also need to learn to pick your battles. Maybe you let your two-year-old wear her headband across her forehead (rather than in her hair), because she *likes* it that way (even though you think it looks ridiculous).

You certainly need to learn to ignore some temper tantrums. Some battles really, really are not worth fighting. Remind yourself that the storm will subside. And tell yourself that maybe, just maybe, letting your toddler kick and scream until he's exhausted will serve some deeply hidden psychological purpose in his inner conflict between autonomy and self-control.

And when the storm is over, be ready to support your toddler. Respond to his frustrations and tell or show him what to do the next time.

Of course, you also will need to squelch some of your toddler's acts of rebellion. You may need to drag your tantruming toddler, kicking and screaming, away from a busy street or perhaps out of the candy aisle. (If you can ignore your toddler's tantrums, you can ignore other parents staring and clicking their tongues.)

And as you find yourself exhausted from setting limits, doubting whether you are doing the right thing and ready to give in (when you know you shouldn't), remember this: Like teenagers, toddlers find limits reassuring—despite their protests and their vow never to admit that you were right (at least not until they become parents themselves).

Finally, one more thing you need to learn is *not* to protect your toddler at times. You need to let *her* learn from the hard knocks of stumbling on the stairs or skinning her knee. Your toddler is only going to learn some lessons through experience.

## TESTING THE LIMITS AND DIVORCE

Learning how and when to set limits can be tricky for all parents and especially challenging for divorced parents. Parenting a toddler on your own can be exhausting. You thought your baby demanded a lot of your attention. Now, you find that your toddler *does not stop moving.* And whatever happened to those long naps, twice a day? How are you supposed to find the time, and the patience, to give your toddler the attention and guidance that he needs?

And when you know it's time to set limits, your own confidence can waver. Without a partner to consult for reassurance, you can end up asking yourself, repeatedly: "Should I say no?" or "Was I too harsh?" or "Am I a terrible parent?"

Let me tell you now—I'll remind you again—you are right to set limits, despite your doubts. You need to say no. This *is* harder to do on your own, but you still need to discipline.

But it is great to get a consultation and some parenting support. When you talk with your ex on the telephone for your parenting conference, you can seek some advice and reassurance. It's not the same as having him right there to help with parenting, but it's something. He may have some tips about keeping your two-year-old busy, or about what discipline techniques work best for him. Or maybe he just listens and sympathizes. He's tired and frustrated at times too.

And, yes, of course, your ex adores your toddler, just as you do. Your story about how he *loved* his new bath toys sounds awesome! He is going to get the same toys for his house too.

Unfortunately, instead of offering support and reassurance, your ex may have different rules at her house. "You let our two-year-old daughter play on your iPad? Are you kidding!? Sure, she's a handful for me too. But I always find time for her. When I'm super busy, I give her something *productive* to do! Don't you own any books?"

Or your ex may have few rules. At your ex's house, it's all play for your toddler. Your son eats what he wants, sleeps when he wants, and does what he wants. And when he comes back to your house, you have to start all over. And *you're* the bad guy!?

In the worst-case scenario, your ex may even undermine you. He *deliberately* gives your daughter sugary cereal, even though you asked him not to. No wonder she no longer eats Cheerios for you— and Cheerios were a concession in the first place.

Coordinating your parenting and your coparenting is not just some nice idea. As I said, you may be able to love your children separately, but you need to discipline them together. Your parenting partnership is basic to raising a happy, well-adjusted toddler. Parents who delay discipline or fight with one another about it will be punished. Maybe not right away, but you will—when other parents complain when your child is four, or when teachers do when your child is eight, or when the police get involved when your child is fourteen.

Later in this chapter, we revisit this central challenge and discuss negotiating rules with your ex, discipline techniques, and toilet training. But first, let's consider plans for sharing time with your toddler.

# Schedules for Toddlers

Attachment security still is the number one parenting concern for toddlers, as I already said. The safe base of a secure attachment encourages exploration. Toddlers need a secure attachment, so they can do their developmental "job" of exploring and expanding their world.

Even though attachment security remains the most important consideration, your schedule can be somewhat more flexible. Why? Toddlers already should have an attachment to both of you. Your stronger circle of security can ease separations from each of you somewhat. You can think of separations from you like long explorations away from a safe base. Toddlers can tolerate exploring farther away from their preferred attachment figure for longer and longer periods of time. And their other parent offers an alternative safe base. Other adults may serve as attachment figures too. But before too long, toddlers need the reassurance that only their primary attachment figure can provide.

But how much more flexible is "more flexible"? Unfortunately, neither attachment theory nor direct research offers a clear answer to this question.

## THEORY AND RESEARCH

As we discussed in Chapter 4, attachment theorists generally recommend few if any overnights away from the primary attachment figure (usually the mother) during the first twelve to eighteen months of life. As we will see in Chapter 6, attachment theorists are much less concerned about overnights for preschoolers. Their recommendations for toddlers are more vague. When asked directly, many attachment theorists suggest that occasional overnights will work for toddlers—perhaps one per week.

Direct research also offers only general guidance about what "more flexible" means. Only three studies have been completed.[1] My graduate students and I conducted the largest investigation. The sample we used was the same one I described for infants. It included 1,527 toddlers whose parents lived apart in the Fragile Families study.

Parents reported raising almost 7 percent of toddlers in joint physical custody, which we defined as spending at least 35 percent of the time with each parent. Another 5 percent of toddlers spent at least one night a week away from their mother, but the amount of time was less than our definition of joint physical custody. About 4 percent had one overnight about every two weeks. More than 5 percent had overnights about once a month. Finally, another 18 percent spent an occasional overnight away from their mother but less than one a month. About a third of the toddlers saw their father only during the daytime. Over a quarter did not see him at all. (Recall that the Fragile Families sample contains many poor, unmarried, minority parents, because it represents the population of large U.S. cities.)

We compared toddlers in joint physical custody with toddlers who had less-frequent overnights or day contact only. We found the highest rate of attachment insecurity (37 percent) among toddlers with joint physical custody. Unlike for infants, however, the increase in insecurity linked to frequent overnights was not statistically reliable.

We also found a possible *benefit* of frequent overnights. At age five, toddlers in the joint physical custody group showed more prosocial behavior than five-year-olds with rare or no overnights. I say "possible" benefit for three reasons. For one, the result shows a correlation, not causation. Families who pick joint physical custody were better parents, more cooperative coparents, and so on *before* they split. So we may just be seeing an effect of who chooses joint physical custody, not a result of toddlers living in that arrangement. Second, we conducted twenty-eight statistical tests in searching for possible effects of joint physical custody. One in twenty should be statistically reliable by chance alone, so we need to be cautious about our one positive result. It may be a chance finding. Third, our research is the only direct evidence of a possible benefit of joint physical custody at this very young age. Even staunch advocates of joint physical custody for very young children have not produced research to back up their arguments.

As I said, two other studies have directly focused on overnights and toddlers. One found no evidence of risks or benefits for toddlers who had some overnights with their fathers versus having no overnights with them. The second found some risks associated with joint physical custody (defined as 35 percent or more time) compared to fewer overnights.

So both theory and research suggest that you can be more flexible with toddlers than infants, but neither is clear about what more flexible really means.

Let me offer you my best effort to be clear. Toddlers generally are able to tolerate longer separations, including some overnights, away from their primary attachment figure. For most families, this may mean about one overnight per week. Two overnights in a row is the maximum number I feel comfortable recommending, and then only in exceptional circumstances. I definitely would not recommend joint physical custody at this very young age, and certainly not a week on/week off joint custody schedule. As at other ages, toddlers are more likely to adjust to more frequent overnights when their parents have a better relationship and the toddler is securely attached to both parents.

## SCHEDULES AND YOUR COPARENTING STYLE: JUSTIN AND NICOLE REVISITED

As we saw in Chapter 4, Justin and Nicole wanted to increase their son's time with Dad as Nathan approached his second birthday. Instead of just one overnight a week at Justin's home, they hoped that Nathan and his older sister, Madeline, could adapt to spending two nights in a row with Dad.

Nicole and Justin made this change when Nathan was about twenty-four months old. It worked well for everyone. The kids started staying with Dad on Thursdays from after childcare until three p.m. on Saturdays. When they first made this change, Nicole came by Justin's on Friday evenings to see the children and make sure all was fine. But the parents soon discovered this visit was unnecessary and perhaps a little disruptive.

Justin's Tuesdays with the children changed a little along with the overnights. He no longer took the afternoon off from work. Instead, he picked up both children from childcare at 5 p.m., had dinner with them, and returned Nathan to his mom's house around 7:30 p.m. Justin continued to keep Madeline overnight on Tuesdays. But he and Nicole decided that Nathan was not yet ready to alternate Tuesday overnights, as they had previously discussed. The parents thought they may try that plan in six to twelve months. Or they may try having both kids spend Wednesday through Saturday with Dad at that time. They both felt comfortable crossing that bridge when they came to it.

As you consider their story, keep in mind that Justin and Nicole not only had a cooperative coparenting relationship. Justin also was involved with the children both before and after he and Nicole split. They were in a better position to make this schedule work than most parents.

## ROTATING OVERNIGHTS AND BIRDNESTING

Still, if your coparenting relationship is cooperative, you may try something like this, or perhaps an even more complicated parenting plan. You may consider birdnesting. Or you may want to swap overnights every couple of days. I certainly do not recommend switching back and forth between homes for most toddlers. (And I don't think I would agree to a schedule like that for my own toddler.) But some psychologists do. And I do know of a handful of parents whose toddlers successfully rotated between homes, spending one or two overnights with each parent. I know another handful of parents who have found birdnesting to be the best arrangement for them and their children.

If you want to try this level of integration for a child this young, I'm nervous but I'm still on board with trying. As I have said, I always put *your* decisions about *your* children first. The research on what works best for toddlers is limited. And it is so important for you and your ex to work together. So if you have a unique schedule you both think will work for your family, I say try it and find out if you're right.

## ANGRY OR DISTANT COPARENTING

What if you have a distant or an angry divorce? In this case, I would not recommend two nights in a row for a toddler. I certainly would not recommend a complicated schedule like Nicole and Justin's. You would expose your children, and yourselves, to too much conflict.

But I am comfortable with you trying an occasional overnight for toddlers. You may begin with one overnight every other week and work your way up into one a week.

The overnights are likely to go more smoothly if you also have some daytime contact in between the overnights. And your toddler surely would benefit from this. Remember that longer separations can undermine attachment security.

You may, for example, begin with overnights that last from five p.m. on Saturday until five p.m. on Sunday every other week. On the off week, instead of an overnight, the weekend schedule may be ten a.m. until five p.m. on Sundays. If possible, it would be great to add in some contact midweek, perhaps a few hours on a Wednesday afternoon or early evening. Eventually, overnights may take place every Saturday, maybe gradually lengthening the time by an hour or two on either end of the visit.

## SEE WHAT WORKS

As always, you should view your schedule as an experiment. Only you can see what *is* working, or not, for your toddler and for you. Of course, trying something new is harder if you have a distant or an angry divorce. This is a big part of the reason why you want to move more slowly if this is you. You want to know that your new schedule is working for your toddler, not wonder if your ex is being truthful about how your little guy does with Dad.

You also should know that in offering these recommendations, I am again trying to err on the side of caution. As with infants, my primary concern for toddlers is maintaining a secure attachment to at least one parent—and hopefully to both. As your toddler's third birthday approaches, her developing sense of time and relationships may allow her to bridge longer separations. Two overnights in a row may work nicely—perhaps even three if her circle of security is strengthened by the presence of older siblings, familiar and comfortable environments in both homes, or highly cooperative parents.

Whatever your schedule, there is something you can do to make transitions easier for your two-year-old. Toddlers cannot comprehend the abstraction of time. This means that you cannot explain your schedule to your son. He is going to need to experience transitions and time in two homes in order to begin to understand how his life is changing. But even then, he won't really understand. For him, the future is the next few minutes, or if he is an older toddler, perhaps the next few hours. He has no way of comprehending what may happen in the coming days or weeks.

Still, you can say things to help prepare your toddler for transitions. Tell her things like, "Daddy is coming soon!" or "Sasha will go to Mommy's house today!" She won't understand "soon" or "today," but she will know that your words mean that she will soon see her other parent. This anticipation should help ease the transition. And when you do this, make sure to put the exclamation point in your voice. Your toddler reacts to your emotions more than your words. You want her to be happy to see her mom or dad. And the happier she is, the easier the transition will be for her.

## DIVORCING IN TODDLERHOOD VERSUS MOVING INTO TODDLERHOOD WHEN DIVORCED

Your schedule for sharing time with your toddler should differ quite a bit—initially—depending on whether you and your ex split during toddlerhood or your relationship ended earlier but your baby has now become a toddler.

If you separate during your child's toddlerhood, you want to move gradually into the typical toddler's schedule for spending time in two homes. Initially, you want to follow a schedule that looks more like the ones I outlined for infants. At first, your plan should include frequent but relatively brief daytime contacts of several hours with few or no overnights. You can introduce more regular overnights, longer daytime contacts, and fewer transitions as your toddler adjusts to your separation and his new home(s), and you do too.

Typically, you can expect that the gradual change to a more typical schedule for toddlers may take place over the course of perhaps two to four months. You may accelerate the transition if your toddler is securely attached and close to you both, or if she is an older toddler who is approaching her third birthday. Slow things down if you have an angry relationship, or if your toddler is still developing her attachment to one of you.

In the end, the timing of your transition to a more typical schedule will depend on your toddler's reactions. Can you both soothe him? Is he constantly asking for one or both of you when he's apart from you? Are transitions going reasonably well, with your toddler showing some separation distress but recovering quickly? Are there any disruptions in his normal patterns of eating and sleeping? Is his tantruming, toilet training, or other behavior regressing? Does he *seem* happy—or unhappy? Is he showing unusual fear or anger?

If you separated when your child was an infant, you should expect to negotiate some changes in your parenting plan as your baby enters toddlerhood. Nothing magical happens on the day your baby turns eighteen months old, so use this as a guideline, not as an absolute. Recall from Chapter 3 that Bethany and Roger miscalculated the timing of the transition for their daughter Bella. They needed to rework their transition plans and slow things down. So think about making some change around eighteen months, but be prepared to maybe try making a change a little later, perhaps closer to two years.

Still, your occasional overnights may become regular as your baby becomes a toddler. You may try something like what Nicole and Justin worked out, but probably at a slower pace (unless you are both really cooperative and involved like they were). And as you begin or increase overnights, you probably want to decrease the frequency of daytime contacts. Doing so usually has the twin benefits of increased convenience and fewer transitions.

The timing of the changes should depend on your coparenting relationship and the extent to which you both are involved in parenting. If you have both been spending time regularly with your infant, he should be ready to try a change sooner, even if one of you hasn't had overnights yet. But if one of you really has not been very involved with your baby, you are going to need to transition into your new schedule as if you separated during toddlerhood.

As always, if you have a cooperative relationship with your ex, you can contemplate more options as your baby becomes a toddler. If you have a distant or angry relationship, you should move more slowly in making changes. If you cannot negotiate changes on your own, seek some professional help around the time your toddler turns two. Try a mediator, a therapist, or collaborative lawyers first, before even thinking about going to court.

You know I want you to stay out of court and make your own decisions as parents. But if your relationship is really adversarial, you still can work on a parenting plan that grows and changes along with your toddler. One thing to consider is to ask a judge to order that your child's turning eighteen months or two years old (or whatever age) constitutes a "change in circumstances." Ask your lawyer. This ruling gives you a legal opening to renegotiate your schedule at that time. Knowing that things can change, even if you have to resort to court, should help you craft a developmentally sensitive parenting plan.

## TALKING TO TODDLERS ABOUT DIVORCE

Your toddler is learning language. This is exciting for you and for her. You can communicate! In fact, your daughter may be ahead of the curve. She may be talking in sentences already—short ones but more than the "telegraphic speech" that is typical at this age. Maybe your daughter is precocious. But be careful not to overestimate what she needs to understand about divorce, schedules, and the like.

Divorce is an abstraction that children cannot begin to understand until they are of school age. So even if your two-year-old's vocabulary is expanding rapidly, don't feel like "divorce" is a term that you need to teach her. She cannot grasp the idea cognitively or emotionally, so don't upset yourself, or her, by trying.

Your toddler's understanding is limited. But be prepared. His words may seem to convey more meaning than they possibly could. He may ask "why" questions like, "Why Mommy not here?" Or he may repeatedly ask about his other parent, for example. "Where Daddy?"

You may answer his questions as best you can. But your toddler still asks the same question again in fifteen minutes.

You may find sequences like this frustrating or perhaps upsetting. *You* may wonder why your ex is not with you, or where he is. But in responding to your toddler, keep in mind that her words mean something different to her than to you. Her understanding is limited, but her emotions are real. Look beyond her words to the emotions behind them. "Where Daddy?" is a request for reassurance, not a geography lesson. Similarly, if she asks, "Why Mommy not here?" your daughter is missing her mother, not wondering why you got divorced. Your best answer to both questions is a happy, "You will see Daddy (or Mommy) soon!" or a warm hug or, better yet, both.

Of course, your toddler will feel less lonesome if he is engaged in fun activities and has your undivided attention. But remember, you cannot be a perfect parent. And parenting isn't a contest. Your two-year-old is allowed to miss his mother or father from time to time. An occasional question about your ex does not mean he or she is the better-loved parent. You only need to worry if your toddler's unhappiness is apparent in constant questions, begging to see his other parent, significant trouble sleeping, or uncontrolled tantrums.

## Parenting and Coparenting Toddlers

Divorced parents of toddlers generally face few big decisions about religion, elective medical care, school, or even things like extracurricular activities. But toddlers present a more basic challenge, and ultimately a more important one. Day to day, how are you going to parent and coparent across households, particularly with regard to your new shared task of discipline?

## PARALLEL PARENTING

As I explained with the Hierarchy of Children's Needs in Two Homes, you and your ex have to work to together, somehow, if you both are going to be really involved in your toddler's life.

Maybe you don't want to work with your ex. If so, I can understand that feeling, whatever your reasons may be. If this is how you feel, one much-discussed alternative is *parallel parenting*. You're a good parent. Your ex is a good parent too. You parent, not together, but in parallel.

I want you to aim higher than parallel parenting. But if this is the best you can do, make sure that your parallel parenting is not like two-year-olds' parallel play. In parallel play, another toddler is there, but each child really is doing his own thing. There is no real interaction or cooperation.

You and your ex need to at least agree on some general goals and a few specific rules, even if you are going to parent in parallel. What foods are OK for your toddler to eat? What should his bedtime be? What are your rules about all the screens in his life, and yours, from televisions to computers to cell phones? What behavior is acceptable in your toddler, and what isn't? What kind of discipline is acceptable for you to use, and what isn't? Are you going to try to toilet train your two-year-old, and if so, how are you going to go about doing that?

And how do you parent in parallel about the unexpected incident that happened yesterday? The antibiotic prescribed for her ear infection? The bruise on her head? The little girl next door that your toddler bit or got bitten by?

All of this means that you need to negotiate with your ex, even though you may wish you didn't have to.

And your negotiations are even more critical now than when your toddler was a baby. You can love in parallel. But you have to discipline together, or your toddler is going to be confused by your different rules and your different goals.

## NEGOTIATING RULES

How are you and your ex going to negotiate the new rules you want to set for your toddler? If you haven't done so already, now is the time to implement the techniques I discussed in Chapter 3. You need to try things like parenting conferences, sending brief e-mails and texts, or perhaps exchanging parenting logs.

I already gave you lots of ideas about how to communicate. So let's focus here on what kind of rules to set.

Let me begin by reminding you to pick your battles, not only with your ex but also with your toddler.

For example, healthy eating is a must, kind of. Your toddler is likely to survive despite his refusal to eat your favorite vegetable, or your ex giving him some processed cereal. (Think *milk*.) And peanut butter really is pretty healthy, even when it becomes a staple for breakfast, lunch, and dinner. (Think *Bread and Jam for Frances*.)

So maybe your toddler forces you to change your philosophy. Maybe instead of all natural, you and you ex decide to draw the line at fast food (or fast food only as a last resort). Or maybe your toddler's diet is really, really important to you. If so, fight this battle, but be prepared to let the next one go. Or maybe, just maybe, you find out that you and your ex really are on the same page about food generally. Diet isn't something you have to discuss much. Nice!

Clothing also can be a matter of contention with your toddler and perhaps with your ex. Sometimes new clothes "really don't feel good!" Are you OK with that? Or your toddler's preferred bottoms and tops may look hideous together. Your toddler's strong preferences are not a plot to drive you insane. Neither is your ex's capitulation to an orange shirt and bright red pants. Is this a battle to fight? Or let go?

What if you want to change some aspect of your toddler's behavior? For example, what if you decide it's time to put your foot down about your toddler waking up and climbing into bed with you in the middle of the night? If so, you and your ex need to do the following:

- Be clear about what the problem is.
- Analyze the problem. Is this normal? A phase? A response to someone or something that needs to be changed?
- Agree on a new rule to deal with the problem.
- Agree on how to deal with your toddler's inevitable rebellion.
- Follow through—both of you.

So let's assume your two-year-old is getting up around two a.m. almost every night. At first, she cried out. You tried to comfort her in her bed. But after half an hour, you gave up in exhaustion. You let her into your bed. This pattern got repeated several times. Now, you're waking up and finding her in bed with you already.

You decide this is a problem for you. You can't sleep well with your daughter kicking. You don't believe in co-sleeping, so you see this as a problem for her too. And you've tried to break the habit, but nothing seems to work.

It's time to talk with your ex. What is happening during overnights at his house? Maybe he loves having his little girl sleeping with him. If so, you're still at step one. You see this as a problem. He doesn't. And if your two-year-old is sleeping with Dad, well, she's sure going to want to sleep with you too.

Or maybe your daughter is sleeping in her own bed at Dad's. Why? It could be something as simple as a night light. Or maybe Dad will lie in *her* bed when she wakes up. Sometimes he even falls asleep there. But he refuses to let her jump in with him unless it's morning.

Of course, he could be seeing and doing exactly what you do. It's easier to let her crawl in with you. And honestly, you may admit this to yourself, if not to your ex: Having her there was kind of nice at first. You don't like sleeping alone. Feeling your daughter next to you was comforting.

Assume you both agree that you are facing the same problem. You both are responsible for encouraging your daughter's habit. Now, you and your ex need to agree on a new rule to try to break the habit. And you need to tell your daughter about the rule, repeatedly: "Kasha is a big girl. Big girls sleep in their own bed."

What are you going to do when Kasha arrives at two in the morning despite your best-laid plans? Well, you and your ex need to set rules for yourselves too. You can agree that it's OK to lie with her in *her* bed (or on the floor if she's still in a crib). But the only time she's allowed in your bed is when it's time to get up.

And you absolutely need to follow through. Sure, you're exhausted at two a.m. It's much easier to put your arms around your little visitor and fall asleep together. But if you do, she'll be there the next night. And when she's back with her mother, she'll do the same thing. So either follow through with your rules or don't set them in the first place.

## DISCIPLINE TECHNIQUES

Another really big thing to negotiate is how you are going to discipline your toddler. How do you feel about spanking? Are you and your ex on the same page? If not, you *really* want to have a conversation. I cannot tell you how many times I have seen child protective services get involved in disputes between divorced parents because one parent complained about the other's use of physical punishment. You do not want this to be you.

I will address using corporal punishment shortly, but I want to discuss other discipline techniques first. If you decide to use corporal punishment, spanking should be your last resort. So let's consider the alternatives.

The best way to keep your toddler out of trouble is to keep him busy. He is a lot less likely to cause problems if he is engaged in some activity. So structure fun times into his day and yours. This may involve a trip to the park, a playgroup, or just a special playtime when he has your full attention.

Of course, your toddler needs to learn to entertain himself some too. You and he will have more success if you create a fun, safe space for him to play. That way, he won't get bored right away. And you won't need to constantly worry about him getting hurt. Make sure that his play space has plenty of toys, especially ones he can use creatively like finger paints or blocks or a sandbox. For years, my kitchen housed a child-sized table loaded with games and drawing materials—and an easel with paints.

Television shows or computer games also make handy babysitters. But I would recommend limiting, but not eliminating, your toddler's screen time. Your standards for screen time are up to you and your ex, of course. But I believe children learn more from engagement in the real world than the virtual world. At the same time, denying all access to a screen (or to sugar or whatever) can create more interest in the forbidden fruit, not less. So my advice is to let your toddler use electronic entertainment, but do so sparingly.

You also want to remember to reward your toddler for being good. If she's behaving well, she can't be behaving badly. So praise her for being a good girl. I know. Some parents overdo it with rewards. Save treats for special occasions. Your attention and approval are the best incentives. If your toddler entertains herself for thirty whole minutes (while you get some housework done), praise her enthusiastically. Admire her coloring. And ask her to color one more picture for Daddy too. When Daddy picks her up, hand him the artwork. Make a big deal about your daughter's wonderful drawing, and her good behavior. Doing so will boost your daughter's pride—and foster consistency and cooperation in your coparenting.

Never forget to focus on the positive. But as I said at the beginning of this chapter, the parents of toddlers must learn to say no. When you do (and you must, even though it can be hard), say no firmly and consistently. Follow through when you need to, or your words will become meaningless.

When you say no, make sure you explain the rule, as well as the reasons for it. Do this in a way that your toddler understands. "No! You hurt kitty. Be gentle. She likes to be petted like this." Explaining your rules and the reasons for them is the essence of authoritative discipline. Doing so also helps your toddler internalize the lesson. He will soon develop self-control, because he knows what to tell himself and why—just as with the hot stove.

Here's a discipline technique that psychologists rarely suggest, although we probably should recommend it more. Well-loved children are sensitive to their parents' disappointment and disapproval. Knowing this, I cannot tell you how often I corrected my children (when they were young) with "the look." I tilted my head, furrowed my brow, and slowly shook my head no. Of course, you have to be paying attention for *your* look to work. If you aren't, your toddler may get your attention by violating rules instead of by following them.

Speaking of paying attention, don't overlook the power of *ignoring* some of your toddler's misbehavior. If your attention is rewarding, losing your attention is a punishment. The best way to deal with some tantrums can be to ignore them. Watch your daughter out of the corner of your eye. (Don't let her catch you looking!) Midtantrum, you may find your toddler checking to see if you are watching. If she sees that you aren't, she'll probably stop. What's the point of putting on a show if you don't have an audience?

Warning: She may escalate her tantruming before she stops. So be prepared to keep ignoring her. Otherwise, you will reward her for tantruming longer and harder. Yikes!

But once she has calmed down, give her some love. You want to teach her appropriate ways to seek your attention. This is a start.

Keeping your toddler busy, rewarding his good behavior, saying no while explaining your reasons, giving disappointed looks, and ignoring tantrums are all good options. But they are not good enough. Unless you have a very well-behaved or shy toddler, you can expect open disobedience and active rebellion in response to some of your rules.

"It's dinnertime." "It's bath time." "It's bedtime."

"NOOO!!!"

You can make these inevitable battles a little easier if you give your toddler a little warning. "One more minute. Then it's bath time." She may not understand your words, but she will understand that it's a warning.

And who doesn't like a little warning?

When she still doesn't come—and I'm talking when, not if—try counting. I always did.

"One." Pause (for maybe five seconds). "I mean it!" Pause. "Two!" Pause. "Don't make me get to three!" Pause. "Two and a half!!"

My toddlers didn't understand the numbers, of course. But they did understand my tone of my voice. I got sterner and louder as I approached the dreaded "THREE!!!" But I never got to three. The unknown always is more frightening than the known. I didn't want my toddlers to know that the world would not end in nuclear warfare at "THREE!!!" Still, I had my share of "TWO AND FIFTEEN SIXTEENTHS!!" Some of these ended with me picking up a recalcitrant toddler and carrying him to the table, tub, or bed. Still, my kids mostly learned to come running, even though they often waited for "TWO AND THREE QUARTERS!!" before moving.

Another valuable discipline technique is *time out*. Time out means time out from getting any reinforcement. For an eighteen-month-old, time out may involve you simply ignoring him, as mentioned earlier. Of course, you need to give him *time in*, lots of your attention, for this kind of time out to work. When he does something wrong, you say, "Time out," and deliberately ignore him. When he's back to behaving well, he gets your praise and attention again.

For older toddlers, time out may mean more than lost attention. You may make him sit in a special chair in a quiet room (or a quiet part of the room you are in) with nothing to do for two or three minutes. Make sure time out is boring, and make sure he stays in the chair. (Time out starts all over again if he doesn't.) And make sure his time out is short. The length of a time out should be equal to your child's age, converting years into minutes. If you want to keep track—and make two minutes seem like an eternity to your toddler—set a kitchen timer. Watch him wait in agony as the seconds tick off oh so slowly.

OK. What about corporal punishment? I am not an advocate of spanking, although I did spank three of my five kids a handful of times. Read on. You'll find a confession or two later in this chapter.

Actually, over half of American parents report using some form of spanking with their children.[2] Most parents are OK with a mild slap on the hand or butt of a young child, provided the spanking is an act of discipline, not of anger. But as I said, if you or your ex *really are not* OK with corporal punishment, you need to have a talk.

If you do spank, save this option as the discipline of last resort. Spank only when other techniques have failed or just aren't going to work. Children typically are much more frightened of the prospect of corporal punishment than the actual spanking. So keep spanking, or saying "THREE!!!," or whatever your ultimate threat is, as just that: mostly a threat.

## TOILET TRAINING

One important challenge that is not small stuff for toddlers is toilet training. If you work together, you and your ex can help your toddler master this key exercise in self-control. If you are not on the same page, well, you know what's going to happen: disaster for you and especially for your toddler. So toilet training is a great example of all of the issues we have discussed. It is really, really important to work with your ex in teaching toddlers self-control.

The first thing that you and your ex need to decide—and agree on—is when to start. Is your toddler interested, seemingly ready for toilet training? You can encourage your toddler's interest by letting her observe your own bathroom habits or by buying a potty. But there is no magic age or way to begin toilet training. Most toddlers show an interest when they are about two years old. Some are ready at eighteen months, and others not until two and a half or later. Many preschools want kids to be toilet trained, so keep this in mind if you are planning on that.

Once you get started, you want to set similar goals—and have similar equipment—in both households. If Dad gives M&Ms for sitting on the potty, Mom's raisins won't be much of a reward. Pick one. Either. Your working together is far more important than a little fruit or a little sugar.

Initially, just encourage your toddler to sit on her potty. So a little reward (the M&M or the raisin) just for sitting is a great idea. This may lead to a happy accident. As she gradually becomes more aware of her internal signals, she may ask for her potty when it's time to go. Get her there in a hurry. And make sure to offer effusive praise when she successfully pees or poops in the potty. Yes, you should find yourself exclaiming with genuine excitement, "You pooped in the potty! What a big girl!"

You do not want to turn toilet training into a power struggle. Back off if your toddler shows little interest. Don't worry if he only sits on the potty for a short time, or if he hasn't peed or pooped in it yet. You may be in a hurry—and thrilled when you're no longer changing diapers. But mastering the art of using the potty lies squarely within your toddler's boundary of autonomy. Remember, the pride of self-confidence and the mastery of self-control work hand in hand in a toddler's development.

As toilet training progresses, make sure to share information ("I'm using Pull-Ups at night") and joys ("Lucy pooped in the potty!") with your ex. Your child's other parent is the only one who can truly join in your elation over these victories. And make sure to share basic toileting information with your ex too. He may not know how important it is for your daughter to wipe front to back. She may not know that little boys usually learn to pee sitting down. And you both should expect accidents to happen, especially at night.

Successful toilet training is a not-so-small triumph. Your toddler learned to use a toilet. And you learned a huge lesson about parenting together with your ex.

## Troubled and Troubling Toddlers

Most toddlers are difficult. Some are *really* difficult, or at least their behavior is. As toddlers, two of my five were biters. Unfortunately, these two were twenty-two months apart. They typically bit each other, or their big sister (twenty months older), when all three were in the tub together. Sure, I could have bathed them separately—if there were forty-eight hours in a day. But that is not the point. Corporal punishment is.

### CORPORAL PUNISHMENT

Time out is impossible with three in the tub. "That's not nice" won't cut it either. For me, a slap on the butt did.

Don't get me wrong. As I said earlier, I am not recommending corporal punishment. Nor am I opposed to a gentle smack on the hand or butt at this age.

I know many parents feel strongly about corporal punishment.

I will never forget the mother who screamed about me in a crowded airplane, "This guy is beating his kid!" I had just slapped the hand of my youngest child, John, who was two and a half at the time. We were on a transatlantic flight and stuck in the middle seat of the middle aisle. John refused to sleep despite being way overtired. Instead, he repeatedly kicked the seats in front of us. Then he tried to climb over the back of our seats to visit the passengers behind us. After several hours of struggle (I would have welcomed brain-numbing screen time for him but there were no televisions on this flight), I gave him the smack on his hand, and said, "Sit still!"

The gentle slap worked for John. I got his attention, which really was the problem with the overtired child. But the smack did not work for the mother in the next seat, or because of her, for me. Fortunately, the woman did not summon child protective services when we landed, although I briefly feared that she might.

What's the moral of my story? Again, make sure that you and your ex agree about corporal punishment. Or child protective services may show up at *your* door.

## TEMPERAMENT

Problem behaviors like biting and bothering other people are common among toddlers. As with infants, however, broader psychological problems are difficult to identify and rarely diagnosed among toddlers. But as we discussed in Chapter 4, your toddler's temperament is an important influence on his behavior. His temperament may exacerbate, or lessen, ordinary challenges.

When it comes to temper tantrums and other acts of rebellion, toddlers who have an easy temperament may not be as easy as they were a few short months ago. They will explore widely and may revolt strongly. Slow-to-warm-up toddlers usually are the easiest, because they are wary about exploring and more sensitive to disapproval. In fact, you may need to encourage your slow-to-warm-up toddler to explore her world and gently confront her fears.

But hold on for dear life if your toddler has a difficult temperament. You are going to have to learn to be *really* good at ignoring ordinary tantrums. You also can expect to have to pick up your screaming toddler, perhaps in an embarrassing public situation. You may have to carry him to some quiet place for a time out. In fact, you may need to hold him firmly in your lap to prevent him from running away from the punishment.

What do you do if you are concerned that your toddler's behavior is becoming a problem? The first person to consult is your ex. He may or may not be running into the same difficulties. Ask yourselves: Is there a problem? If so, what is the problem? Then, what do we do about it?

Your answer will determine how you respond. A confused child may need clearer rules and routines. A frustrated child may need more patience and understanding. A temperamentally difficult child may need firmer limits. Whatever the problem, your challenging toddler needs you and his dad working together as a team, even though you live in different homes.

## Other Relationships and Your Toddler

As with infants, older siblings may be a part of a toddler's circle of security. So if you have older children, you may be able to consider a parenting plan for your toddler that is a bit accelerated developmentally. For example, you may think about moving to two overnights in a row a bit sooner. But unless your older children have an every-other-weekend schedule, you still will need different plans for your toddler and for them.

Your children benefit from the support of siblings, grandparents, and other people. You need some support too. Hopefully, your ex is a good coparent, and knowing this, you can relax when the children are with her. You also can use some support when your kids are with you. Maybe your parents are helping out. If so, see my discussion of grandparents in Chapter 4. Or you may have a good friend, perhaps another single parent, who helps you out. You need someone with whom you can commiserate, someone to do things together with you and your kids, or perhaps someone willing to swap a little childcare.

Speaking of childcare, do not waste time and emotional energy feeling guilty if your children are in childcare or if you need a sitter from time to time. Raising children is hard work in a two-parent family. And you are on your own. So accept your limits, be grateful for the help, and put the guilt away. Besides, your children will benefit in the long run. Most kids love childcare settings, because they get to be around other children. And your kids may love the young babysitter who occasionally watches them at night. Plus, a night out will make you a better parent the next day—and probably for the next week too. So do not be shy about using or getting the help you need.

If you split when your toddler was a baby, your life may now include romantic relationships. One advantage to dating at this age is that, unlike older children, your toddler will not ask nosy, angry, or embarrassing questions about your date, which is a relief. I deal with those issues in later chapters, especially the one on adolescence.

But it is not too early to hear my standard advice about new romantic relationships. Go slowly—for your children and for yourself too. You may want and need romance in your life. If so, it's great that you are dating. But whatever your situation, you have been through a lot emotionally. You are vulnerable. Give yourself time.

And you don't want your toddler getting too attached to someone who may not be around for too long—or who may not be the greatest influence on your children. So take my advice and go slowly with romantic relationships.

## CHAPTER 6

# Preschoolers:
# Play Is a Child's Work

Childhood begins with the preschool years (ages three to six), my favorite age. Your baby is no longer a baby. She's a little kid! Her preschool years can be, and should be, a magical time of fun, friends, imagination, excitement, and boundless curiosity.

Who cannot love a developmental period when a child's main "job" is to play? Play *is* a child's work. Preschoolers learn all kinds of lessons from their play. Play teaches preschoolers to get along with friends, to share (even when you don't want to), to use your imagination, to find joy in just about anything, to focus, to discover the excitement of learning new things, and with a little bit of help, to pick up when you are done.

Children should play more. We all should play more.

Preschoolers need new tools to help them do their work. Preschoolers need friends, so they can discover the limits of selfishness. They need friends to learn that when you do something wrong or hurt someone, you should say, "I'm sorry." Preschoolers also need friends to help them develop compassion. Your daughter learns empathy when she feels the pain of a friend's skinned knee. She discovers that other people care, because her friends comfort her when she is bruised too.

And preschoolers need friends because friends are *fun*. Friends keep your preschooler occupied and happy. It is less work for you, not more, when your preschooler has a friend over to play. They keep each other busy and entertained—and they eventually tire each other out. Yes!

Preschoolers need other tools to fuel their imagination. They need toys, dolls, dress-up clothes, stories, art materials, books, songs, or just an empty cardboard box to help them discover new worlds—and their own creativity. They need balls to bounce, ropes to jump, trikes and bikes to ride, walls and trees to climb. Yes, today's preschoolers even need a computer (of some sort), so they can begin to explore the virtual world. And preschoolers also need adults to teach them, playfully, the days of the week, how to count to ten (or higher!), the alphabet, and maybe even how to begin to read.

I want all parents, married and divorced, to let preschoolers be little kids, not try to make them into little adults. I want you to protect these magical years, when elves, the tooth fairy, and monsters under your bed are *real*. Sure, monsters can lurk in the dark of your preschooler's imagination. But the creations of a preschooler's mind are mostly magical. Your preschooler, and you, should revel in the enchantment of play and fantasy.

Remember my Hierarchy of Children's Needs in Two Homes? My ultimate goal for your children is at the top of the pyramid: Kids get to be just kids. A big part of letting your preschooler be a kid is keeping reality at bay.

I bet you would like someone to do that for you too.

The preschool years are the essence of childhood. You *have* to protect that innocence, for these special years and beyond.

How? Remember the lessons *you* learned in preschool.

You teach your preschooler to "be nice." You need to play nice too.

And everyone needs to learn to share, even if, like your three-year-old, you don't really want to. You can share information about your son's growing activities, interests, and fantastic stories. You can share his favorite toys between homes—as well as the burden of transporting forgotten treasures to your son's other home. You also can share his new friends, and their parents too.

If you do this, you will allow your preschooler to share too—to share her love with you both, instead of feeling like she has to divide her loyalties, not just her time.

## Play Is a Child's Work

We think of preschoolers as little kids, not babies, because children become so much more independent around their third birthday. Infants and toddlers depend on their parents for continual protection and entertainment. But more and more, preschoolers can take care of and entertain themselves. Preschoolers still need supervision, of course. But unlike babies, they don't need constant oversight and direction. Their emotional, social, cognitive, and physical growth allow (and motivate) preschoolers to play on their own.

Friends surely are the most important new "toy" for a preschooler to play with. You no longer are enough to entertain your three-year-old. Preschoolers *need* playmates. Yes, you can and should play with your preschooler. But as much as you may try, you are not three!

You probably noticed how, even as a baby or toddler, your son reacted differently when he saw another child, or even just heard a child's voice. He tuned in, maybe got excited. Someone to play with! Peer play is a hardwired social motivation, just like attachment is. Watch two puppies or two kittens chase each other, wrestle, and groom. Kittens are desperate to play. So is your little girl.

Attachment relationships, special bonds with adult caregivers, are still important to preschoolers (see Chapter 4). At the end of the day, and many times during many days, your three-, four-, or five-year-old still needs your comfort and protection. Your preschooler still needs your love, very much. But he no longer needs you always to be in his immediate proximity. He doesn't need you hovering. Most of his world is familiar now. He no longer needs a safe base as much as he used to. As a toddler, he pushed the limits. He pretty much knows his boundaries now, at least within the limits of the familiarity of his homes and school.

Plus, preschoolers have become experienced in using multiple attachment figures. Their hierarchy of attachment typically includes both of their parents, teachers, and other adults too. And peers give preschoolers a reassuring companion when exploring unfamiliar territory.

Actually, peer relationships are the most important new world for your preschooler to explore. Children (and puppies) learn much from peer play. Peer play teaches children critical social lessons, like patience and how and when to regulate strong emotions. Children learn that being angry or selfish or mean *hurts* people. They get hurt too, when their friends are mean. Peer play teaches preschoolers basic lessons in kindness and reciprocity that are essential in relating to others later in childhood and, really, throughout life.

And preschoolers' individual likes and dislikes distinguish them. Your son's preferences bond him with some peers and separate him from others. Thus begins your child's long exploration of his identity as an individual, as well as a part of a group.

Children also develop physically and cognitively through play. Preschoolers perfect fine motor skills by stacking blocks and painting pictures. They improve large motor skills by chasing after one another and climbing on play structures. Preschoolers practice language skills when interacting with peers. Social competition— something else preschoolers must learn to regulate—motivates preschoolers to learn to ride a two-wheel bike (or at least try) and to master their ABCs.

Toddlers engage in parallel play. Toddlers like having other children around. But they mostly do their own thing. A preschooler's play becomes reciprocal. Preschoolers engage in back-and-forth interaction:

"No! You're the daddy. *I'm* the baby. You say, 'Night-night, baby.'"

"All right. But next time I'm the baby!"

"OK. Now say it!"

"Night-night, baby."

"Goo-goo, ga-ga. Night-night, Daddy!"

Cognitive growth allows preschoolers to play reciprocally. Preschoolers begin to see the world not just from their perspective but from other perspectives too. Their new perspective-taking abilities allow preschoolers to play Daddy or baby or fireman or whatever. They gain more perspective when rehearsing social roles whether playing Mommy or teacher. Preschoolers also develop perspective, and patience, when they play in a group and have to take turns, as they do at preschool.

Your preschooler's ability to begin to see others' perspective can lead her to ask meaningful questions: Why can't Daddy sit with us at the picnic? Are you lonely when I'm at Mommy's house?

I'll suggest some ways to answer these kinds of questions shortly.

Preschoolers also become increasingly attuned to other people's feelings. This includes their friends and adults. Your preschooler may try to comfort a friend in tears, or to correct a peer who is being disruptive. When you are upset, your four-year-old may want to comfort you too. But because you are your preschooler's attachment figure (see Chapter 4), your sadness or anger may confuse her. She may react to your emotions with mixed emotions. She is worried about you, but she's likely to be scared and confused too. *You're* the one who is supposed to comfort *her*. What is she supposed to do now? As a result of her confused emotions, she may not know what feeling to act on.

The preschool years teach simple yet vital lessons that we should work hard to preserve not only for preschoolers, but also as life becomes more complicated for older children, and for ourselves as adults too. Play nice. Share. Have fun. Pick up your mess.

## PRESCHOOLERS' PLAY AND DIVORCE

Your preschooler's world is expanding, which means that your world is growing too. You are likely to find now, and in the years to come, that you become friends with many of the parents of your children's friends.

You want to keep your divorce in the background, not the foreground, with most other parents, and with your preschooler too. You want your focus to be on your child. You want to be positive, happy, and upbeat. You want her caught up in these happy years of play and discovery. And you want to join her in her happiness—even if you feel lonely or hurt or angry when you're alone at night.

Your task in protecting your preschooler from the dark side of your divorce is trickier than it is with younger children. Three-, four-, and five-year-olds become attuned to their social and emotional world, including you. True, even infants and toddlers are upset by their parents' loud, angry fights. But you can hide a lot from babies. Preschoolers are tuned in not just to your fights but also to your feelings. They want to know why you look sad. They want to know why you are being mean to Mommy or Daddy. They want to know how come their other parent is not at their preschool event.

So you may need to learn to pretend a little. You do this so your five-year-old gets to be a kid. Let him worry about mastering a two-wheeler, not about you looking sad or being lonely. Put a smile on your face, and your misery on the back burner. Who knows? Setting your unhappiness aside may not just help your preschooler. Maybe you will feel a little better too.

# Schedules for Preschoolers

By the time they reach preschool age, children are emotionally capable of spending overnights apart from each of their parents. Experts agree on this point, including attachment theorists who are concerned about overnights for infants and toddlers.

So you can breathe a sigh of relief as the parent of a preschooler. You can put one controversy behind you. Overnights are OK for your child. But as you steer past one debate, beware of another dispute dead ahead. Should you and your ex share joint physical custody? And if you are going to share physical custody, what should that arrangement look like for a three-, four-, or five-year-old?

## JOINT PHYSICAL CUSTODY FOR PRESCHOOLERS?

Before we move forward, let me point to a big yellow sign of caution. As with infants and toddlers, there is not much direct research to help us answer big questions about joint physical custody for preschoolers.

How much is not much? One. Only *one* study has examined how preschoolers fare in joint physical custody.

The one study is the same investigation I mentioned in Chapters 4 and 5. Using a national sample of Australian children, Jennifer McIntosh and her colleagues found signs of attachment insecurity among infants who had overnights weekly or more.[1] These researchers also found indications of similar difficulties among toddlers who shared 35 percent or more overnights between two homes (joint physical custody). But they found no more—or fewer—emotional struggles among four- and five-year-olds living in joint physical custody versus other arrangements. Again, this one study found no risks, or benefits, associated with joint physical custody for preschoolers.

American psychologist Marsha Kline Pruett and her colleagues conducted the only other direct study of custody arrangements and preschoolers.[2] She found that having some overnights (versus no overnights) during the preschool years predicted better psychological adjustment at age six in a sample of girls. Having any overnights did not predict better (or worse) adjustment among boys. Again, these investigators did not study joint physical custody.

Two other studies deserve brief mention. Each study found more insecure attachments among preschoolers whose parents were divorced. One evaluation attributed the increase in insecure attachment to less sensitive and responsive parenting in divorced homes.[3] The second found that the difference in attachment security was explained by divorced parents' lower incomes and education.[4] Neither study looked at whether insecure attachments might be tied to joint custody, overnights, or any aspect of the parenting plan.

Not much to go on, is it?

So my guidance to you about joint physical custody has to rely on limited direct research—plus general knowledge of preschoolers' development, my extensive clinical experience, and studies of older children.

Of these, research on older children perhaps is most relevant. So let me summarize the main points about older children living in joint physical custody that I detailed in Chapter 3.

- Joint physical custody does not necessarily mean 50/50 time.
- On average, children whose parents share joint physical custody are better adjusted than children in families where one parent has sole custody.
- Part of the "benefit" of joint physical custody surely reflects the fact that better parents with better coparenting relationships—and probably better adjusted children—try joint physical custody in the first place. That is, joint

physical custody does not necessarily create happier families. Instead, happier families are more likely to choose
joint physical custody.

- Still, part of the benefit of joint physical custody probably
is real. But no matter what, the benefit of joint physical
custody for children is small, at least as best we know
with our limited research.

- Despite the potential upside, joint physical custody appears to benefit children only when (1) it is logistically
practical, (2) parents cooperate to make it work, and (3)
the arrangement fits an individual child's personality.

- In the wrong circumstances, particularly when parents
have an openly angry relationship, joint physical custody
can harm children rather than help them.

## DIVIDING THE WEEK

If you are considering joint physical custody for your preschooler,
you need to think carefully about whether your family circumstances
seem right for making the arrangement work for your child. You
also need to remember my advice about experimenting to *see* what
actually works for your child (see Chapter 3). You don't want to lock
yourself or your child into a plan that seems great on paper but just
doesn't work in practice.

Assuming you want to try joint physical custody, let me offer a
suggestion. You should consider altering off-the-rack joint custody
schedules to fit the unique needs of your preschooler. In particular,
you want to explore dividing the week as a way of sharing time more
evenly, instead of following a week on/week off rotation.

Why? A week is a *very* long time when you are a preschooler.

Preschoolers are beginning to develop a sense of time. By the
time they are in kindergarten, many children can recite the seasons
in a year, the days of the week, and perhaps the months in a year.

Five-year-olds also may understand that certain times of the day hold special meaning. Eight o'clock means bedtime, for example.

But preschoolers' growth in understanding concrete markers of time does not mean that five-year-olds grasp the concept. In fact, most children do not really understand what time is (or learn how to read an analog clock or use a calendar) until about second grade. It is no coincidence that time concepts typically are taught in school in second grade.

Preschoolers mostly live in the now. But they know that time extends beyond right now. School will end, and they will go home. They did not go to school yesterday. They will go to school tomorrow. Sometime, winter will come, and they may see snow again.

Their new cognitive and emotional appreciation of time helps preschoolers manage longer separations from you and from your ex too. But you need to remember that a little time is still a *long time* for a three-, four-, or five-year-old. Forget about child development research or guessing about your preschooler's experience. Think back to how long time lasted when you were little.

For me, the time between when school ended and I had to come inside for dinner, a couple of hours, was a *long* time. A whole weekend seemed endless (until Sunday night). A week seemed to last forever, particularly as I looked forward from Monday to a whole week of school. And as I write this, I'm recollecting my eight-year-old experience. Time already had begun to speed up by then. I'm sure time moved much more slowly when I was four.

Because time passes so slowly in the eyes of preschoolers, many experts and parents prefer schedules that divide the week rather than alternating weeks. One example is the 2-2-5-5 schedule, where your child is with one parent every Monday and Tuesday and with the other every Wednesday and Thursday, and he alternates three-day weekends with each parent.

Another common schedule involves dividing the week in half, Wednesday after school until Saturday afternoon with one parent,

Saturday afternoon through Wednesday before school with the other. You're right. Those overnights do not work out to 50/50. If that bothers you, reread what I said about 50/50 in Chapter 3. (This is the schedule I followed with my daughter Maggie during her school-age years, even though I got "only" three nights out of seven.)

In addition to shorter separations, an advantage of dividing the week is that children (and parents) track time based on days of the week, not based on every other week. Meetings you have that take place every other week require effort to track. So does swapping from Mom's to Dad's every other week—even for older children who understand time far better than preschoolers. Mondays and Tuesdays at Dad's is pretty easy to figure out, even if you've only just learned the days of the week.

Whatever your schedule, your preschooler will benefit from predictability in the arrangement. Some flexibility is good and necessary. But too much flexibility can seem like chaos, especially to a preschooler who has been waiting *a long time* to see one of his parents.

And remember that preschoolers tie time to concrete experiences. Reread the preceding examples. Eight o'clock means bedtime. Winter means snow. You can help your preschooler bridge time between homes by anchoring the abstraction in something concrete. For example, consider making a calendar with Mom's days and Dad's days colored in. Your five-year-old doesn't really know how to use a calendar. But she can count the number of blue days until there's a red day. And who knows? Your colorful calendar of Mom's days and Dad's days may help your daughter learn the days of the week and the months of the year. It surely will alleviate some of her anxiety about her schedule and transitions between homes.

## JUSTIN AND NICOLE GET TO 50/50

As I discussed in Chapter 5, when their younger child, Nathan, turned two years old, Nicole and Justin increased Dad's time with the kids, as they had planned to do. They added Thursday overnight to Justin's Friday overnights with Nathan and his five-year-old sister, Madeline. The kids also continued to spend dinner on Tuesdays with Dad.

Justin originally had only Madeline for Tuesday overnights following dinner. But as Nathan approached his third birthday, he started begging for "his turn" to spend an overnight just with Dad. In response to Nathan's "requests" (they were more like demands), Justin and Nicole agreed to try alternating Tuesday overnights with each child. The switch worked beautifully. Madeline and Nathan eagerly made special plans with Mom or Dad for "their night." Over the last several months, everyone had begun to look forward to Tuesdays.

Now, Nicole and Justin wondered. How could they move toward 50/50, like they had planned, but preserve the special one-on-one time they had created? Originally, they had talked about the kids being with Justin from Wednesday through Saturday, and Nicole Saturday through Wednesday. But the success of their Tuesday "alone" nights complicated that idea. After considering and rejecting several alternative schedules, Justin finally said, "Why don't we just keep alternating Tuesday nights?"

Nicole's immediate reaction was anger. "How is that fair? You get Wednesdays added on and *keep* Tuesdays too? We had talked about pushing your time with the kids together. You were supposed to drop Tuesdays once Nathan was old enough. Now you want to have your cake and eat it too?!"

"But our times with the kids *would* be pushed together if I kept Tuesdays," Nathan retorted. "Tuesday, Wednesday, Thursday, Friday with one kid one week, and Wednesday, Thursday, Friday the next week. You'd have Saturday, Sunday, Monday, Tuesday one week, and then Saturday, Sunday, Monday the next. That would keep our one-on-one time and be really close to fifty-fifty."

It wasn't until our next meeting that anyone realized that Justin's idea wasn't close to 50/50. It was exactly 50/50. As you may remember, that's the way I like to do the math about dividing time—afterward, if at all. Worry about equal, or what's fair, after you have figured out a plan that seems like it's going to work well for your children.

As you also may remember, Nicole always was less focused on 50/50 than Justin. But she eventually agreed to the plan—with a few conditions. First and foremost, she wanted to be clear that if it didn't work, they'd have to come up with something different. Second, she wasn't sure low long Justin's plan would work. She was concerned that as Madeline moved through elementary school, a Tuesday night transition would disrupt her schooling. Kindergarten and first grade might work out all right. But starting in second grade, schoolwork got pretty serious at Madeline's new elementary school. Nicole doubted that Justin's proposed schedule would work then.

Finally, Nicole wanted to talk about one thing she did *not* like about the old or the new schedule. She never had a weekend off—or a whole weekend with the kids. She didn't want to rearrange the entire schedule just for this. But she did want the kids to stay with her, or with Justin, for a whole weekend every once in a while. Ideally, she thought this might happen about once every two months. She didn't want to set anything in stone, or even to count weekends. She just wanted a little flexibility.

To her surprise, Justin agreed to all of Nicole's conditions. And he didn't agree just to compromise. He actually shared Nicole's concerns. He even suggested that when the kids spent a whole weekend with him, Nicole should keep them both the following Tuesday night. That way she'd have a little more time to catch up with the kids after her weekend away.

I was present when Justin and Nicole worked out their new schedule. But I didn't do much. Nicole and Justin clearly had figured out how to coparent—even when their big decisions involved some conflict.

And I'm sorry, but I cannot tell you how long their new schedule lasted. I helped guide Justin and Nicole in raising their children as babies, toddlers, and preschoolers. But they never needed my help again. That makes me happy, of course. But I wonder—and I really kind of miss seeing them.

## EVERY OTHER WEEKEND AND OFF-WEEK NIGHTS

As I have said before, Justin and Nicole are an exception, not the rule, when it comes to coparenting. If you're an exception too, that's awesome—for your preschooler, for you, and, I think, for your karma.

But you may have an angry or a difficult, distant divorce. If so, your preschooler is likely to be better off if she spends less time with one of you. That way, she will be less involved in your disputes.

If this is your situation, consider this. Despite all the talk you hear about joint custody, the most common parenting plan still is a traditional one. The children live mainly with one parent and spend every other weekend with the other parent. If this is you, one piece of good news is this: Unlike infants and toddlers, your preschooler is developmentally ready for every other weekend. She should be able to easily manage two overnights in a row.

For many parents with an angry or distant divorce, the innovation in parenting plans is not joint physical custody. The innovation involves visits on the *off week*. The off week is when you don't have your children for the upcoming weekend. Off-week visits typically include an evening meal with some playtime before or after. As long as it isn't too disruptive, some parents turn this visit into a midweek overnight on the off week.

## EVERY OTHER WEEKEND PLUS THURSDAY OVERNIGHTS

If you have a difficult divorce but want significant time with your children, you may consider a variation on the every-other-weekend schedule. The children spend every other weekend with one parent.

But the weekend begins on Thursday night, instead of Friday, and lasts through Sunday afternoon. On the off week, the children spend Thursday overnight with that parent too.

Another way to describe this schedule is every other weekend plus every Thursday overnight. That's a pretty simple schedule for children to comprehend, even preschoolers. And it gives both parents at least some involvement with day-to-day schooling. Plus, the schedule meets the criteria for joint physical custody according to many definitions, including my own (see Chapter 3). It divides time about 70/30 (72/28, to be precise).

This schedule may be a compromise for you to consider if you both want lots of time with your children but have an angry divorce. You also may like this schedule if one of you faces many work demands. Or you may think it's important for your children to have stability in one home during most of the school week. This schedule gives you that too. I have seen it work well for many families.

Whatever your weekly schedule, you may consider modifying it during the summer school holiday. I know a number of parents who do that. Maybe you try week-to-week joint physical custody during the summer. Or maybe the parent with less time during the school year has the children more during the summer. Or maybe each parent gets three or four weeks of vacation time with the children, even if your vacation involves staying at home.

## HOLIDAYS

Summer vacation is one piece of an essential and often emotional aspect of your parenting plan. What are you going to do about the holidays?

You may not want to even *think* about this, but you need to. Sooner or later, it will be Christmas Eve or your son's birthday. You don't want to be wondering or arguing about what you are going to do. You don't want kids not knowing either.

A starting point is to list all potentially important holidays. Big religious holidays like Christmas or Passover are obvious. So are Thanksgiving and spring break. But Mother's Day, Father's Day, and everyone's birthday may be important too. Halloween is a really big deal for most preschoolers and school-age children. And your extended family may have traditions, like gathering over Memorial Day or Labor Day. List everything you can possibly think of.

Once you have figured out what's important, you need to consider how to allocate holidays. You essentially have five options:

- You can alternate holidays. You get Thanksgiving one year; your ex gets it the next.
- You can divide holidays. Your ex is Christian. He gets Christmas. You're Jewish. You get Passover.
- You can share holidays. You get your kids from the beginning of school break until noon on Christmas Day. Your ex gets them from noon on Christmas until New Year's Day.
- You can celebrate holidays together. You both attend your son's birthday party and go out for a family dinner together afterward.
- You mix and match. You divide Christmas week, but you alternate who gets the first half (including Christmas Eve) from year to year. You always celebrate birthdays together. And you each pick two weeks for separate summer vacation with the kids by March 15.

Once you have a plan in place, here are a few more tips on managing holidays:

- Your children deserve their celebrations even if you feel cheated out of yours. Encourage them to have a blast with their other parent.

- Get into the spirit of the season. Make a New Year's resolution to let go of anger and treasure all that you have.
- Love means far more than money. Your time, attention, and emotional presence are much more important than lavish gifts.
- Holidays are not a competition with your ex or for your children.
- Coordinate. A brief e-mail can ensure that you don't duplicate presents or plan back-to-back feasts for stuffed and confused children.
- Work things out in advance with your own extended family, whether that means saying no, spending the holidays differently than usual, or asking for help.
- Establish traditions, even new ones that may be "off time" or different from the past. Year-in, year-out traditions will be remembered for a lifetime.
- Consider celebrating together with your ex, particularly if your separation is recent.

Let me offer a final note about schedules for preschoolers. I have focused on how you may change your schedule. I have assumed that you are moving into the preschool years while divorced. But the schedules I have outlined still apply if you are separating during your child's preschool years. And if you are separating now, you can move quickly into your schedule, whatever it is. Yes, you still may want to ease into a schedule a bit, especially if your preschooler is younger, confused, or upset. We all like a little time to adjust. But unlike infants and toddlers, your preschooler is emotionally equipped to manage separations of a few days from both of you.

# Divorcing during Preschool versus
# Moving into Preschool When Divorced

If you separated when your preschooler was an infant or toddler, you may want to revisit your parenting plan around his third or fourth birthday. Maybe you have a cooperative coparenting relationship, and your goal has been to gradually work into a 50/50 schedule. If this is what you have been planning, you should be able to get there (or close) now, as Justin and Nicole did.

But remember, your children don't count minutes. You shouldn't focus too much on time either. There is no need to change a plan that is working well and gives you both significant parenting time but isn't exactly 50/50.

## TALKING TO PRESCHOOLERS ABOUT DIVORCE

You also can move into a new schedule more quickly because, unlike with babies, you can tell your preschooler what is happening and a little bit about why. Your guidance can help prepare him, emotionally and practically, for the changes ahead.

You can, and should, talk with your preschooler about your divorce. She can understand your words if you keep them simple. She also can grasp some of the emotions and practicalities. If you tell her what is happening, she will be a little better prepared for the changes to come. She also will be ready for innocent questions her friends may ask: "How come your Mommy and Daddy have different houses?"

You should talk with your preschooler. But what should you say?

In *The Truth about Children and Divorce*, I wrote an entire chapter about talking to children. You may want to have a look. You may also want to flip ahead to Chapter 7, where I go into a little more detail about how to talk to children. But let me offer you some essential guidance here.

## KEEP IT SIMPLE

First and foremost, you want to keep your explanations to your pre-schooler, or really to children of any age, simple and practical. As a point of reference, think about how you might answer the question "Where do babies come from?" Your preschooler is not interested in, or capable of understanding, a lecture about reproductive biology or safe sex. She just wants you to confirm that babies come from Mommy's tummy.

You want to offer a similarly simple, child-focused explanation about your separation. Abstractions like divorce are beyond a five-year-old, so you don't even try to explain them. Your five-year-old also is not interested in, or capable of understanding, much of what went wrong in your marriage. Instead, keep it simple and practical. The heart of your message may be:

*Mommy and Daddy are going to live in different places. Mommy is moving, but Daddy will stay here. Tomorrow, Mommy is going to show you her new home and your new home. You are going to have your own room and your own stuff in both of your homes. And you are going to spend lots of time with both of us. You will go back and forth every few days. We're going to set up a calendar so you can see where you will be. Of course, your teddy will go back and forth with you. You will stay in the same school and have the same friends. It's true. Mommy and Daddy disagree about some important things. That's a big part of the reason we decided we can't live to-gether anymore. But one thing we will always agree about is how wonderful you are and how much we both love you.*

## EXPLAINING WHY YOU ARE DIVORCING

How much do you tell your preschooler about the reasons for your divorce?

Not much. In my example, the only explanation is, "We disagree about some important things." Another simple explanation is, "We love being parents together, but we aren't happy as husband and wife." Or maybe, "We love each other as your mom and dad. But we don't love each other anymore as husband and wife." If you use this last explanation, make sure to tell your son that a parent's love will never end—even if husbands and wives sometimes stop loving each other.

What if you disagree about getting a divorce or the reasons for it? What if one of you had an affair? These are really complicated questions. Read my chapter in *The Truth* for some guidance. I also discuss this a little more in the next chapter. But the bottom line is this: Your preschooler needs a simple, consistent message. So if you and your ex disagree about what happened, you still need to agree on an age-appropriate sound bite to tell her.

## EMOTIONAL REFERENCING

When talking with your preschooler, you want to keep strong emotions out of the discussion. You particularly want to guard against appearing out of control emotionally or sending strong but contradictory emotional messages.

Why? Your preschooler has a limited understanding of your words and your relationship, or any relationship. But her radar is tuned in to your emotions. She will sense your intense sadness or anger. She will dial in to your feelings, even if you try to hide them, and certainly if you don't.

Your emotions also tell your preschooler how she should feel. At five, she has no idea how to react to your separation. When they don't know how they should feel, preschoolers (and younger and older children) engage in what psychologists call *emotional referencing*. They look to how *you* are reacting to gauge how they should feel.

Of course, you want your daughter to realize this is sad. It is. So you can show some sadness. But you mostly want her to feel safe and secure, despite all the changes. You want her to be happy, still. She will feel sad but still safe, secure, and basically happy, if you *show* her how she should feel. Show her some of your sadness, but definitely show her that your emotions are in control. In your words and actions, tell her that everything is going to be all right. Do this even if you are not 100 percent sure within yourself.

And keep anger and blame out of it. Anger frightens a preschooler, and blame confuses him. Whom should he believe? Whose emotions should he reference? Of course, you are allowed to be hurt and angry. But the goal of talking with your preschooler isn't to make him as hurt and angry as you are.

## SIMPLE ISN'T EASY

I know. Simple doesn't mean easy. Telling your preschooler about your separation is going to be one of the most painful moments and memories in your life.

Your simple message isn't easy for your daughter either. She may not really understand what you are saying—practically or emotionally. Or she may be so upset that she's really can't hear your words.

That's OK. This is just a start. You can and should talk to her again, later. That night, alone in her room, you can answer her questions or clarify her misunderstandings. But helping her with her emotions is the big reason why you're talking to her. Snuggle with her. Reassure her that everything is going to be all right. And, of course, tell her again (and again) how much you love her, and Dad does too.

## SELF-BLAME AND FEELINGS OF RESPONSIBILITY

Preschoolers sometimes blame themselves for divorce. Even if you tell your preschooler, "This is not your fault," she may still say, "It's my fault."

Why does she do this? Preschoolers are egocentric. As they try to understand and influence their world, they focus on themselves. So if something bad happens, a four-year-old can wonder, "What did I do wrong?" Preschoolers also engage in magical thinking. Your daughter may not only think she caused your divorce. She may believe she can fix it. She just has to figure out how.

Don't be confused by her self-blame or magical thinking. Your daughter doesn't need a lesson in logic—or details on why everything is your fault (or your ex's). You can reassure her that this is not her fault, and especially that this is not something she needs to fix. But focus on the reassurance, her emotions, not her intellectual understanding. You cannot "cure" a four-year-old's egocentrism. But your preschooler will have a lot less to try to fix, or to blame herself for, if she feels like everything is going to be OK.

So tell your preschooler, "This is not your fault." But make sure you add, "And fixing this is not your job. It is our job. It's a grownup's job. Dad and I are going to take care of everything, even though we are going to live apart. And we're definitely going to take care of you."

## WHY DON'T YOU AND DAD LIVE TOGETHER?

What if you separated when your child was very young or were never married? Now that she's a preschooler, you may want to explain a little bit about your family. Or maybe your five-year-old will ask, "How come you and Daddy don't live together?"

If this is you, you face far fewer complications than explaining an impending separation to your preschooler. You are discussing *old* news. Whew! The emotional volume of your divorce should be turned way down by now. And your urgency to explain everything that happened, and why, should have dissipated. (If you separated recently, this is a helpful perspective. Looking back from years into the future, how are you going to wish you managed this?)

If you divorced years ago, really all you need to tell your pre-schooler is a little bit about how and why your family is different—and that she has a great family even if it is different. But I don't need to give you a script about what to say. Just listen to the *Barney* song, "My Family's Just Right for Me." Have your daughter listen too. Barney says there are all kinds of families. Families are about love, no matter who lives where. And Barney wants to emotionally reassure kids. You should too. Tell your daughter, "Like Barney says, our family is just right for us. It's all about love!"

## PARENTING AND COPARENTING PRESCHOOLERS

Choices about schools are one of the three major decisions shared in joint legal custody (see Chapter 3). So if you share legal custody, you and your ex must agree about what preschool your child attends.

Picking a preschool may be the first big decision you and your ex have to make together. So your choice of preschool not only is a big decision. You also may be figuring out how to make *any* big decision with your ex.

I discuss this same issue in the next chapter, where we consider the even bigger decision of picking an elementary school for your child. You may want to flip ahead to read that section now. For now, here are my basic tips:

- Give yourself time. This *is* a big decision.
- Gather information. Visit different schools, ideally to-gether with your ex.
- Share information. Share not only what you learn formally

but also your impressions, as well as whatever you hear from other parents.

- Discuss the problem you are trying to solve, not just your preferred solution. What are your goals and concerns for your child? For example, you may see her as shy. You may think she'll do better in a small class with a warm teacher. Maybe you have found a great fit for her. But don't just argue for that school. You and your ex need to agree on your goals, so you can find a school that best meets your child's needs. Keep an open mind. Maybe there is an even better solution or a different one.

- Don't avoid disagreement. You do not want to turn picking a preschool into a conflict that requires the United Nations to send in troops. But you do want to be able to voice your opinion, feel heard, and discuss various pros and cons. That way, you will feel better about the whole process, even if you end up settling for your second choice.

- If you cannot come to agreement, get outside help. Mediators, therapists, collaborative lawyers, and school consultants are out there for a reason. This may be the time to seek some professional support.

Of course, you can pick a preschool all by yourself if you have sole legal custody. Maybe having that authority sounds attractive. But unless you have a terribly contentious divorce, I think that you still would be wise to consult with your child's other parent.

Why? You want his support for your child's preschool experience—and beyond. Your ex is more likely to be supportive if he has had some input about picking a school, even if the final decision remains yours. Plus, you may find it helpful to hear a second opinion about this big decision. And if you ask your ex for his ideas, you should also be able to use him as a sounding board for your thoughts and concerns.

And if the shoe were on the other foot, you surely would like to have input.

You may not have a cooperative divorce. But this doesn't mean you can't cooperate sometimes, particularly when making big decisions.

Sharing legal custody is the norm today. So you probably have an angry divorce if you have sole legal custody. Inviting your ex to help you pick a preschool could be a step toward normalizing your relationship.

This may be the most important reason to ask for his input. Maybe you have good reasons to be angry now. But do you want to remain angry with your children's mother or father throughout your children's life? If you do, it's going to be a long, difficult row to hoe, for you and especially for your children. So think about extending an olive branch, even if you don't really want to. I've never heard regret from parents who take the high road—even from parents who travel the high road alone.

## CHILD-RELATED EXPENSES

Picking a preschool raises financial issues that are a part of coparenting across two homes. Now or soon in the future, you should be receiving or paying *child support*, money exchanged between parents to help offset the added costs of raising a child. Every state has a formula for calculating child support. (Yes. Formulas differ across states. So child support amounts can differ quite a bit depending on where you live.)

You should be able to find your state's guidelines online. Many states have online calculators that only require you to plug in various numbers to determine a child support figure. Or you can ask an attorney, mediator, or state child support agency for help in calculating child support amounts for your family.

Child support is designed to cover the basic costs of raising a child. This includes things like the added cost of housing, feeding, and clothing children, as well as health insurance and work-related childcare. Formulas also typically consider each parent's income, and your child's standard of living during your marriage.

But there is a big gray area in child support. Are parents required to share certain discretionary costs that some parents view as essential? Examples of these gray areas include the following:

- The cost of children's extracurricular activities. Piano lessons and travel sports can get quite expensive.
- College tuition. This is a huge topic that I discuss in Chapter 8, on adolescence. But I could have raised the issue of college tuition in the infancy chapter, because that's when you should start saving.
- Tuition for private schools, including preschool.

Most public school systems do not offer free preschool, except perhaps for low-income families. Are you and your ex supposed to share this expense?

You *could* ask a judge to decide who pays for the costs of preschool. But the legal expenses probably would be far higher than your daughter's preschool tuition. A much better approach is to address this topic in the agreement you reach with your ex with the help of a mediator or attorneys. You can detail what "gray area" costs you will share and how you will share them. For example, I often specify that the costs of extracurricular activities will be shared in proportion to each parent's income or according to some designated split, such as 50/50 or 75/25.

When I write agreements, I also usually put in a maximum amount of expenses to be shared. You may limit total costs for extracurricular activities to two thousand dollars a year, for example. As an alternative, your contract may indicate that you and your ex must agree about whether your child participates in extracurricular activities. If you agree, you and your ex know in advance how much it will cost you. This can be a real help—or it can be an impediment. Your arguments about extracurricular activities may really be fights about money, not whether your daughter should participate in travel soccer.

Reading this, you may have had an "aha!" experience: Gray-area expenses can complicate legal custody decision making. Yes, they can.

Circling back to picking a preschool, you know that the tuitions at different preschools can vary, sometimes by a lot. So when you are trying to make this joint legal custody decision with your ex, money may be a factor. Actually, that is fine. Money affects married parents' decisions about preschool too. But when it comes to the well-being of your children, parents can be reluctant to say, "That's too expensive." As a result, you may take on debt that you really can't manage. Or you may end up arguing about which school is better—when you're *really* arguing about money.

So that's why I addressed costs head-on here. In discussing preschool with your ex, you need to talk about money head-on too.

And, sorry, this problem is *not* resolved if you have sole legal custody. With sole legal custody, you may get to pick your child's preschool. But this does not mean that your ex has to pay for it (except if your agreement indicates that he will). And unless they make or have inherited a great deal of money, it's pretty rare for someone to agree to pick up the tab for school, no matter what it costs.

So now you know another reason why you may want to involve your ex in picking preschools, even if you have sole legal custody. He's more likely to contribute to paying for a preschool that he has helped pick.

## DAY-TO-DAY PARENTING

*How* you make decisions, not what you decide, almost always is the most important part of day-to-day parenting. Your preschooler will benefit if you and your ex share pretty similar expectations about things like bedtimes, reading books versus playing with the iPad, and getting dressed by yourself. But the important thing isn't whether bedtime is 7:30 or 9:00 p.m. The most important thing is that you two pretty much agree. This means you will need to communicate somehow.

Whether in person, over the telephone, or by texting, keep your interactions with your ex focused on your child. If not, well, you aren't coparenting. Big decisions like picking a preschool are almost certain to require face-to-face interactions. You may visit schools together, meet for coffee to discuss options, or perhaps use a mediator to help you review options and weigh pros and cons. Reserve texts or e-mails for sharing basic information about practicalities like preschool field trips or minor medical issues like colds.

Apart from sharing big decisions and little details, effective coparenting requires you and your ex to discuss many ordinary but important questions. How is your son adjusting to school? What kids are best for playdates? Is your son getting enough sleep? Are transitions between homes creating difficulties? As I described in Chapter 3, scheduling a weekly parenting conference call is one of the best ways of managing these kinds of parenting essentials.

Of course, preschoolers still need you to set limits. So discipline is another potential topic for your weekly parenting conference. I won't revisit how important it is for you and your ex to agree both about your rules across homes and about the discipline techniques you use. I discussed these topics in detail in Chapter 5. If you jumped ahead to this chapter because you have a preschooler, make sure to go back and read that.

## IS THIS NORMAL BEHAVIOR OR IS THIS ABOUT THE DIVORCE?

Parenting conferences are not just about making decisions. You also want to use this time to share fun stories about your preschooler.

You want to discuss your concerns too—and hopefully alleviate or at least better identify your worries.

Divorced parents continually face vexing questions during this stage, and at every stage, of their children's development. The specifics differ, but these questions often boil down to this: Is your child's challenging behavior part of normal development or a sign of something deeper, perhaps owing to the upheaval of your divorce?

Let's consider imaginary fears as an example of this dilemma. At some point, your preschooler is going to wake you up, screaming in terror about monsters in the dark. You'll do your best to comfort her. Then you'll tuck her back in bed. In the morning, you'll ask her if she had a bad dream. But then the same thing happens again three out of the next four nights. You start to get worried, and exhausted. Is something wrong?

I remember a legal case involving imaginary fears from decades ago. I had created and was studying a mediation program in a Virginia court. We dealt with all kinds of legal and physical custody disputes. In this case, a dad filed a legal complaint against his ex for the alienation of his four-year-old daughter. (Alienation involves often controversial claims that one parent has turned the children against the other.) In essence, the dad was taking his ex to court for telling their daughter false and frightening claims about him and his home.

In mediation, I soon discovered Dad's evidence for Mom's alienation. His daughter had developed new fears when sleeping at his house. She couldn't sleep, hated the dark, and worried about (and sometimes searched for) monsters in her bedroom. She had never shown the slightest anxiety about being at his house until recently. To him, only one thing could have caused this: His ex clearly implanted false, irrational fears about Dad in their four-year-old daughter's impressionable mind!

The mediation was brief. Mom was incredulous upon learning for the first time about why she was in mediation. Then she started laughing. (The fact that our mediation service was free may have improved her humor.) She told her ex that their daughter showed the same fears at her house too. The little girl started waking up maybe two months ago. For the last several weeks, Mom had let her four-year-old daughter climb into bed with her most nights. That way, they both got some sleep.

Upon hearing this news, Dad looked relieved and perhaps more than a little embarrassed. He also looked a little skeptical—until I confirmed that imaginary fears are common among four-year-olds. I told both parents that they both should reassure their daughter when she got scared. Her fear was real even though the monsters weren't.

The parents readily agreed to comfort their little girl, and to get her a glass of water the next time she woke up in the middle of the night. After some discussion, they also decided *not* to allow her to climb into bed with either of them. The parents agreed that letting her into their beds solved the immediate problem. But the short-term solution eventually would create a new and bigger difficulty.

The parents also agreed that the next time something like this happened, they would talk with each other first.

When your preschooler wakes up in the middle of the night, are you going to accuse your ex of turning your child against you? I know how upsetting it is to see your children so frightened. I also know that you worry about the consequences of divorce for your children. After all of my years of training, three decades of experience, and five children, I know how difficult it can be to sort out what is normal from what is the sign of something deeper.

And I know the best place to start to sort out all of these worries. If you can keep your own imagination in check, you can and should talk with your ex. He may have a helpful perspective. He may remember that imaginary fears are a scary consequence of your preschooler's wonderful new world of imagination. He may have strategies that work for him in helping your child feel safe and sleep through the night. Or maybe all he can do is commiserate, worry too, and perhaps help you decide to seek some expert advice.

## Troubled and Troubling Preschoolers

What bigger problems should you worry about with your preschooler?

Mental health professionals rely heavily on what people say about their thoughts and feelings when diagnosing problems like depression. But preschoolers cannot say, or perhaps know, much about how they feel. This makes it difficult to accurately identify anxiety or depression at this age. Think about it. Even if he *is* depressed, your four-year-old is unlikely to tell you, "I feel hopeless. Can I see a therapist?" For these reasons, anxiety and depression are identified rarely—and sometimes overlooked—at this young age.

Instead, experts focus more on what young children do than what they may (or may not) say. Two important conditions can reveal themselves in a preschooler's behavior: attention deficit/hyperactivity disorder (ADHD) and autism spectrum disorder (ASD).

ADHD and ASD are problems too complex to describe in detail here. But I can give you a little information. That way, you'll get an idea of whether you may want to find out more.

Some parents refer to ADHD as ADD (attention deficit disorder). But ADHD is the correct term. Children with ADHD have trouble paying attention. They struggle to stay on task. They also may find it impossible to stay still—they can be fidgety, sometimes *really* fidgety. Finally, children with ADHD also can be impulsive. They may act before they think. Some children with ADHD show all three symptoms. Others have problems mainly with attention, which is where the old ADD term came from.

ADHD usually is identified in the elementary school years. For this reason, I focus on it in the next chapter, on school-age children. In recent years, professionals have diagnosed ADHD more and more among preschoolers. But let me warn you. Unless your child is *very* ADHD, you should be a bit skeptical if the term is applied to your four- or five-year-old. When it comes to preschoolers, there is not a lot of research to back up the diagnosis of ADHD—or its sometimes controversial treatment with medication.

Autism spectrum disorder (ASD) involves a wide range of impairments. Symptoms can vary from mild difficulties in social interaction and unusual, focused interests to extreme social disinterest, inability to communicate, and all-encompassing, repetitive behavior.

Experts have cast a much wider net in making the ASD diagnosis in the last two decades. Still, research shows that children with ASD respond well to highly structured behavioral interventions, particularly treatments that begin as early as possible in a child's life. So if someone has suggested that your preschooler may have ASD, this is definitely something to investigate and perhaps treat—as soon as possible.

Here's something else to keep in mind. Children with ADHD or ASD typically respond best to structure. They often find change difficult. So if your child has one of these conditions, an intellectual disability, or almost any emotional difficulty, you may need to consider a schedule that gives your child a "headquarters" in one home. You both can still be involved in your child's life. You just may need to keep schedules simpler.

Even as I say this, I can think of several children with ADHD or ASD who have done well with joint physical custody. (The case of Robert and Michele in Chapter 7 is one example.) That's great for them, and for their parents too. As always, the key is to find a schedule that fits best for your unique child and for your family. Just keep in mind that for kids with emotional challenges, the best fit may be a little different, a little simpler.

Finally, let me raise another possible concern, one that falls somewhere between normal and potentially troubling. Because peer rela-tionships become so important, parents of preschoolers often worry about their children's developing friendships. You may be concerned if your preschooler is getting few invitations for playdates. If so, you might consider whether your child perhaps is being overly aggressive or shy or acting immature. His preschool teacher should be able to offer some insight into his social interactions—and help steer appro-priate playmates in your child's direction.

If playdate invitations are sparse, another thing to consider is how you relate to other parents. Parents are gatekeepers of their preschooler's friendships. If you are always depressed, complaining, asking for help, or competing with your ex, parents may be avoiding you, not your child.

As a bottom line, remember this. The critical number of friends for your child, or anyone, is one. Keep this in mind, too, if someone else in your child's preschool has a child with special needs. You will do much for another family, yourself, and your child if you make occasional playdates with that child.

## Other Relationships and Your Preschooler

As your preschooler's social world expands, so does yours. This means that you and your ex will need to share relationships with your child's friends, and their parents. And if you don't share nicely, you will create problems for those other families—and for yourself and your child too.

### YOUR PRESCHOOLER'S SOCIAL LIFE, AND YOURS

Helping your child make and maintain friends can be tricky, for her and for you. She (or you) may be shy and feel left out. He (or you) may be a bit too aggressive and repel potential playmates. And sometimes arranging playdates can seem like a social competition, not just for your child but for you too. The stay-at-home moms may band together—and arrange for their kids to play together. And you work full time. And you're divorced. Or maybe you're a dad, not another mom. You may wonder: Is it OK to ask a mom over for coffee so your kids can play together?

Whether you're Mom or Dad, you may find that you are getting fewer invitations from the couples you used to spend time with. Now that you've split, you just don't fit in, or at least that's how old friends seem to treat you.

Some social problems may be in your preschooler's imagination— or yours. You may *think* you are being snubbed. But maybe that play-mate (or parent) is a little shy too. So extend your own invitation for a playdate. Encourage your four-year-old to do the same.

Of course, people with similar interests do tend to band together. There may be a social clique of parents whose kids play together too. Do you *really* want to be a part of that group? Does your child? Maybe you'd be better off making friends with other single parents. Or maybe you want to cultivate one or two group members who are more open and friendly. You may be surprised how eager other parents can be to help—if you ask (and do your best to reciprocate).

What about your ex? As I said, you need to share, or at least try. This includes sharing at least some of your children's friends and their parents. You don't have to all be friends together. Just be OK when your child's friends play at your ex's, or when other parents get along with your ex too.

## GOING PUBLIC

An important part of sharing friends and acquaintances is being careful what you say to other parents about your ex. Sure, other parents may seem really interested when you tell them stories about your divorce. You make the Kardashians sound boring! Train wrecks hold a macabre fascination. But really, no one wants to deal with the mess. If you give other parents too much information, you may discover they really were more interested in the gossip than in you. They may fan the flames with rumors, act hostile toward your ex, or maybe grow tired of your stories. None of these reactions is going to help your child, let alone you.

You and your ex may have different versions of your history: his divorce, her divorce. But like keeping his-and-hers towels separate, you do *not* want to share dueling explanations about what happened with other parents. Conflicting stories put friends, and ultimately your child, smack in the middle. And other parents will get out of this uncomfortable spot by avoiding you.

So I suggest that you find one or two great friends to vent to, or maybe a therapist. But with most acquaintances, especially the parents of your children's friends, don't share intimate details about your divorce. Just give them a benign sound bite. "It's been tough, as you can imagine. But we're really trying to work together as parents."

This sort of simple explanation discourages gossip. Ho-hum. Boring. It also makes your ex look better. And you look better too. Maybe I'll have you and your son over for a playdate or two so I can hear the gory details about your divorce. But I'm more likely to be friends, real friends, with the parent who puts her kid first, who makes her kid feel comfortable, and who makes my kid and me feel comfortable too.

## PUBLIC EVENTS

Your preschooler's world, and yours, is bigger in another way now too. You will begin attending events like school picnics with your child—and probably with your ex. Yup. Your divorce is going to be on display in public.

The best way to manage your family's public face is to act like one big happy family (even if it is an act). You and your ex can sit together, focus on your children, and engage each other in polite, superficial conversation. I am always impressed when I discover that those really nice parents I recently met are divorced. "Wow," I think. "They're doing things right."

You want to be those parents.

If this is your first public gathering, talk with your ex in advance about how she wants to handle things. If you split recently, maybe all you can manage right now is a polite greeting. You feel like you have to sit apart.

If you do sit apart, make sure your child—and other kids and other parents—feel free to move between you. You aren't in a contest over your child, or anyone else. So don't turn a school picnic into one. This is only the beginning. Hundreds of events await you in your child's future. Get off to the best start you can. And make it your goal to have each new gathering be a little bit more comfortable than the last one, for you and for everyone else.

### DATING

If your marriage ended when your preschooler was an infant or toddler, hopefully you have your own social life now too. That's great, but as I've mentioned before, my standard advice with a new romantic relationship is "go slow," for your child and for yourself.

My advice holds for children (and parents) of all ages. With preschoolers, a special concern is that your son can get attached quickly to new adults in your life (and his). Breakups of short-term relationships may be hard on you—and harder on your five-year-old. So your new partner should not spend much time around your children until you're sure this is a serious relationship. Keeping your private life private also will help avoid unnecessary conflicts with your ex.

If you have split up only recently, the preceding advice applies tenfold.

## SIBLINGS

Finally, one thing can be simpler with preschoolers. If you have older children, you may not need a different schedule for them and your preschooler (as you do for infants and toddlers). A week still is a long separation for a young preschooler. But traveling in a pack may provide enough emotional security for a four- or five-year-old to help her bridge the longer time apart.

If you are considering a week on/week off schedule for your preschooler and her older siblings, you may want to reread the case of Bethany, Roger, and Bella from Chapter 3. Sometimes you need to adapt your plans, even when you are doing your best to be sensitive to your child's developmental needs.

## CHAPTER 7

# School Age: Reading, Writing—Right and Wrong

S chool age (six to twelve years old) begins with first grade and ends with puberty. This is a time in development when we expect children to get down to business. That business, of course, is schoolwork. We expect school-age children to devote time and energy to mastering the basics of reading, writing, and arithmetic.

Psychologists often divide this long period of development into early school age (ages six to eight) and late school age (ages nine to twelve). At times, we will too. Certainly, first, second, and third graders are different from fourth, fifth, sixth, and seventh graders. But the overriding focus on learning is shared throughout this stage of development.

Of course, school is the focal point of children's education. But as children move through elementary and middle school, we expect them to learn on their own too. We want school-age children to do their homework, read ("Get away from that screen and read a book!"), and follow their independent interests. Those independent interests may involve joining a club, pursuing a hobby, or just tracking a favorite sports team.

And school-age children continue to learn through play too, including sports and other physical activities. Play teaches school-age children about give-and-take in peer relationships. Sports can teach them about trying hard, working as a team, and being gracious in both victory and defeat. Independent play feeds imagination and ultimately creativity. Play also helps children relax and maintain balance. "Work hard, play hard" is a standard to cultivate during school age, and, I think, to live by throughout life.

School-age children learn many social and emotional lessons through their work and play. They learn to be away from their parents for long periods of time. They learn to independently control their behavior, attention, effort, and emotions. As with the three *R*s, our expectations for self-direction and self-control increase as school-age children grow. Until the storm of puberty wrecks the calm, we expect older school-age children to maintain their focus, follow the rules, and not object (or at least not too strenuously).

School-age children also learn what actions are right or wrong. They learn to judge themselves. And they learn to judge other people too, including their parents.

Because of her cognitive growth, your twelve-year-old understands what divorce means—intellectually, if perhaps not emotionally. Her knowledge about the meaning of divorce, for her and for you, makes helping her both easier and harder.

Your task is easier, because you do not need to tell your twelve-year-old what divorce is. She knows. But your task is harder, because you may need to address your twelve-year-old's feelings *about* your divorce, not just help her through it. For example, you may need to respond to your daughter's anger as she judges you for getting divorced, or perhaps for being responsible for your divorce.

## Reading, Writing—Right and Wrong

Around age six or seven, children's cognitive abilities take a sudden jump. The famous Swiss developmental psychologist Jean Piaget called this shift the stage of *concrete operations*. Children in the stage of concrete operations can understand concepts and the rules that govern them.

Unlike a four-year-old, for example, an eight-year-old understands that numbers are about more than size. (Four is bigger than three!) She knows that numbers can be used to quantify many properties of many things, from shoe size to money to the distance to Grandma's house. She also understands, in a concrete way, that numbers can be manipulated. And she knows some of the rules for transforming them. By age eight, she can add and subtract and maybe even multiply. Numbers also help her understand time. She can use a calendar to calculate how many days (or weeks) until summer vacation—or until she sees Dad again.

Their cognitive development allows school-age children to understand difficult social and emotional concepts too, at least in concrete terms. For example, a four-year-old typically views death as reversible. I remember when, as preschoolers, my kids asked repeatedly when Blackjack, our pet cat, would come back—even though they helped bury him. But an eight-year-old understands that death is universal, inevitable, and permanent. At age eight, he cannot appreciate the abstraction of death. He's not about to grapple with death's ultimate religious or biological meaning, or the general struggle of searching for meaning in death. Instead, at eight, he knows that death is a powerful force, something he cannot control and likely fears.

As death becomes a real idea, your eight-year-old may develop new concerns that you may die. He fears your death, because he now knows that one day you *will* die.

Today, many early-school-age children develop similar fears that their parents will divorce. Divorce is not universal or inevitable. But divorce can seem awfully common and unpredictable to an eight-year-old. It can become something to fear.

Children grow emotionally, as well as intellectually, when they enter school age. Unlike cognitive development, which is marked by a qualitative shift into concrete operations, psychologists generally view the school-age child's emotional growth as more gradual. Still, school-age children fully experience some new emotions for the first time. One important example is the emergence of the "moral emotions," including guilt, shame, and sympathy.

Another example is the development of anxiety. Infants and toddlers experience fear, of course, as do preschoolers who use their imagination to create new things to be afraid of. School-age children certainly know fear too. But their new understanding of time can lead them to fear the future, perhaps disproportionately. That's the definition of anxiety. Fear is realistic and present focused. "That dog is scary!" Anxiety is out of proportion to reality and future focused. "I think something awful is going to happen!"

School-age children also become better at controlling their emotions. One adaptive change is their growth in *emotion regulation*. School-age children are better able to "use their words" (or other emotion-regulation strategies) instead of acting on their emotional impulses. A nine-year-old's ability to control his emotions starts to become essential to his success in school, sports, and relationships.

School-age children also get better at masking their emotions. Sometimes, it seems, they try to hide their feelings almost as soon as they recognize them. Children particularly struggle to cover up negative emotions that seem to signal weakness. Taunts like "crybaby" or "scaredy cat" capture that social disapproval. The derisions also convey the message "Don't let your feelings show." And the heckling indicates that many children—the "crybabies" and the "scaredy cats"—struggle in trying to hide their feelings from their peers.

Covering up your emotions can be adaptive in some social situations. But hiding your true feelings can be maladaptive too, particularly if you are a ten-year-old dealing with difficult feelings. Perhaps your parents' divorce makes you deeply sad, angry, or embarrassed. Maybe you feel all alone. How can someone help you if you refuse to share what's troubling you? You may not want to talk with your parents. But you have to talk to someone.

A school-age child's cognitive and emotional development both bear on another important quality that emerges during these years: moral judgment. Most psychological research on children's moral development focuses on self-control, the internalization of rules and the reasons why you should follow the rules. In everyday life, we call this the development of a *conscience*.

But a small body of work has examined the important topic of how school-age children judge others, not themselves.

In studying the three *R*s, school-age children first make rote associations: 1 + 1 = 2. Jane runs. Dick runs. Jane and Dick run. Eventually, they master complex rules, for example, about grammar and long division.

Children's views of others' actions as right or wrong also develop with age. Preschoolers and early-school-age children judge others based on outcomes. If you do something that hurts other people, you're "naughty," even if you did it by accident. To a six-year-old, some kids (and adults) are nice; others are mean. Mean people hurt you, physically or emotionally. Nice people don't.

By late school age, children learn intricate rules about appropriate social behavior. Often these rules are based on principles of fairness that parallel the rules of sports or games. In making a moral judgment, intent becomes critical. There's a big difference between something that happened by accident and breaking the rules on purpose. You *have* to follow the rules. If not, you are *cheating*.

## READING, WRITING—RIGHT, WRONG, AND DIVORCE

The school-age child's growing understanding presents divorced parents with new opportunities and new challenges. Once children enter the stage of concrete operations, they can begin to grasp abstract concepts like marriage and divorce. But their understanding is concrete, anchored in their experience. Marriage is a ceremony, a plan to have children, and to live together forever. Divorce is . . . "getting unmarried," an explanation my daughter Julia gave me when she was six years old. (She was trying to figure out what I do for a living, I think.)

Growing knowledge and life experience enrich late-school-age children's understanding of concepts. Most eleven-year-olds know quite a bit about marriage, if you can get them to talk about it. They know that marriage is a commitment. They know about marriage ceremonies. They may be able to discuss the details of weddings at some length, perhaps including their own fantasized plans. Late-school-age children also know that marriage involves a deep emotional connection.

But they do not yet understand romantic love.

Eleven-year-olds know that divorce is the legal ending of a marriage. One parent moves out. There may be a lot of fighting. Kids often end up in the middle.

But they do not understand their parents' profound feelings of pain, loss, fear, and failure.

Your school-age child's intellectual understanding of divorce means you can and should talk to him about it. But as I discuss later in this chapter, he still mostly wants to know concrete details. He wants to know how divorce will affect *his* life and relationships, not what it has done to yours.

And he mostly wants to focus on *his* emotions too. He may be twelve, but he still knows it's your job to take care of him, not vice versa.

And he's right.

## Schedules for School-Age Children

Getting judged by your school-age child may be painful, devastating, or merely annoying. Whatever it is, her judgment complicates things.

But some things about divorce are easier with a school-age child. For one, school age is the best age for sharing joint physical custody. There are a number of reasons why.

One reason is that your relationship with your seven-year-old son is well established now. His attachment to you and his dad is still important. Love always is most important. But unlike when he was an infant or a toddler, your seven-year-old has the mental and emotional tools to allow him to bridge time. He knows you love him, and he'll be excited to see you in a week.

And while your eleven-year-old daughter is busy, well, she's not a teenager—yet. Teenagers, of course, develop their own, strong opinions. One thing a fifteen-year-old may decide is that joint custody is too complicated for *her* life. But when she's eleven, you're still pretty much in control of your daughter's schedule. At least you have some veto power. Plus, you have the responsibility of getting her wherever she wants to go. Part of that responsibility can be getting her back and forth between your house and your ex's.

Joint physical custody can work well at other ages. But school age is the sweet spot.

Another reason why school age is the best age for joint custody is that a couple of dozen studies support the potential benefits of joint physical custody for school-age children, as I discussed in Chapter 3. We know that school-age children can thrive in joint custody. For them and for your relationship with them, joint physical custody can be the best schedule.

And sometimes joint physical custody is the worst arrangement for a ten-year-old. I won't repeat all the reasons why. You can flip

back to Chapter 3 if you want to review the details. But let me remind you that children do best in joint physical custody when:

- It is logistically practical (you live pretty near to your ex).
- The back-and-forth fits with your child's unique personality (something you can only judge once you try a schedule).
- Most important, you have a pretty cooperative relationship with your ex (something you *can* work to achieve).

Please don't think that by raising these concerns, I am trying to talk
you out of joint custody. Actually, I am trying to talk you *into* joint
physical custody. I want you to make joint physical custody work for
your children by making the conditions right to make it work.

You *can* keep trying to work with your ex. You *can* tweak a
schedule. You *can* make extra effort to make the back-and-forth less
disruptive for your orderly child. And, yes, if parenting and coparenting really are your priorities, you *can* move closer to your ex. You
also can turn down that promotion that would move you far away.
Or you even can approach your ex about finding a new job too and
moving across the country six months after you do.

I have helped many parents negotiate each of these compromises.

Assuming you are willing to find a way to make joint physical
custody work, here is your next decision. Should you try week on/
week off, divide the week, or create your own unique parenting plan?

## WEEK ON/WEEK OFF OR DIVIDE THE WEEK?

If you prefer a week on/week off schedule, that arrangement can
work well during school age.

Except in unusual circumstances, school-age children can manage longer separations from their parents. Intellectually and from
experience, a seven-year-old understands what a week means. So
you need not worry about most of the concerns I raised about how

time moves so slowly for preschoolers—or my related thoughts about creating a schedule for preschoolers by dividing the week instead of alternating weeks.

And your seven-year-old also has practical tools that can make it easier to go for a while without seeing you. He may know how to use FaceTime, a telephone, or Skype. If he doesn't use social media tools yet, you can rest assured that he will learn in a hurry. Virtual interactions are not the same as real contact, but they can help him (and you) bridge longer times apart.

But just because you *can* do week on/week off doesn't mean you *want* to.

Week on/week off has advantages. It gives you a nice block of time with your children. The schedule also requires your children, and you, to make fewer transitions. And week on/week off also can work well if your work involves frequent travel. You can arrange (most of) your trips on the weeks when your kids are with your ex. You can be home when your kids are with you.

Still, you also want to consider the possible advantages of dividing the week instead of alternating weeks with your school-age child.

A week can feel like a long time of no contact for you and your daughter. If she's only six or seven, a week may seem particularly long. Some parents deal with this by including midweek visits in a week on/week off schedule. A midweek dinner may work great. But there goes the advantage of fewer transitions.

Your work schedule also may make dividing the week more attractive. Maybe you always need to travel at the beginning of the week. Or maybe you are on call or have late meetings on Mondays and Tuesdays. If so, a 2-2-5-5 schedule (or some other schedule for dividing the week) may work just great for you. Your daughter is with her mom on Mondays and Tuesdays. She is with you on Wednesdays and Thursdays. And she alternates three-day weekends with each of you.

But in my mind at least, the biggest advantage of dividing the week is that most of us schedule our lives around the days of the week. This includes your children and the schools they attend. So if your son's third-grade field trip is scheduled for the second Thursday in October, he can make an easy calculation about whom to talk to. He's always at Dad's on Thursdays. That's a big advantage, I think. But if week on/week off has other big advantages for your family, well, calculating who he is with the second Thursday in October is not *that* hard.

It isn't the schedule. It's what works best for your child and your family.

And remember, of course, that what works best for your child and your family may not be exactly 50/50.

## HOME-CRAFTED JOINT CUSTODY: ROBERT AND MICHELE

In Chapter 1, I briefly introduced the parents of two school-age children. The dad, Robert, was adamant about getting equal time with his children. He had two children: a nine-year-old son, Robert Jr. (who had mild autism spectrum disorder), and a six-year-old daughter, LaKeesha. He entered mediation insisting on 50/50. As he made clear, he was unwilling to consider anything other than joint custody.

The mom, Michele, did not object to joint custody. She knew Robert was a loving father, and his children needed him. But she worried that her kids also needed a "headquarters," particularly for the start of the school week. She was especially worried about Robert Jr., who could struggle with change because of his emotional problems.

Michele said that she had always organized the kids for school. And her consulting job gave her the flexibility to continue to do this. Robert's surgery schedule, on the other hand, was anything but flexible.

At first, Robert took Michele's concerns as a personal attack. He thought she was saying she was the better or more important parent. He thought she was saying she was flexible and *he* was rigid—not his schedule.

I gave both of the parents some time to air their concerns. I even allowed them to snipe back and forth for a while. I didn't really jump in until they both turned to me in frustration. As I recall, Robert said, "So now you see why mediation will never work!"

"Actually," I said, "now I see why mediation *has* to work."

I explained to Robert and Michele what it felt like being in the middle of their disputes. I suggested this wasn't a comfortable spot for me, or, I doubted, for their children.

They could not argue with that.

I told them they had to do better if they wanted joint custody to work for their children. As a first step, I said, we had to refocus our discussion.

I educated Michele and Robert about joint custody—both legal and physical. I shared my strong opinion that trying to do everything exactly 50/50 was taking the wrong approach. We needed to think about the bigger picture. I told them that while they may end up with 50/50, joint custody is defined more flexibly in both research and the law. And most important, we needed to focus on their *goals* for Robert Jr. and LaKeesha first. Then we could figure out the best schedule for trying to achieve those goals.

Much of what I said about joint custody was news to Robert. He thought he wanted it. But as it turned out, he wasn't exactly sure what joint custody meant.

And while Robert and Michele differed in their initial proposals, they actually agreed about their goals. They both wanted their kids to be happy and healthy. They both wanted to be involved in their children's lives. They agreed that it would be great to have some one-on-one time. They agreed that experimenting with a schedule made sense, rather than fixing something in stone when it may not work. They agreed that their children, especially Robert Jr., bene-fited from structure. They agreed that Robert's surgery schedule was demanding and rigid, particularly at the beginning of the week. And, after considerable debate, Robert even agreed that Michele was in a better position to give the kids a "headquarters" for the start of the school week.

After four sometimes tense mediation sessions, we came up with a unique, home-crafted definition of joint custody for them. Michele and Robert would share joint legal custody, of course. But they now knew what joint custody involved—legally and in day-to-day par-enting. Robert and Michele also would share joint physical custody. But the schedule they agreed to try was not 50/50. It was 32/68, as Robert angrily pointed out shortly after we first hatched the plan.

According to their proposed schedule, the kids would be with Dad every other weekend from Thursday through Sunday, as well as every Thursday overnight on the off week. On Wednesdays on Rob-ert's off week, he would alternate overnights with each child. For the first off week, Robert Jr. would be with his father for Wednesday (alone) and Thursday (with LaKeesha). The next off week, LaKee-sha would be with her father for Wednesday (alone) and Thursday (with Robert Jr.).

The schedule gave Michele the "headquarters" she wanted for the kids. And Robert grudgingly admitted that the headquarters idea made sense. The plan also gave Robert the significant time that he wanted with the kids. And as I noted in Chapter 1, Robert was both surprised and thrilled when LaKeesha told him after a few weeks, "I like the schedule, because we have the same amount of time with you and Mom."

In her mind and experience, 32/68 was equal. She didn't count minutes. But she knew she still had a mom and a dad.

And everyone loved the "alone" time. You should really think about creating alone time too.

Both Robert and Michele viewed the schedule as an experiment, one that was subject to change. And it did change, but not for three years.

About a year after his divorce from Michele, Robert got involved in a serious dating relationship. Not one to waste time, Robert remarried within two years of his divorce. His remarriage to Destiny was great, he said (to me privately). But their family life was complicated. Destiny had an eighteen-year-old daughter and a thirteen-year-old son. The boy, Kordell, was two years older than Robert Jr., who was now eleven.

Destiny had a week on/week off schedule with her children. Kids were moving in and out of Robert and Destiny's home all the time. It was crazy, but they made it work.

At first, Robert's remarriage created concerns for Michele. She and Robert had a distant relationship. Yet they coordinated things well enough to make their kids' lives happy and whole. What was going to happen now?

But Michele soon discovered that Destiny was a great stepmother. When important issues arose in their children's lives, Michele spoke to Robert. But when it came to the kids' day-to-day activities, she found herself communicating more, and better, with Destiny.

Over these years, one happy outcome for the family was Robert Jr.'s progress. He had become much more organized and independent in his schoolwork. He continued to have "different" interests. And he could be somewhat insensitive socially. But Robert Jr. really was doing great. He attended regular classes, did well enough in most of them, and excelled in subjects that grabbed his attention. And when Robert Jr. developed an interest, it was intense. He was particularly involved in a school science club called BACON (Best All Around Club of Nerds). He had become a science star. His success gave him joy, confidence, and a role in his school.

Another happy development was Robert Jr.'s great relationship with his stepbrother, Kordell. Robert Jr. idolized Kordell and did his

best to imitate him. His dad said this relationship was the best possible social skills training for Robert Jr. And Kordell genuinely liked
Robert Jr. too. He accepted Robert Jr.'s quirks, but he also gave him
feedback on how to act. Robert Jr. wasn't hurt by the advice. Whatever Kordell said was gospel to him.

Their relationship was so good, in fact, that Robert Jr. asked his
dad *and* his mom if he could have the same schedule as Kordell.
Robert Jr. *always* made his wishes clear. And he didn't worry about
hurting his mother's feelings. Sometimes a degree of social insensi-
tivity can be a good thing.

I learned all of this information from Michele and Robert, but
not because they needed help with parenting. Instead, they had
scheduled an appointment with me to sort out details about how to
share the proceeds from the sale of their family home (where Michele
had been living). During our financial discussions, they announced,
matter-of-factly, that they had decided to switch Robert Jr. to a week-
to-week schedule, as he'd asked. LaKeesha wanted to stick with her
schedule, and the parents had agreed to continue that for her.

Michele and Robert made it sound like the change was no big
deal. So I didn't make a big deal out of it. But I quietly was elated.
They may not have had a great relationship. But they got it. They
had negotiated a *parenting* plan. They were in charge of their children's lives; the legal system wasn't. And in making decisions, big or
small, they found a way to put their children's interests first.

In fact, they continued to make changes to meet their children's
needs, as I discuss in the next chapter.


## IS A DISTANT DIVORCE GOOD ENOUGH FOR JOINT CUSTODY?

The case of Robert and Michele raises an important question. Do
parents with a distant divorce have a good enough relationship to
make joint physical custody work for their children?

As you may recall from Chapter 3, an Australian study found

that 59 percent of parents with a cooperative relationship maintained joint physical custody compared to 21 percent with a distant divorce and 19 percent with an angry divorce.

You know that parents with a cooperative coparenting relationship can make joint physical custody the best arrangement for their children. You also know how much I worry that angry coparents make joint physical custody the worst.

It is trickier to suggest when a distant divorce is good enough for joint physical custody. But let me try to offer you some guidance. Distant divorces come in many flavors, but I think there are two main varieties, kind of like chocolate and vanilla.

Plain-vanilla distant divorces involve parents who just don't have much to do with each other. Maybe they don't like each other much. But mostly they just have gone their separate ways. When together, they may have been more roommates than a couple. These parents may not share many joys of parenting, but nothing big gets in their way either. If this is you, you can make joint physical custody work. You just have to muster the energy to make the effort.

The other main flavor of a distant divorce is melted chocolate. The ongoing heat in this relationship is responsible for the mess. These couples use distance to keep their anger and pain in check. Distance is not a bad strategy for managing conflict. Certainly you would rather be cool to your ex than constantly bickering with him. But beware if you are unable to detach. Joint physical custody can give you or your ex many opportunities to turn up the heat. So you need to structure your coparenting carefully, perhaps with ongoing professional help, as Robert and Michele did. Or maybe you need to reconsider whether joint physical custody is going to work for your children.

As you weigh whether you can truly disengage, consider this. Fighting for your children may be an act of love. But not fighting for your children is even more loving. Remember the biblical story of

Solomon, where a false mother and a real mother were vying for custody? The false mother was willing to divide the baby in two. The real mother would rather give up her baby than do that.

## Divorcing during School Age Versus Moving into School Age When Divorced

If you separated when your child was younger, revisiting your parenting plan isn't an automatic just because your child is beginning school. Yes, your six-year-old can manage longer separations. So you may want to think about moving to week on/week off if you have reasons to prefer that schedule. But the schedule that you followed during preschool may continue to work well, especially through the early-school-age years. "If it ain't broke, don't fix it" is a great motto for many things in life, including your parenting plan.

If you separate when your child is school age, developmental issues need not affect your consideration of different schedules. As I said earlier, school age is the best age for joint physical custody—and for other schedules too.

In general, school-age children are pretty adaptable. They are focused more on their life than yours, but they still count on you to manage it. So as long as you keep your eight-year-old's life on track, well, his life should be on track.

Actually, you may be surprised how quickly your child adjusts to your separation. As long as you protect her from your conflicts and both remain a presence in her life, your daughter won't be devastated by divorce, at least not for too long. Instead, she will realize that her life hasn't become horrible or really even changed all that much. So she will get back to doing what eight-year-olds do. She will learn her lessons in and out of school. She will continue to play, be happy, and generally be a kid.

### TALKING TO SCHOOL-AGE CHILDREN ABOUT DIVORCE

She may adjust quickly, but you do face the painful task of telling your six- or ten-year-old that you are separating, and why. Brace yourself. This is going to be emotionally wrenching. This moment often becomes a memory that children and parents never forget. So you need to do your best to convey the right message, even though there is no way to sugarcoat things.

### HOW TO TALK TO CHILDREN

How you talk to your school-age child matters. If at all possible, you and your ex should speak with him together. You want to keep anger out of the conversation, of course. But it is all right to express some sadness. Showing some sadness is a good thing, really. This *is* sad.

As I described in Chapter 6, your child will engage in *emotional referencing*. He will look to your emotions to guide how he should feel. So don't just tell him how he should feel. Show him. Turn down the "temperature" of all of your emotions. (Turn off the anger and blame.) Be sad but in control. You want your words and actions to convey that you will take care of your child—and yourself.

You definitely don't want a ten-year-old feeling that you are so sad that he needs to take care of you. You want him to feel free to be sad but also to go on. When he goes back to school on Monday, you want him focusing on school, not on your divorce. He may be a little distracted, of course. This is going to take some time.

Just as with preschoolers or adolescents, you want to keep your explanations short, child-focused, and emotionally reassuring. Discuss practicalities like where you and he will live, go to school, and so on. Hopefully, you can reassure him that most of these things will stay the same in his life.

Whatever you say, give your child time and space to process. As your child grapples with the devastating news, focus on her emotional understanding more than her intellectual understanding. Help her understand how she feels, not what happened or why.

Search for emotions she may harbor but cannot express, as well as the ones she does. School-age children learn to hide their feelings, as I described earlier. So your nine-year-old may be grappling with a lot of sadness under a calm surface or with much pain under an angry one.

I'm not suggesting you pry. Kids have a right to their own feelings. Besides, maybe your daughter can't talk to you (or your ex) because she sees you, or both of you, as the source of her pain. In her mind, maybe you messed up her life.

So just give her *permission* to be upset. It's OK for her to be angry, or sad, or whatever, including that she really is fine.

If she is obviously struggling but just won't talk, you may consider getting some outside help. Find a therapist, someone who knows about divorce as well as about children. Make sure the therapist is willing to talk with you, as well your daughter. Of course, your daughter's sessions will be confidential. But you want feedback, even if it may be hard to hear. And it may help for the therapist to see the two of you together at some point—and maybe more than just the two of you.

## GETTING JUDGED

As I said earlier, your school-age child's development may introduce a new dimension into his understanding of your divorce: moral judgment.

Your twelve-year-old may blame you, or your ex, or both of you for getting divorced. The solution to getting blamed is *not* to follow an all-too-natural impulse: When you are blamed, shift the blame. Actually, the right thing to do is just the opposite. You need to accept responsibility for your mistakes. And you need to deal with the consequences, including, perhaps, asking your children for forgiveness.

Not all school-age children attribute blame in the same way. Six-, seven-, and eight-year-olds really want everyone to get along—on the playground or in divorce. If you cannot or will not get along, your child may think you (or your ex) are mean. And he is likely to be upset. He may get angry with you, or perhaps feel that he needs to get you to be nice.

Or—and beware of this—he may think that *he* can fix things. How? By being the perfect child. That's what my daughter Maggie started to do. She was seven when her mom and I split.

What did I do? I did my best to make her life happy. And I reminded her of her job: to be a kid. Flip back to my Hierarchy of Children's Needs in Two Homes in Chapter 2 if you need a reminder.

And, fortunately, early-school-age children are forgiving. If you fix it or if you start to behave better, all is good in his world again, including in his relationship with you.

Older school-age children may not be as forgiving.

In her mind, a twelve-year-old *knows* what divorce means. And she may be judgmental about it. It's not fair! Certainly, divorce is not fair to her. Your twelve-year-old also may ask who broke the rules. But she does not really want to know that your ex had an affair, or really who is to blame. More likely, her appeal to the rules is an attempt to fix things. Deep down—or very much on the surface—she hopes that following the rules will make things better. If you *promise* to follow the rules, maybe you will even get back together.

Reconciliation fantasies generally are more common among early- than late-school-age children. But they are not uncommon at any age.

Parents have reconciliation fantasies too.

Reconciliation would be a solution. Unfortunately, it is typically not a realistic solution.

## EXPLAINING THE REASONS FOR DIVORCE

Most twelve-year-olds really do not want to know the detailed reasons for your divorce. But some kids ask. A few demand to know what happened. And sometimes one parent demands that the children be told what happened. Or maybe you just think you need to say something.

If you are going to talk about what happened, remember what your child wants to hear, which is not much. Offer a simple explanation: We just were too unhappy. We couldn't get along.

Or you may want to tell your child that you no longer love each other—as husband and wife. You still love each other as his parents. And, of course, you always, always will love her as Mom and Dad.

What if one of you has done something really wrong, or your divorce is one-sided? If your ex is unwilling to give you a pass, which may be understandable, you may need to accept responsibility, including with your children. There still is no need to go into details. All of this is painful enough. You just need to be clear. You need to "own" your mistakes. Examples of you accepting responsibility include the following:

- I wanted this, even though Mom didn't.
- I fell in love with someone else.
- I have a problem with drinking. I am going to try to get help, but my drinking wrecked our marriage.

You can expect your child to be angry with you if you admit to mistakes. If you are the one who messed up, you can expect to receive the brunt of his anger.

But taking responsibility is the first, necessary step toward earning his forgiveness.

If he's twelve, your son is unlikely to be quick to forgive. That is tough, for sure. But you did make a mistake, right? Accept responsibility. Tell him that you have your side of the story, but that's adult stuff, not kids' stuff. Don't try to justify your actions, explain them away, or shift blame onto your ex. These are all Band-Aids. And they really are more for you than your child.

Instead of justifying yourself, repent. Tell your son you are sorry. Tell him that you hope he will forgive you—one day. Tell him you want to make amends. And, most important, *make* amends. How? Not by lavishing your son with gifts, fun activities, or other bribes. Instead, why not show your regret by being the best parent and coparent you can be?

And remember this too: Whether you did something wrong or were wronged, you have a responsibility to try to minimize the impact on your child—and on your own functioning as a parent. You need to do this for all kinds of reasons, including so your children can begin to forgive and move on.

You want him to forgive, even if you were the one who was wronged. You want your son to forgive his father, even if you think you cannot.

## Parenting and Coparenting School-Age Children

Parenting and coparenting a school-age child can be both easier and harder than with younger children. It's easier because your eight-year-old is busy at school for six to eight hours a day. She's also more independent, flexible, and able to adjust if the routines in her two homes are somewhat different.

But it's harder too, because you face some big decisions. For one, you need to agree on an elementary school. And you have to make sometimes difficult decisions about extracurricular activities. You have to pick between the things you prefer, the activities your ex prefers, and, oh, your daughter's preferences too. Plus, you and your ex *do* need to coordinate across homes. You especially need to work together on bigger issues, like getting homework done. And you need to figure out how to get your daughter back and forth to soccer practice on your days—and on her days with her mom too.

## CHOOSING AN ELEMENTARY SCHOOL

Picking where your child will go to elementary school is a big decision. And the choice can be controversial. You and your ex may live in different school districts. So picking an elementary school may affect your parenting plan—or your convenience (or hers) in maintaining your current schedule. You may have different opinions about schools, teachers, or the makeup of the student body. One of you may prefer private over public education. If so, you not only face a big decision, but you also may need to find a way to pay for, or share, a hefty tuition bill.

If you share joint legal custody, choosing a school is one of the big decisions you must make together with your ex. And as I suggested in earlier chapters (in regard to other legal custody decisions), you may be wise to include your ex in the process, even if you have sole legal custody. If you do not have legal custody, you would like to be asked, I'm sure. If you have sole legal custody, you may reserve the right to make that final decision yourself. But if your ex has some input, he is more likely to support the decision. Her father's support certainly is something you want for your daughter's education. Asking him for his thoughts may even improve your strained relationship. So consider reaching out, even if you have an angry divorce. Yes, I *know* I've said this many times. I hope you are getting the message.

Don't avoid conflict if you and your ex disagree, particularly if you share joint legal custody. Public or private? Your district or hers? Neighborhood school or magnet school? You need time to sort this out. This *is* a big decision. Gather information. Visit several schools separately or, even better, together. Talk with other parents. Share information and impressions with your ex.

Try to keep an open mind. And do more than just take a position for or against some school. Identify and discuss your underlying concerns. *Why* do you prefer one school over another? What problem are you trying to solve?

If you are worried about your son's academic or social skills, share your worries. Your ex may not even be aware that you see this as a problem. If you can focus on the problem, not your preferred solution, you two should be able to think more creatively together. Problems typically have more than one solution.

You can voice your underlying concerns even if you are reluctant to share them. Maybe you cannot afford tuition. Is your ex willing to pick up (most of) the cost of a private school? Maybe you don't have time before work to drive your son to a distant but good school. Can your ex help out with the morning driving? Maybe your ex teaches at a great elementary school. You may love the school but fear that you will be unwelcome in "his" school. Talk with him!

You cannot solve that problem, or any problem, without identifying it. So bring up your concerns, even if it's difficult. And if you are still stuck, get a mediator, therapist, or school consultant to help you sort things out. Picking an elementary school *is* a big decision. Face your issues now instead of stewing about them for years to come. Even if you have to compromise, which is likely, you will be better prepared to solve new problems that arise if you have identified your concerns in advance.

## EXTRACURRICULAR ACTIVITIES

Picking a school is not the only big decision you face with a school-age child. Sooner or later, your son is going to get involved in extracurricular activities. That's great for him. He's going to have a lot of fun, and benefit in all kinds of ways, from playing sports or learning to play a musical instrument, or from clubs, scouting, or whatever he gets into.

But making decisions about extracurricular activities can get complicated. These decisions involve a gray area in joint legal custody. The law typically does not *require* you and your ex to share decisions about extracurricular activities. Yet, as I discussed in Chapter 3, many parents find themselves in court, litigating over soccer versus piano. I even have heard of judges who award sole "sports custody."

This seems to me like a desperate effort to clear the courtroom. I hope it seems that way to you too. You can do better.

One helpful thing you can do is make advanced plans. I often meet with parents who have trouble deciding about extracurriculars (and scheduling other special events) at the beginning of each "semester"—in late summer for fall plans, in January for the spring, and in March or April for summer.

These meetings can be difficult. Some parents are adamant about violin lessons or travel lacrosse. But with or without professional help, you will be better off discussing your differences in advance. You do not want to sign your son up for football, get him excited, pay five hundred dollars—and then get into a war with his mom about whether football is a great idea, or a horrible one.

Yes, I know the expression. "It's easier to ask for forgiveness than permission."

Tell *that* to the judge.

There is another practical reason why you both want to get on board about extracurricular activities. Extracurricular activity schedules rarely map neatly onto your own.

You do need to respect your ex's time. But you don't want your daughter to miss her piano lesson every other week. Maybe you can make an activity work if you offer to help with transportation. Or maybe you need to make sure to include your ex in the activity (especially if you are the coach). Or you may have to trade off your favorite extracurricular activity for hers. You and your ex can compromise. Your son can try Boy Scouts *and* take violin lessons. But at least for the current semester, you have to let go of drama class, and your ex must give up on soccer.

And, of course, let's not lose sight of what your *child* wants. He may not like scouting, even though you were an Eagle Scout. Or he may *love* scouting. So please do not stand in your son's way just because scouting is his dad's thing. Or perhaps you don't know whether your son is going to enjoy piano. You (and he) will never know unless he tries.

Your children need you *and* your ex to encourage them. If your ex thinks piano is ridiculous, you know your son will lose interest. Even if his dad says nothing negative, your ten-year-old will pick up on his lack of enthusiasm.

If you or your ex agree to try something new, and your kid learns to love it, success! Remember, your child is not the only one who can learn and have fun through extracurricular activities. You both will be thrilled to see your daughter nail her recital, score a goal, or star in her school play.

So even if you have differences, find some extracurricular activity to encourage—and encourage it wholeheartedly. Your daughter may surprise you with her interest in dancing. And you may surprise yourself. Ballet turns out to be pretty cool after all, particularly when your daughter loves it so much.

## TEACHING CHILDREN RESPONSIBILITY

Parenting and coparenting school-age children involves more than making big and semibig decisions about school and extracurricular activities. You may not need to coordinate every little thing across your school-age children's two homes. But as I said earlier, you do want to coordinate important things, like making sure that homework gets done and grades are on track.

As they grow older and become more independent, perhaps the most important lesson school-age children can learn is responsibility. Your eleven-year-old can and should learn to be responsible for his schoolwork, practicing his clarinet, and his own behavior, even when he is unsupervised.

He also can learn responsibility at home. You almost certainly want him to do some regular chores like picking up his room, babysitting younger siblings, or helping to make dinner. You want your school-age child to learn responsibility now, because responsibility is a hard lesson to learn for the first time as a teenager.

## PARENTING ALONE BUT TOGETHER

Children learn responsibility not from any one task but as a result of being held accountable. How do you hold your children accountable for their chores—and for so much else?

As you recall, my Hierarchy of Children's Needs in Two Homes highlights the importance of authoritative parenting, being loving *and* firm but fair in discipline. Authoritative parenting comes naturally to some people. Others need to learn how to be authoritative. You may not be good at saying no. Or maybe you feel so guilty that you can't. You may just want to have fun with your son when he's with you. So you avoid conflict by avoiding discipline. Or perhaps you leaned on your ex to be the disciplinarian. What do you do now?

Whatever your issue, if you have trouble saying no, you need to learn how to be a firm hand when needed. What a great opportunity to develop something that you probably wish you were better at anyway.

Even as you struggle with your lessons, you still can rely on your ex for help. True, you can no longer say, "Wait until your father gets home!" But you can say, "Do I need to talk with Dad about this? Should I call him up right now?" Your kids may not like that. But secretly they will be reassured that you are on the same team.

Your love is basic to authoritative parenting too. And your ex also can support you there (and vice versa). Tell your kids, "I love you and I'm so proud of you, and I know Mom feels the same way too." Everyone wins when you say that. And if your kids confide only in one of you, well, you and your ex can talk in confidence too. There is *no one* better to share your concerns with than your kids' other parent.

Mom and Dad can still be a team, even though you have become free agents.

Of course, you may not like everything your ex does as a parent. You may think she is too involved with the kids. So you step back to give them the space you think they need. Or you may think he is too strict. So you compensate by indulging your children.

A little of this is fine, but if it's becoming a pattern, you have a problem—with your ex, with your children, and with your own parenting.

When I see parents trying to compensate for one another's perceived parenting flaws, I think about one of my favorite pieces of playground equipment: the seesaw. There are two ways to make a seesaw balance. You can both move farther out. Or you can both move closer to the middle.

You and your ex do not need to occupy exactly the same spot on your parenting seesaw. But you know your kids will benefit if you keep things in balance by moving toward each other, not farther away.

## Troubled and Troubling School-Age Children

We expect school-age children to focus their attention and master the three Rs. But some children flounder in school. The mismatch between the structure of the classroom and a given child's strengths and struggles can make for big problems. If your child is one of these kids, he may be diagnosed with attention deficit/hyperactivity disorder (ADHD) or perhaps a learning disability (LD).

## ADHD AND LD

I briefly introduced ADHD in Chapter 6. There I suggested that except in unusual cases, it is premature to identify ADHD during the preschool years. But it is common, and hopefully helpful, to diagnose ADHD among school-age children. In fact, symptoms must begin by age twelve in order to make the diagnosis.

Children with ADHD have trouble sustaining attention. As a result, they often fail to stay on task in the classroom. They also can be overactive. The problem is not so much constantly running around, but more being "fidgety," like squirming constantly in your seat. And kids with ADHD also can be impulsive. They act before they think, for example, blurting out an answer before a teacher finishes her question.

Some kids have trouble with just attention. Parents sometimes refer to these kids as having attention deficit disorder (ADD), a term professionals no longer use. Other kids have more problems with overactivity and impulsivity. Still other kids struggle with all three symptoms.

If your child is diagnosed with ADHD or his school suggests that you get him evaluated, you will want to get more information than I can give you here. You should be aware that some experts think we overdiagnose ADHD and overuse medication to treat it. You also should know that medication is the most effective short-term treatment for ADHD. And you should know that, unfortunately, medication mostly helps to improve children's behavior in school, not their learning. On top of that, there is no evidence that medication produces long-term benefits for either behavior or learning once you stop taking it.

Now you at least know some of the questions you want to investigate, as you learn more about this common and vexing problem.

Children with learning disabilities have normal intelligence but fall behind in a specific subject area, most commonly reading. Experts and school systems often differ in how they define LD. The argument essentially boils down to how big the gap must be between ability and achievement before a child qualifies for the diagnosis.

There is no single go-to treatment for LD. A first step is identifying the problem. Frustrated kids with LD can think they are stupid. And they typically are greatly relieved by the diagnosis.

Often what helps most is a combination of approaches. Tutoring in problem subjects is common. And tutors or other experts also may be able to help kids with LD develop individualized, more-effective learning strategies. Finally, most schools offer special testing accommodations for kids with LD, perhaps even for standardized tests. For example, a school psychologist may suggest that a child with LD should have extended test time. Or perhaps the psychologist would instead recommend that the student take tests in a quiet room.

## HOW CAN YOU HELP YOUR ADHD OR LD CHILD?

Genetics play a big role in both ADHD and LD. There is not much you can do about that. But one thing you or your ex may be able to do is empathize. There is a good chance that one of you had similar problems. What was that like? What helped? A little reflection on your own history may give you some ideas about your child's experience. You can gently share your insights with him—and with your ex.

Even though they struggle with the structure of the classroom, kids with LD or ADHD actually benefit from having more structure, not less. So another thing you can do is *really* get on the same page with your ex—and with your child's school. Your son may benefit from more regular feedback between school and home. For example, you or a mental health professional may ask his teacher to send home daily or weekly "report cards." These report cards don't have grades. Instead, they offer specific information about whether your son met expectations for behavior, attention, and learning. You, in turn, reward positive steps and make up for missed assignments at home. Obviously, this increased communication is going to help only if everyone works together.

Another consideration is that some kids with ADHD or LD need the structure of a "headquarters" in one home. If you think this may help, you can modify your parenting plan to cut down on transitions or provide a more consistent start to the school week. The case of Michele and Robert, discussed earlier in this chapter, is one example of a schedule that provides a "headquarters" but still gives you both a lot of time with your child.

## BEHAVIOR PROBLEMS? DEPRESSION?

One more thing for you to consider is the possibility that what seems like ADHD or LD isn't. Sometimes attention, behavior, or learning problems result from chronic misbehavior or depression. So if your child's teacher raises concerns about your child's behavior, attention, or learning, you want to think carefully from the outset. Could the real problem be something else? Is my son rebelling—or out of control? Is my daughter depressed?

You particularly want to consider behavior problems or depression if you have an angry divorce, or if you are barely working with your ex in a distant divorce. As my Hierarchy of Children's Needs in Two Homes shows, you need to do more than to be authoritative parents, separately. Your kids need you to work together, not against one another.

Either depression or behavior problems or both can result from your failure to give your school-age child what he needs. The good news in this bad scenario is that you *can* do something about this. As I have said earlier, the trick often is finding a way to love your kids more than you hate your ex.

## TALK TO TEACHERS!

You definitely want to talk with her teacher if your daughter is having problems in school. Just as you and your ex need to work together, kids need parents and teachers to be on the same side.

Sure, your daughter may not love her teacher. You may not either. You can empathize. And you also can remind your daughter that sometimes in life, we all need to deal with situations that are less than ideal. Her fifth-grade classroom may be one of them. Give your daughter tips on how to cope. She may end up learning a lesson that's a lot bigger than fifth grade.

If you have separated recently, or are about to, you also want to talk with your child's teacher. Let him know a little bit about what's going on at home. Maybe your daughter is showing problems in school that you haven't heard about yet. She may be acting up or spacing out. Now you and he know what's going on. Your daughter isn't out of control or depressed. She's just going through a rough spot.

Or maybe your daughter is doing great in school. Still, she may turn to her teacher for advice. He will be in a far better position to listen and offer suggestions if he knows what your daughter is going through at home.

In fact, your daughter's teacher may be able to help *you*. She may know that the new school counselor just started a group for kids of divorced parents. Research shows that children benefit from these groups. Groups for school-age children with divorced or single parents encourage kids to recognize and voice their feelings. They also help children realize that they are not alone, even though they may feel like they are.

# Other Relationships and Your School-Age Child

Your child's relationship with his teacher is important for how school goes this year. And perhaps that relationship may influence your son for many years. Think about it. What teachers (or coaches or other adults) had a big impact on your life? There isn't much you can do to make something similar happen for your child. But if your child gets lucky, you can try to facilitate the relationship. Don't try to join in, though. Sit back and enjoy their relationship vicariously.

### DATING

School-age children can make dating tricky for you, particularly if you separated in the last year or so. A seven-year-old may want you all to herself, worry about your ex, or hope you'll get back together. Twelve-year-olds may feel the same way. But instead of showing her true feelings, she judges you. You're *disgusting*!

Of course, your twelve-year-old may feel the same way about her dad's dating—and complain to you about it.

And keep this in mind. A lot of kids have trouble getting angry with their divorced parents. They *are* angry. But they don't want to get mad at you or their mom. They need you. Or maybe they think they need to protect you. Or they fear you will get mad back. They worry that their anger will drive you away. Or maybe your daughter is afraid of rocking the boat after her family is finally calming down.

So where does their anger go? Here's a "safe" target: your significant other. Lucky him.

If he hangs in there (and who wants him if he doesn't?), you may let him know what's really going on. He will be able to absorb your daughter's anger more easily if he sees her hurt, fear, and confusion. Maybe he can even help her recognize those feelings in herself. That's huge for your daughter if he can. And it's huge for you too.

Keep these same things in mind if you are hearing horrible things about the woman your ex is dating. You may want to believe she's as bad as your daughter makes her sound. But maybe, just maybe, your daughter's comments reflect more about her inner turmoil than your ex's choices in women.

This may be a good time to remind you of two things I have said many times already.

When kids complain, listen and respond to the emotions that underlie their complaints, not just to whatever it is they are being snarky about.

And when it comes to dating, go slowly, for your children and for yourself.

Of course, if you separated when your child was a baby or a toddler, you *are* going slowly. Maybe you are going *too* slowly. That possibility is at least something to consider.


## SIBLINGS AND STEPSIBLINGS

Our relationships with our brothers and sisters can be something special, even if they may not always look that way from the outside. Parents (and courts) almost always want to keep siblings together for this reason. Still, you should consider what I've said repeatedly. Think about building a little one-on-one time with each of your children into your parenting plan.

School-age children learn responsibility by taking care of younger siblings, among other tasks. So expect your ten- or twelve-year-old to entertain or babysit a little brother or sister. She can be a really big help from time to time. Or she can be a big help on a regular basis for some of the time. But guard against expecting too much from her. Remember, your twelve-year-old daughter is a kid too.

Stepsiblings may be a part of your life, and your child's, if you have been divorced for some time. If so, remember my advice to stepparents. Work on being an adult friend to your stepchildren. Let—and expect—their biological parent to do most of the hands-on parenting, including most of the discipline.

What your stepson calls you is one indicator that you are an adult friend. Most stepparents today do not expect to be called Mom or Dad. They know that kids already have a mother and a father. So I suggest that your stepson call you by your first name.

If you have a blended family, where both you and your wife have kids from a previous marriage, parental roles can get even trickier. *Who* does *what*? I still stand by my advice. Biological parents parent. Stepparents are adult friends. But along with everything else, you may need to blend your roles a little more in a blended family.

What can you do to help your children and stepchildren get along? Give them space—literally and figuratively. Kids love having the privacy of their own room. Remember this when house hunting (if you can afford the extra space). If the stepsiblings in your home get along so well that they *beg* to share, well, make an exception to my rule. Pat them, and yourself, on the back.

As for figurative space, give the kids the opportunity to work things out for themselves. Avoid any temptation to micromanage. The good news is that unless someone is really troubled, kids generally find a way to get along. In fact, they may break down barriers with each other a lot faster than with you or your new wife.

## OTHER RELATIONSHIPS

Of course, there are many other relationships that may be important to your children. Let me offer you a quick take on a handful of them.

Maybe you are not the parent who is remarried. Maybe your ex is. If so, allow, yes, even encourage, your son to have a relationship with his stepmom. It may help if you have a little relationship with her too. You may think about asking her out for coffee. But check with your ex first, so he will know what you are doing. This also will give him a chance to prepare his new wife, and hopefully encourage her to grasp your olive branch.

Or maybe you are recently divorced. You are wondering what to say about your divorce to your son's teacher (as I advised) or to other parents at your son's school. If so, read the section "Going Public" in Chapter 6. What's the heart of the message? Don't offer these people anything more than an innocuous sound bite. Take the high road, and you will do more than feed their curiosity. You will earn their respect.

What about your child and your mom? Or your child and your ex's sister (your child's aunt)? When it comes to extended family, my basic rule is this: Each parent should be in charge of managing their children's relationships with their own biological relatives. Sure, you can still be nice to your in-laws. But almost everything is between your ex and his family now.

Really, deciding the right thing to do often boils down to this: Put yourself in your child's shoes. What would you want? How would you want your parents to act?

You will not go too far wrong if you truly take your child's perspective.

## CHAPTER 8

# Adolescence: Autonomy and Relatedness

Adolescence (thirteen to eighteen years old) begins with puberty and ends with high school graduation. Or maybe adolescence ends with the beginning of college, leaving home for good, or landing a job with benefits! Today's "extended adolescence" can continue into, and perhaps through, the twenties. Twenty-somethings may rely on their parents during a period of graduate education or questionable job security. That is one reason why I discuss emerging adulthood in the next chapter.

Here we will bring an end to adolescence with high school graduation or a teenager's nineteenth birthday, whichever comes first. Many states use this same definition as the end date for child support.

What is adolescence all about? Well, here is what Mark Twain had to say about this sometimes trying period of development:

*When I was a boy of fourteen, my father was so ignorant I could hardly stand to have the old man around. But when I got to be twenty-one, I was astonished at how much the old man had learned in seven years.*

Twain's quip wryly captures adolescents' disdain for their parents. The remark also gives parents hope that their teenager's scorn may one day turn into respect. (My father quoted Twain to me repeatedly, and without effect, during my teen years. But I guess he ultimately made an impression.)

Breaking away from parents is the key psychological and (to a lesser extent today) practical task of adolescence. The teen years are about gaining independence—and hopefully learning to exercise your new freedoms wisely.

Teenagers learn to be responsible for their own schoolwork. The exercise of this responsibility often is helped along by repeated reminders from parents, occasional threats or real punishments, and, perhaps, earned rewards.

Adolescents also gain the freedom to manage their own relationships, with few limits. Think about it. Curfews or rules for behavior *that you directly observe* are hardly restrictive, despite your teenager's protests to the contrary.

Out of sight, a great many teenagers also feel free to experiment with sex, alcohol, and drugs, among other things. And then there is the prototypical emblem of autonomy, the privilege that fosters all other freedoms: the driver's license.

Yes. Many of today's teens are well behaved and compliant, perhaps overly so. If you have a particularly studious adolescent, you may need to update Mark Twain's remark. Add several years both to Twain's age when breaking away begins and when it ends. Your focused adolescent may delay gratification—and autonomy seeking—while pursuing her long-term goals.

Other teens fail to seek independence or flounder in their efforts to do so. If this describes your adolescent, make sure you are not an obstacle in the path of your teenager's autonomy. As I discuss later in this chapter, you particularly do not want her to fail to break away because she thinks she needs to take care of you. You want your teen to know you can take care of yourself. That way, she's free to focus on herself.

## Autonomy and Relatedness

Teens often reject and ridicule their parents as a part of seeking independence from them. But adolescence really is about achieving autonomy while *maintaining* relatedness.

Teenagers are preparing to leave the nest, but they still need a nest.

Sure, adolescents insist that they are hipper, cooler, and smarter than their parents. Yet parents should remember that teens act more grown up than they may feel. Adolescents are driving their independence on a learner's permit, no matter how cocky they may act behind the wheel.

We parents of teenagers (I have three as I'm writing this) also need to remind ourselves, repeatedly, of this: The security of our love is what allows teenagers to, well, be teenagers. Not unlike what happens with toddlers, the secure base we offer allows our adolescents to explore. Our teenagers can and do test themselves away from (and against) us, because they know that we love them. True, they, or we, may not feel terribly loving in the midst of the trial. But the promise of Mark Twain's observation is this: As the storm subsides, both teenagers and parents will recognize that they maintained a connection that the fury of adolescence transformed but did not break.

### AUTONOMY, RELATEDNESS, AND DIVORCE

Divorced or together, most parents find a teenager's quest for independence challenging. As they did during the terrible twos, teenagers test the limits. A short list of things that mean freedom to your adolescent and headaches for you includes messy rooms, broken curfews, unanswered texts, dating, driving, dubious sleepovers, drugs, alcohol, and lax grades or college preparation.

Teens test you. But they still need limits. So you must set them.

Of course, it is hard to say no. Your teenager may badger you or tower over you. He may say, "Dad lets me do this. Why are you such a tyrant?"

But your adolescent son will respect you more, not less, because you have limits. Deep down, he even will know that your rules reflect your love and concern.

So stick to your guns. Then call your ex. Get some support, plot a strategy, and plan to act as a united front.

Chances are that your fifteen-year-old was just trying to push your buttons when he said, "Dad lets me." If so, that's important for you—and his father—to know. Ask your ex to check in with your son about what he said about his dad's rules. Your teenager will be stunned, a little scared, and secretly pleased that you two are talking. He will also learn that he can't manipulate you by "guilting" you.

If his dad *is* letting him do more than you, you and your ex need to get on the same page. Your ex may need to get tougher. Or you may need to loosen the reins. Really, it probably doesn't matter who changes. What matters is that you work together, at least on big issues like curfews, schoolwork, dating, and driving. That way you are in charge, even if you loosen your rules. If you and your ex contradict each other, neither of you is in charge. Your adolescent is.

Maybe you already are a united front. I hope so. Teens will play you against each other if they can. When they succeed in conning you, their "success" usually is to their short-term benefit—and contrary to their long-term interests.

## PARENTING AN ADOLESCENT AUTHORITATIVELY

Remember my Hierarchy of Children's Needs in Two Homes? It applies to adolescents too. You want to be an authoritative parent to your teenager, loving yet firm but fair when it comes to discipline. You did this when she was younger. And your teenager still needs you to be authoritative. She needs you to be loving and firm, even though she's pushing the boundaries, even though the rules of the game are changing.

Of course, disciplining a teenager can be difficult. She will protest, loudly and repeatedly. She will try to push your guilt buttons. She will break the rules behind your back. She will sulk and withdraw. She may scream that she hates you.

And you need to be a parent despite all of her games. You need to try to outsmart her, even though you know you won't always succeed.

But you expect discipline to be a challenge with a teenager.

## STAYING CONNECTED BY LETTING GO

What may really upset you is if you find yourself struggling with the unexpected: feeling the love. Loving your daughter used to be the easy part of being an authoritative parent.

Teenagers can be hard to love sometimes.

You may feel hurt or abandoned when your adolescent pulls away from you. You may have too little time with her already, sharing her with your ex. Now she spends her time—supposedly with you—hanging out with friends, snuggling with her boyfriend, involved in endless extracurricular activities, or just in her room, with the door closed.

Or maybe your son has decided he wants to spend more time at his dad's now that he's sixteen. Sure, it stinks that your son isn't around as much. You love just having him near you, even if his friends are over, or if he's watching television. But maybe your son asked for the change because he and his dad are not as close as you two are. And hopefully it's a really good thing for him to spend more time with his dad.

Even if you think your ex is not a great influence on your son, you need to remember this. Letting go, little by little, is critical to maintaining your connection with your teenager.

Your son is *not* rejecting you, although it can feel that way. Sure, he's venturing out. He is seeking his independence, as he should. But remember that autonomy is a part of relatedness, not a threat to it.

Your son is trying out his wings. He is supposed to do that. Cheer for him, even from a distance. And keep the nest ready too, just in case he needs it.

And as you let go, you still can foster your connection in little ways. Your son loves your apple pie, or whatever special treats you make. And few teenagers can resist the offer of a driving lesson. So buckle up in the car, and within yourself. Feel secure in his love for you, so he can feel secure in your love for him.

## Schedules for Adolescents

From a developmental perspective, adolescents are capable of managing a wide range of parenting plans, including every other weekend, dividing the week, week on/week off, two weeks on/two weeks off, or if needed, the school year in California and summer in Massachusetts.

But adolescence introduces two major complications for crafting a parenting plan:

- Teenagers "have a life," that is, their own busy schedules.
- Teenagers have opinions too, sometimes strong ones.

If you are crafting or thinking about revising your parenting plan, you need to think carefully about your teenager's schedule, as well as your own. As I said in the previous chapter, school-age children are busy. But parents are primarily responsible for managing a school-age child's schedule. This is not so for teenagers.

Your studious teenager may take grades really seriously. She may be getting extra help after school, studying with friends, and cramming late into the night. She also may be juggling sports, clubs, and other extracurricular activities. Maybe she loves everything she does. Maybe she loves being busy. Or maybe she just thinks her college applications must look perfect.

Or maybe school is a priority for your daughter. But friends are priority number one. She doesn't know what she's doing this weekend. It's only Wednesday—or maybe it's "only" seven p.m. on Friday, with texts flying and plans evolving.

Whether she is busy for good reasons, or not, the question for you is this: Week on/week off (or whatever) may work great for you. But does the schedule work for your teenager?

One way to make joint physical custody work during adolescence is to devise a schedule that gives your teenager longer blocks of time in each home. But maybe juggling her own schedule is complicated enough for your daughter. Maybe juggling between two homes is too much.

## COMMON RESIDENCE CHANGES DURING ADOLESCENCE

Whether it is because adolescents "have a life" or for other reasons, research shows that parenting plans for adolescents can get complicated. For one, parents are less likely to negotiate joint physical custody for teenagers than younger children. There is no single reason why this is so. Some reasons surely include adolescents' own busy schedules, the relatively short amount of time teenagers have left at home, and teens' ability to maintain relationships with both parents in many ways, including electronic communications and driving to Dad's to hang out.

Research also shows that joint physical custody is unstable over time. If a child lives primarily with Mom or Dad, chances are things will stay pretty much the same. With joint physical custody, it's a coin flip. Things are about as likely to change as they are to remain the same. That's not a bad thing. You know that I want your parenting plan to evolve to meet your children's changing needs. But be prepared. Things can evolve rapidly in adolescence, particularly with joint physical custody.

While most teenagers live mostly with their moms, evidence also shows that compared to younger children, more adolescents live mostly with their dads.[1] Why? Some teenagers may want to get to know their father better. Perhaps some fathers feel better equipped to parent teenagers. And if their teen is challenging, some mothers may benefit from the support—and the respite—of managing day-to-day parenting alone.

Evidence also shows that contact with their other parent becomes a lower priority for adolescents.[2] If you are this parent, I know the diminished interest can hurt. Still, let me offer an adolescent observation about this fact: Duh! *Of course*, parents are a lower priority in the eyes of teenagers. Surprise. Teenagers are focused on themselves.

And remember what I said earlier. Whether he is living mostly with you, mostly with your ex, or in joint physical custody, often the best way to hang on to a teenager is to let him go (little by little). Embrace this paradox. Insist on seeing him, of course. He should make an appearance at dinnertime—or sometime during the weekend he is supposed to be with you. But don't insist on seeing him too much or exactly the way you used to. If you do, your son will remind you how that feels to him. He will snarl at you, or mutter to himself, "I'm *not* a baby."

Your adolescent will take care of the autonomy. Pick your spots to preserve the relatedness.

## DO TEENAGERS GET TO DECIDE WHERE THEY LIVE?

As a part of her newfound autonomy, your teenager may have an opinion about your parenting plan. This raises another important question. How much input should a teenager have in choosing where she lives?

What should you do if your sixteen-year-old-daughter says that she is tired of the back-and-forth? She wants to quit joint custody and stay at her mother's.

Mine did.

When she was sixteen, Maggie told me she had had enough of joint custody. Among other things, she told me that when boys asked, she wanted to give them only one phone number. (This was in the days before cell phones.) She said that she loved me. But she wanted to live mostly with her mother.

Maggie's reasoning about boys sounded like a teenager's, which actually made her arguments more convincing. But what influenced me more was the fact that Maggie asked for the change. We were really close. She wouldn't bring this up lightly.

When she first raised the topic, I didn't say yes. And I didn't say no. I said, "This is a big decision. We need to talk."

Maggie didn't particularly want to talk, but we did. (Hint: If you want to talk to your teenager, try taking her for a long drive. Why? You don't need to make eye contact. There are plenty of little distractions, but no big ones—just make sure that you leave *both* of your cell phones at home. And as long as you are moving, she cannot run away.)

After several emotionally wrenching discussions, including a couple with her mom, I agreed with Maggie that her reasoning made sense. She wanted a headquarters. Her mother's home was the logical choice.

So I allowed Maggie to make the change.

This decision was really, really hard. I felt like I was letting go of

Maggie before I was ready to. Even now, thinking about it makes me sad. But then, and now, I think it was the right decision. And I learned a few lessons that I hope are worth sharing.

- Listen to your teenager's opinions. Listening does not mean that you agree. Listening does not mean that you will acquiesce. Listening means that you will hear him out and take your teenager's opinions seriously.
- Your teenager's reasoning matters. A good reason for wanting to change his schedule may be that your son wants to simplify his life. A good reason may be that he wants to spend more time with his dad. A good reason may even be that your son's relationship with you is not so good right now. (Depending on the circumstances, this may be a not-so-good reason too. But either way, it certainly is a reason worth listening to carefully.) Of course, your teenager may have bad reasons for wanting to live with his other parent too. Bad reasons include that there are no rules at his dad's house, or Dad promised to give him a car.
- It is all right to show some emotion to your teenager at a time like this. I cried during one of those painful discussions with Maggie. I don't think I overwhelmed her. I was sad but under control. I certainly never said or suggested anything like, "How can you do this to me?!" But I hope my tears showed her how much I cared for her. I hope they conveyed that this *was* a big decision. I am not sure that Maggie saw me cry again for fifteen years—on her wedding day. I'm glad I cried then too.
- If you make a change, you should insist on maintaining some regular contact with your adolescent. A change in the schedule is not the end of your relationship, even if it may feel that way in the moment. Maggie and I agreed that she would still come for dinner Wednesday, Thurs-

day, and Friday evenings, just as she had been doing. She just wouldn't spend the night.

- In the end, make the final decision your decision, not your teenager's decision. This is really important. I *let* Maggie make the change to live mostly at her mother's house. I didn't say, "This is your decision." I said, "This is my decision. And I'm going to let you make the change." The difference involves far more than semantics. Making this your decision helps you maintain your parental authority. More important, making the decision yourself takes the responsibility off your teenager's shoulders. Maggie didn't want to hurt me. She just wanted to take care of herself. I know it was hard for her to voice her opinion. I think (and hope) I made it easier on her by taking the decision out of her hands and making it myself.

- Letting go really can be the best way to hang on. I hated no longer having Maggie for all those overnights. But I am convinced that if I had insisted on maintaining joint physical custody, I would have won the battle but lost the war. If I had demanded that the schedule stay the same, Maggie probably would have complied. But I think it would have driven a wedge into our relationship. Instead, we remained (and remain) close. Even today, I think this painful talk so many years ago helps Maggie to feel that if she needs to, she can talk to me about tough stuff.

## SHOULD YOU ASK?

What if your teenager hasn't voiced an opinion? Should you ask?

Yes, I think you should ask. In this case, you and your ex probably should *not* talk to your teenager together. That's a lot of pressure. He may feel like you are asking him to choose between you, to pick who he loves the most.

Instead, talk with him alone, at a time when you can command his attention. (Remember my advice about a long drive.) Ask him what he thinks. Keep your voice and your manner calm and non-judgmental. Be prepared to hear what you may not want to hear—and tell him that you are ready to hear whatever. This is about him, not you.

Rather than asking what he wants in an open-ended way, it probably will help if you give him an idea to react to. Tell him that you and your ex are considering week on/week off. Let him know that you both want his input about your ideas.

And while you probably don't want to do this together, your ex certainly should know that you spoke with your son. And your ex should make sure to talk with your son too.

If you are the parent who is going second, you should speak to your son in the same accepting way I already described. But begin by telling him that you know he already spoke to Dad. Tell him that you aren't trying to argue with him or change his mind. Say that you just wanted to talk with him yourself, so you can hear his opinions directly from him—and share some of yours.

You know you are doing things right if your son gives you and your ex the same answers.

If he gives you different answers, you have a problem. Your son doesn't have a problem. *You* do. Maybe your ex isn't being honest. Or maybe you are only hearing what you want to hear. Or maybe your son is telling you both what he thinks you want him to say.

In all of these circumstances, the problem is this: Your teenager isn't free to speak up. Someone isn't listening. Most likely that some-one is *both* of you.

If you automatically assumed that the problem was your ex, I urge you to think again, and more deeply. You may be right. But you may not be.

Finally, if your adolescent does not voice an opinion when you speak with him, don't force him to. Maybe he doesn't have an opinion. Maybe he wants you to decide. Maybe he doesn't want the pressure or the responsibility. If so, that's fine. At least you asked. Now you and your ex are free to make the decision, as best you can.

As I said, whether he voices no preference or a strong one, this still is an adult decision. Make sure he knows that from the beginning. Make this your decision, not his, even if you decide to do exactly what he wants. He's the kid. You are the parent.

# Divorcing in Adolescence versus Moving into Adolescence When Divorced

You need to be prepared for almost anything if you are divorcing during your child's adolescence. He may be furious. He may withdraw and look sad. He may act indifferent. He may be embarrassed. He may pull away from one or both of you. His moods may change dramatically from day to day.

## TEENAGERS MAY RESIST CHANGE

If you are separating now, when the time comes for crafting a parenting plan, your teenager may resist change. He may want to stay right where he is—in the home that he knows. If he's an older adolescent, these feelings may be especially strong. He may not care which of you lives at home with him, or if you birdnest, taking turns moving in and out. He just doesn't want your divorce to mess up his life.

Can you blame him?

If he's a junior or senior in high school, you may consider letting him stay where he is. To take some of the emotion out of this big decision, consider this: What would you do if you were still married, but at the beginning of your son's senior year in high school, your employer moved you across the country? Would one of you consider delaying the move, so you could remain in the family home and let your son complete high school? Would you consider allowing your son to live with a friend or relative until he graduates?

Those would be big decisions, of course. But even if you could find no acceptable solution, I don't think you'd be surprised by your son's wish to stay at home. It is reasonable for a seventeen-year-old to want *his* life to stay the same, despite his parent's new job. If you found yourself in this situation, surely you would give some thought to your son's wishes.

So don't be surprised—or too hurt—if your son doesn't want his life disrupted by your divorce either. His feelings likely are much more about his life than yours.

As I have said, in divorce or in relocating your family, you are still the parents. You still make the tough decisions. But you do want to listen. Try to understand your adolescent's point of view. And, perhaps, you may decide to give him a little more independence than you thought you were prepared to give him.

## CHANGES IN *YOUR* LIFE

If you separated when your teenager was younger, the transition to adolescence does not automatically mean you should change your parenting plan. Your teen may be perfectly happy to continue with a familiar pattern. For example, if your teen moved into adolescence living with joint physical custody, well, she is used to life in two homes. She is likely to be more accepting of the back-and-forth than an adolescent whose parents just separated.

Still, be prepared for your daughter to voice new opinions at some point, even if your parenting plan has been stable for years. She is going to develop new attitudes about many things. You should hardly be surprised if her living situation is one of them.

One thing that may affect your teenager's point of view is a big change in *your* life. For example, what if your job does require you to move? If this happens, your daughter may rather move in with Mom full time than go somewhere new with you. If she voices this preference, your relationship probably is not the problem. She just wants to stay with her friends and graduate from a familiar high school.

Your new romantic relationships also can have a big impact on your teenager's opinions. As I discuss later in this chapter, adolescents can have an especially hard time accepting their parents' partners, including remarriage. In fact, sometimes a new relationship can trigger a teenager to request to change where she lives. That's what happened with Michele and Robert's daughter, LaKeesha.

## MICHELE'S COHABITATION AND LAKEESHA'S RETREAT

I introduced the case of Robert and Michele in Chapter 1 and revisited them in Chapter 7. These parents had two children, LaKeesha and Robert Jr., who was three years older than his sister and had mild autism spectrum disorder.

When I first met them, Robert demanded 50/50 time with his six-year-old daughter and nine-year-old son. In mediation, he grudgingly settled for 32/68. The parenting plan involved joint custody. But it gave the kids a headquarters with Michele at the start of the school week. Despite the 32/68 division, the kids viewed the arrangement as involving equal time—much to Robert's relief.

The parenting plan worked great for three years. But Robert Jr. asked to switch to week on/week off when he was twelve. Robert's remarriage to Destiny and Robert Jr.'s great relationship with her son, Kordell, prompted the change.

At the time, Robert and Michele altered the parenting plan on their own and with little conflict. LaKeesha wanted to keep her 32/68 schedule the same, and her parents agreed to do that too.

That's where we left off in Chapter 7. But things continued to evolve for this family. The big change centered on Michele's new and intense romantic relationship with her boyfriend, Ari.

Unlike Robert, Michele did not rush into dating following their divorce. Instead, she focused on her children, her work, and herself. She got into therapy, and she got a lot out of it. Therapy helped her slow down and reflect. She learned to recognize, express, and explore her many conflicting emotions. She grieved the loss of her marriage. She went through a midlife crisis. She rethought her values. She improved her parenting and her relationships with her own parents. She got reenergized in her work. It took a few years, but eventually Michele felt ready to move on into the world of dating.

From my point of view, Michele did just about everything right. She took my advice and moved slowly in exploring new relationships. But unfortunately, just because you do things right doesn't mean that things work out right.

At age forty-six, Michele found dating pretty awkward. Plus, the men she encountered, particularly those she met online, seemed like either predators or lost souls. She started to despair of ever meeting Mr. Right. Her marriage to Robert had huge problems. But Michele always admired his drive, his convictions, and his strength. She was a strong woman. She was sure that she needed a strong man to balance her.

She thought she had found that man when she met Ari.

Ari's motto was "work hard, play hard." A successful businessman, he was recently divorced, but his children were grown. He and Michele met on a dating website, and they clicked immediately. Ari found the time to take Michele on exciting adventures, whether that involved going camping or flying to Europe.

After fifteen months of a whirlwind relationship, a romance more exciting than Michele ever imagined, she made an uncharacteristic decision. She agreed with Ari that he should move in with her.

LaKeesha recently had turned fourteen, and she was *not* infatuated with Ari. LaKeesha *hated* Ari, although she lacked the courage to tell her mother that. (It had taken a while, but LaKeesha had developed a good relationship with Robert's wife, Destiny, years earlier.)

Part of the problem was that Ari was taking LaKeesha's mother away from her. But that was the least of it, according to LaKeesha. LaKeesha said that Ari acted like *her* house was *his* house. She claimed that Ari sometimes acted like he thought he was her father too. She especially hated when he tried to "boss her around." Other times, LaKeesha felt that Ari treated her like a maid. And he was such a slob! There was no way she was going to pick up after him, even though she had long helped her mom clean the house.

And the worst part of it was that her mother didn't seem to notice. Michele thought Ari was so funny. And—disgusting—her mother was always hanging on him. She acted like the teenage girl that her mother insisted LaKeesha should *not* act like.

LaKeesha's anger turned into rage the day she overheard Ari speaking with her mom. Ari asked Michele if she had ever considered sending LaKeesha to boarding school.

LaKeesha said she had wondered all along. Now she knew it. Ari was trying to get rid of her.

That idea was getting to be fine with her.

LaKeesha knew her brother hated Ari too. But Robert Jr. was not someone she could confide in. Instead, she started talking to a school counselor. One day, she told the counselor she wished she could live with her dad. After about six weeks, her wish turned into a plan.

LaKeesha approached her father about making the change. Robert said that he was open to the possibility. But he said that LaKeesha needed to speak with her mother first.

She did. And Michele blew up. She and LaKeesha fought for two months. LaKeesha said most of the arguments involved her mother defending Ari, not listening to her. (Michele didn't say this to La-Keesha. But she later told me that she felt like she was being forced to choose: her daughter or the man she had been searching for.)

During her fights with LaKeesha, Michele began to wonder, eventually out loud, "Is your father turning you against me?" This insinuation infuriated LaKeesha even more. But Michele became more and more suspicious. She talked with a lawyer and a therapist. They each raised the possibility of parental alienation.

During this time, Michele's distant relationship with Robert grew icy and then angry. Robert said he tried to talk with Michele about LaKeesha's point of view. But she refused to listen. After a few more months, he went to see a lawyer too. He wanted to see if he could win custody of LaKeesha.

Fortunately, Robert's lawyer asked about mediation. That's when they returned to see me.

Unfortunately, the family's problems were entrenched by then.

I met with Michele and Robert alone a couple of times. We got nowhere. Well, I guess at least I learned what had happened.

At their request, I then held a meeting with LaKeesha alone. I told her I was working with her parents. She vented her emotions and her opinions. LaKeesha was clear. She wanted to live with her dad. She was upset. But she also offered clear, understandable reasons to back up her opinion.

With LaKeesha's permission, and her parents' too, I followed up by telephoning her school counselor. The counselor confirmed La-Keesha's wish to live with her father. Her desire had remained firm for many months. The counselor also agreed that LaKeesha's reasoning was sound. And she thought LaKeesha was a remarkably mature girl. She knew LaKeesha was a superior student.

Armed with this information—and LaKeesha's permission to share it with her parents—I again met with Michele and Robert. While she still resisted the information I relayed, toward the end of our second meeting Michele said that she might accept a *temporary* change. But she wanted to hear LaKeesha's opinions directly one more time—in the safe setting of mediation.

Before our family meeting, Robert and Michele discussed a new schedule that Michele might be willing to try. At this time, I also coached the parents: Make sure that the final decision is yours, not LaKeesha's. And I told them to let LaKeesha know this. You are listening to her, but you are the ones making the final decision. (I explained why this was important, for reasons I have already shared with you.)

Our family meeting went well. LaKeesha was clear, and she kept her anger in check. Michele was tearful but in control emotionally—and, ultimately, accepting. Robert mostly remained quiet. But he made it clear to LaKeesha that he wanted and expected her to maintain her relationship with her mother despite any new schedule.

Near the end of the meeting, Mom and Dad told LaKeesha that they agreed. She could live with Dad until the end of the school year, four months away. She would spend every other weekend with Mom (during Robert Jr.'s weeks; his schedule would not change). In addition, every Wednesday, LaKeesha and Mom would spend several hours together in the evening alone. No Robert Jr. and no Ari.

There is so much more to this story. But the details are too complicated. So let me give you the highlights.

The new schedule lasted for over a year. Ari lasted about six months. (He was "playing hard" with other women.) During a two-week vacation the following summer, LaKeesha and Michele repaired their relationship, which gradually had been improving following Ari's exit. Robert Jr. went off to college despite his autism spectrum disorder (a separate long and happy story). And LaKeesha started her junior year in high school with a brand-new schedule. She asked if she could follow Robert Jr.'s former week on/week off routine. Her parents readily agreed.

And through it all, Michele and Robert's relationship thawed from angry back to distant. And it seemed to be warming beyond that. As life's mistakes piled up, Robert and Michele seemed to be more forgiving of the ones they had made with each other.

## TELLING TEENAGERS YOU ARE SEPARATING

If you split during her adolescence, obviously you and your ex need to talk with your teenager. In Chapter 7, I discussed at some length how to talk to a school-age child about divorce. You should read that, because you really want to talk to your teenager in the same way.

I won't repeat all of the details. But here are a few standouts.

- Talk to your daughter together if at all possible. Let her know you are on the same team: her team.
- Plan what you will say in advance, together with your ex. And stick to the script—while, of course, reacting to your teen's emotions and questions.
- It's OK to let your sadness show. But stay under control. With words and actions, convey that you both are going to be OK. You may be feeling other emotions. You may be angry or hurt or guilty. But just show your sadness. Sadness is a feeling you and your ex share. And it's a feeling you can share with your children, without making them uncomfortable or putting them in the middle.
- Share some of your ideas about a parenting plan. But unlike with younger children, your schedule does not need to be detailed or firm. Actually, your ideas probably shouldn't be set in stone. Tell your teenager that you are going to want to hear her ideas too—not now but sometime soon.
- Keep the conversation short, child-focused, and superficial, despite your child's age or her questions, even pointed ones. She has no need or real desire to know the details of

your private life. Yes, she may be old enough to see R-rated movies. But keep this PG, or better, G.

- Follow up with individual "check-in" conversations, maybe later that night or in the next day or two. In a week or so, you may want to solicit her thoughts about a schedule. When you do, follow my tips from earlier in this chapter.

## TALKING TO TEENAGERS ABOUT A LONG-AGO DIVORCE

If you split when your child was younger, moving into adolescence probably means more discussions about your family circumstances— at least at some point. Your son may want to know more about what happened. If he does, answer his questions as best you can. But still keep things superficial, simple, and G rated. He isn't asking because he wants to know the gossip. He's asking because he's trying to understand you, his family life, or maybe himself.

So keep your son's perspective in mind when answering his questions. A good starting place may be to ask him why he is asking you these things. Maybe he heard something about a friend's parents, and now he's curious about you. Or maybe someone asked him a question about you, and he didn't know how to answer. Or maybe he's struggling with trying to understand what happened long ago, and what your divorce means for him and his own relationships.

Each of those circumstances and a dozen other possibilities should lead you to give pretty different answers to similar questions your son may ask. Your different answers are tied together by the fact that you are responding to your teenager's needs. Your personal history is available on a need-to-know basis. So find out what your son needs to know, and why. And then give him an edited version of history, one that is appropriate for children. Teens *are* children.

## TALKING TO A TEEN ABOUT HER STRAINED RELATIONSHIP WITH YOUR EX

Another type of questioning may arise if, over the years, your teenager has not had a good relationship with her other parent. If so, your adolescent may ask you about her mother's difficult moods or her father's apparent lack of interest in her life.

In responding, it is essential that you, again, keep your teen's perspective in mind. She isn't looking for you to criticize her mother or father. She is asking for your help. She wants you to help her understand.

How can you help? Well, you may want to encourage her to talk with her other parent. Maybe you can help her formulate the words to say. Perhaps you can offer the support that will give her the courage to initiate a conversation.

Or maybe your daughter doesn't want to talk to her other parent. Maybe she has tried that already, and it didn't help. Or perhaps she isn't ready to take that step yet. Maybe she's just looking for your thoughts and observations.

In this case, you may offer your daughter a little bit of your perspective. Maybe her father has always struggled to make relationships a priority over work. Maybe her mother seems to be dealing with a long-standing depression but cannot seem to admit this to herself.

But be gentle in offering observations like these. Your goal is to support your teenager, her other parent, and their relationship. You want to help your adolescent understand better, be hurt less, and perhaps be more patient or more accepting with her mom or dad. You do *not* want to undermine your ex in your adolescent's eyes. Remember the evidence I discussed in Chapter 2? If you put down your ex, in the long run, you will turn your adolescent against you, not him.

# Parenting and Coparenting Adolescents

Having a teenager, particularly an older adolescent, can make life simpler for divorced parents. You may no longer need a weekly telephone conference with your ex. There just isn't that much to talk about, or at least that often. And you probably don't need to exchange as many texts or e-mails. Your daughter is (mostly) in charge of her own schedule now. So you and your ex can worry less about many details of her day-to-day activities.

And if your son is driving, well, that's a worry and a relief. Of course, you want him to drive carefully. But your seventeen-year-old can pick up a forgotten laptop or just pop by for a quick visit. He also can help drive younger siblings in exchange for using the car. Yes! Some clouds really do have silver linings.

Divorced parents of teenagers may need to interact less in other ways. For example, your teenage daughter now should be in charge of taking her own medications. You don't need to remind your ex. *Your daughter* needs to take responsibility for taking her antibiotics, her insulin, or her birth control pills.

Yikes! Birth control pills?

Teenagers in charge of insulin can be a "yikes!" experience too.

## FEWER ISSUES, BIGGER CONSEQUENCES

Even as you and your ex spend less time on day-to-day details, the stakes go way up when parenting teenagers. So you do still need to keep in touch. Separately and together, you both need to monitor your teenager's independent actions—even from a distance.

And the two of you need to talk, maybe in detail, about potential trouble spots.

Hopefully, you can present a united front not only about discipline but also on bigger issues. Here are some big issues that should grab your attention.

- Sex
- Alcohol (and drugs)
- College

Of course, parents differ in their opinions and approach to these (and other) big issues. But that is my point. You want to be ahead of the game. You want to discuss these complicated issues in advance with your teen—and with your ex too. In the end, your teen may still challenge you. But at least you will be better prepared.

And you and your ex will be *a lot* more effective if you are a united front, or at least if you are delivering compatible messages. These are topics of huge importance to your teenager's well-being. Your approach now also may affect how your daughter deals with these issues for the rest of her life.

Parents are not the only ones who disagree about sex, substance use, and college. These are topics that can challenge core values, religious beliefs, and politics. So my advice for all three topics is that *you* need to develop a strategy. I cannot tell you what your strategy should be.

But let me offer a few ideas about possible approaches. I start with sex, where I must be most tentative, and end with college, where I have more to say about an essential but more neutral topic.

### SEX

Religious, political, and personal views about sex vary greatly, of course. My goal here is not to change or challenge your opinion. Really, I am mainly trying to help you think. How can you translate your own beliefs about sex into a plan of action for talking with your children—and your ex?

My own views about parenting, sexuality, and adolescents boil down to a few key points.

- I want to influence my adolescents' sexuality. I want my sons to respect girls and themselves. I want my daughters to be careful, safe, and yet comfortable with their own sexuality. (I believe male and female sexuality differs substantially, and this difference is at the heart of a lot of sexual negotiations. But that's a topic for another book.)
- I want my teenagers to control their sexuality.
- And when they are ready, I want my children to thoroughly enjoy sex, intimacy, and love (including same-sex relationships if that is where they find love).

Balancing the yin and yang between control and enjoyment is a huge challenge, I think. How can parents or religions or cultures teach children that sex is "bad," something you have to guard and control? And then, one day—the day your teenager is mature enough or maybe on her honeymoon—sex suddenly becomes "good," a wonderful bond between a couple that produces the greatest gift, children?

And here is something else to make this challenge even harder: Sexuality ultimately is going to be your teenager's decision.

My position that sex is a teenager's choice is largely a practical matter. American teens are surrounded by sexual messages and imagery. Teenagers also have all kinds of opportunities to be sexual. And based on research, we know that a great many teenagers are sexually active. About half of American boys and girls report having had sexual intercourse by age seventeen.

Part of my position about adolescent decision making also is philosophical. My personal concerns about youth sexuality are more focused on health. I am particularly concerned that young people develop healthy attitudes about their own sexuality and about their sexual partners. I realize that you may hold strong moral and religious views about sex. I am not trying to dictate your morality. I am merely trying to be honest in sharing my own.

Finally, I do not anticipate being able to discuss sexuality in great detail with my children. The range of willingness to discuss sexuality that I have encountered with my teenagers begins with great reluctance and extends to great resistance.

Hopefully, you can do better.

Given all of the above, my message about sexuality to my teens has boiled down to this:

- Sex is great.
- Sex is so good that you need to make careful decisions about it.
- Sex in the context of a loving relationship can be wonderful.
- Sex in the context of a relationship that is unloving is likely to be hollow, or horrible, or worse.

Again, you do not need to agree with *me* about sex. Actually, it's pretty instructive if your views about sex and teenagers are different from mine. *What if I were your ex?* We would be giving our teen pretty different messages. Maybe that would be OK. Teenagers need to sort much of this out for themselves. Or maybe that thought scares you to death.

So here is the bottom line. If you want to influence your teenager's sexual decision making, you and your ex need to get pretty much on the same page, whatever page that is.

## ALCOHOL AND DRUGS

What about alcohol and drugs? You may think that your teen doesn't drink or use drugs. And you may be right. Or you may be wrong.

Here are a few findings from a recent in-person survey of a nationally representative sample of 10,123 teenagers:[3]

- Seventy-eight percent of seventeen- and eighteen-year-olds reported using alcohol. Half of boys and 40 percent of girls said they used alcohol regularly. The researchers judged about 2 percent of each gender as having a serious alcohol problem.
- Over 60 percent of fifteen- and sixteen-year-olds reported using alcohol (about one quarter regularly), as did over 40 percent of thirteen- and fourteen-year-olds (about 10 percent regularly).
- Almost 80 percent of seventeen- and eighteen-year-olds reported having the opportunity to use a range of illicit drugs (from marijuana to cocaine to prescription drugs). Forty-six percent of boys and 38 percent of girls reported using some illicit drug. Fifteen percent of boys and 9 percent of girls used illicit drugs regularly.
- About two thirds of fifteen- and sixteen-year-olds and 40 percent of thirteen- and fourteen-year-olds had the opportunity to use illicit drugs. About one quarter of fifteen- and sixteen-year-olds reported using some drug, as did about one in ten thirteen- and fourteen-year-olds.

When it comes to alcohol, I am a pragmatist, especially given numbers like these. I expect teenagers to drink, including my teenagers. Given this expectation, I hope my teenagers will drink responsibly. But how can they learn to drink responsibly? They never take a class like driver's education. (Drinker's education?) They don't get a learner's permit to drink.

I have tried to offer a little of this education at home. I have always offered a glass of champagne, even to my young teenagers (on special occasions). My older teenagers are welcome to have a beer or a glass of wine with the family. I hope this experience helps them manage drinking when they encounter alcohol with their friends.

When they drink excessively, which I also expect will happen sometimes, I want my teenagers to avoid danger. My hard and fast rules include the following:

- Do not drink and drive. If you are intoxicated and need a ride, call me—no matter what time it is. I will give you a ride. There will be no repercussions.
- Be careful about putting yourself in a potentially dangerous situation with a member of the opposite sex. And treat a potential romantic partner like you would treat your brother or sister. If you wouldn't be OK with someone acting like that with your sister, you better not act that way yourself.

As for illicit drugs, my message is this: Don't be stupid. There are a lot of dangerous drugs out there. You can get into big trouble, legally and otherwise. And your friends will tell you a lot of myths about drugs, including weed. All drugs make you dumber, not smarter. And while I cannot stop you from trying illicit drugs, I do not condone any of it.

You may not like my messages. If so, that's fine. Honestly, I am kind of ambivalent myself. As I said, I am just giving you something to react to.

Maybe now you know what messages you *don't* want to convey to your teenagers.

My question for you is: What *do* you want to tell them?

And as you are trying to answer that question, talk to your ex, so you two can deliver the same message. Maybe the two of you also can work together to monitor what your teenager says, and more important, what he does when it comes to alcohol and drugs.

## COLLEGE

As we transition from alcohol and drugs to college, I should share another personal value. I expect my children to work hard in school. I expect them to get the grades they are capable of earning. I expect them to go to college. (I have three in college here at the University of Virginia as I am writing this. And, no, I get no break on tuition as a professor.)

If they are not doing their job in school, my children are in *a lot* deeper trouble regarding curfews, alcohol, or whatever. If they do their job, well, they earn some freedom.

But my goal in discussing college is not to address value questions. My goal is to raise money questions. In round numbers, the current cost of four years of college (room, board, and tuition) is roughly $100,000 at a public school and $250,000 at a private one. And the rising costs of college have long outpaced the rate of inflation.

Do I have your attention?

How are you and your ex going to pay for your children's college education?

I should have asked this question in earlier chapters. (Actually, I did, briefly.) Hopefully, you asked yourself this question when your child was born. Because that is when you should start saving for college. I don't care if it's $100 a month. You should get in the habit of putting some money into a 529 account—for your infant or your teenager. (A 529 account is a college savings account that offers tax benefits. Different states have different plans. Do your research. Tax benefits and investment costs can vary.)

If you and your ex divorced long ago, I hope you not only thought about savings for college. I hope you added a provision about college expenses to the legal agreement you made way back when. And I hope you saved, so you can hold up your end of the bargain.

If you are getting divorced now, I urge you to think about including a provision to address college expenses. You can be an ostrich and put your head in the sand. But when you pull it out, college expenses will still be there—but bigger because of inflation.

You definitely should apply for aid. But let me suggest that unless your son is a truly gifted athlete or scholar, or you are truly poor, you need to consider more of a plan than "He'll get a scholarship."

Unless you are wealthy, you and your ex are going to need to have a *long* conversation about college costs. You need to discuss your values about a college, particularly public versus private. You need to discuss your values about how much you think you should support your children's education. You need to discuss whether your children should have "skin in the game" and pay part of their own expenses, and if so, how much. On your own, you need to estimate how much you may have to pay, how much you can afford to pay, and probably how you can alter your budget so you can start saving more now.

There are essentially two approaches to converting this difficult exercise into a contract with your ex.

One approach is that you can each agree to pay some percentage of the costs of room, board, and tuition at a given university, perhaps the flagship public college in your state. For example, you may agree that you, your ex, and your son each will be responsible for one third of the costs of attendance at the University of Michigan, no matter where your son actually goes to college. Make sure to name a college, because the cost variation can be huge. And make sure to talk to your teenager about your values, and your agreement, long before he starts the application process. He may want to go to Brown. He may be good enough to get in. But is he prepared to either get a scholarship or take out loans to cover the difference in costs between Brown and Michigan?

A second approach is to agree on a savings plan. You may do more than *resolve* to contribute $100 per month to a 529 plan. You may sign a contract that you and your ex will each make a monthly contribution in that amount. This kind of an agreement gives you more control over your financial commitment, but you need to do the math. Even if you contribute $200 per month ($100 each) from birth through your daughter's eighteenth birthday, you will come up far short of the costs of paying for a public college education. You certainly will be better off than if you save nothing. But you may be committing your daughter to be responsible for a much bigger percentage of her college education that either you or her mom are committing to.

Even if you are not sure you can do much to contribute, talk to your ex and eventually your children about college and college expenses. I know many divorced parents who *should* have been able to help their children with college. But they cannot. Some planned poorly. Some thought their ex, or his parents, would pay. Some spent the equivalent of a college education on lawyers. A few refused to help their children because they resented the support they paid to their ex.

If you cannot help much with college expenses, well, that is a reality for many parents. You just don't want to put yourself in this position because you took the ostrich approach toward planning.

## Troubled and Troubling Adolescents

With all the things that can go wrong, parents naturally focus on keeping teenagers out of trouble. But adolescents also can be too well behaved. Today, many teens are overburdened with schoolwork, extracurricular activities, and pressures to succeed. They worry about getting into a top college, maybe with a scholarship.

All of this is great if your teen thrives on the challenge. But the pileup of demands can contribute to serious problems with anxiety or depression. These problems become far more common during adolescence, particularly among girls. In recent years, depression and anxiety have become more prevalent in general. Many experts attribute the upswing in adolescent depression and anxiety to the rising and sometimes unrealistic expectations that parents and schools hold for teenagers' success.

Your teen may be too good in another way. Some hyper-responsible teens end up taking care of their parents as well as themselves. These caretaker teens become a lonely or depressed parent's best friend. Or they become the adult, constantly mediating between warring parents, perhaps in an effort to protect younger siblings. Whatever the specifics, caretaker adolescents are "parentified." They take on responsibilities that a parent should be fulfilling.

## GROWING UP FASTER

It is normal for kids from divorced families to grow up a little faster. As a result of caring for younger siblings or having to help to manage the household, your teenagers may learn to be more responsible than many kids their age.

Exposure to their parents' flaws also can cause kids to grow up faster. Eventually, we all learn that our parents are people. They are human. But adolescents whose parents divorce may come to this revelation at a younger age. They may see that Dad makes bad choices. Mom's feelings are hurt too easily. Such observations can burst a protective bubble, the illusion of parental infallibility. As a result, a sixteen-year-old may become a little more jaded but also a little more mature more than her peers.

The pain of divorce also can cause kids to grow up faster. The pain hurts, of course. But living through pain also can make adolescents both tougher and more sensitive. Their resilience gives them substance and depth beyond their years.

All of these ways of growing up faster can be healthy. Really, they can be character building. But you do *not* want your teen to grow up faster as a result of you neglecting discipline. You do not want her to assume too much autonomy too soon. That is pseudomaturity, not depth.

## PARENTIFIED OR CARETAKER TEENS

You also do not want your responsible teen to become your caretaker. It is one thing to assume more responsibility for practical tasks like babysitting or chores. But it is something different when teens do a parent's *emotional* job. You do not want your adolescent to become your confidant. You do not want her to hear your confessions about your disappointments with dating, or whatever. You do not want her to feel like she has to fix your unhappiness.

From the outside, teens may look resilient when they serve as an emotional support for a parent. You may think of your son as your rock. But whether it involves becoming "the man of the house" or your new best friend, caretaker kids suffer from the weight of developmentally inappropriate responsibility.

Under a surface of competence, hyper-responsible kids often are anxious about making everything better—or depressed about their failure to do so. Even when they "succeed," parentified teenagers still lose. They learn an impossible lesson: *I am responsible for other people's happiness*. And they carry this belief into other relationships: "My boyfriend is always angry. I must be doing something wrong. I have to make him happy."

Resilience is about getting to be a kid, despite divorce. Parentification is about assuming responsibility for something that you cannot be responsible for: someone else's happiness.

Sooner or later, your parentified child will fail. She cannot make you or her boyfriend happy. No one, not even a mental health professional, can be responsible for another person's happiness. Ultimately, we all have to be responsible for our own happiness. I teach hyper-responsible teens and new graduate student therapists to be *responsive*—to care, to *try* to help. But there is a world of difference between being responsive and feeling *responsible*—feeling like you *have* to fix someone who is not helping himself.

Of course, you are allowed to be sad, worried, whatever. But you want your teen to know that *you* will take care of yourself. That's your job, not your teenager's. Your fifteen-year-old's job is to take care of *her* life. You need to do your job so she can focus on hers.

## YOU MAY *NOT* BE THE PROBLEM

Before leaving the topic of troubled adolescents, let me be clear. You may *not* be the problem. Whether the problem is large or small, your teenager's psychological struggles may not be your fault.

This is a book about divorce. So I naturally focus on how divorce can contribute to children's emotional upheaval. In doing so, I am trying to help you to do things right. I am offering you warning signs. I am suggesting things you can try to correct to see if a change may help your troubled or troubling child.

But I am *not* saying that every one of your adolescent's problems is your fault.

Mental health professionals often seem to blame parents, or bash them, for causing all of children's emotional struggles. Of course, it always is good to ask, "What could I do differently?" But sometimes the answer is "Nothing."

One reason why the answer may be "Nothing" is that your teenager's struggles may be *normal*. You can't "cure" adolescence. And you wouldn't want to. Like you, your teenager will learn from life's challenges—and from his mistakes. Bumps and bruises, whether physical or emotional, teach all of us important lessons. Yes, you may agonize, wondering, "Is this normal or is it the divorce?" But that is a familiar question. You have worried about it at every age. (I already addressed it at some length in Chapter 6.)

Another possibility is that your teen's difficulties may be due to peer relationships, not you. Of course, you may try to help him fix things with his peers. But that may be an impossible task. You may be unable to change your son's choice of friends or how his peers treat him. Maybe *he* has to figure that out.

And, of course, genetics play a big role in shaping personality, problems like depression, and even difficulties like substance abuse. You may already be aware of a family history. If so, don't waste time blaming yourself—or your ex—for bad genes. That changes nothing. Instead, help your adolescent find the professional help he may need.

And your son shouldn't waste time blaming bad genes either. Instead, his task is to find a way to cope effectively. If he inherited diabetes (or whatever physical disease), you wouldn't let him say, "It's unfair," and give up responsibility or hope. You would be sympathetic, but you still would expect him to manage the illness.

He may need to learn ways to manage his moods or his behavior too—as best he can. Part of being responsible for himself may include taking medication or seeing a therapist regularly. Or maybe his immediate task is to accept that he has a problem.

Genes may account for some of your teen's unique challenges. But genetic inheritance is about predisposition, not predestination. It offers an explanation, not an excuse.

## Other Relationships and Your Adolescent

In many ways, teen life is all about relationships. And adolescent relationships are a source of joy and drama.

*Joy and drama* almost certainly describes your relationship with your teen. She fights for autonomy. You ask for just a little relatedness. And her friendships? They are loving, supportive, and everlasting. Until they become cruel, competitive, and ever changing. Then there is romance. She frets about boys. She discusses boys endlessly with her friends. When she dresses for the school dance, she looks like she is twenty-one. And if she develops a serious romance, the bond can become powerful, passionate, and, sadly, painful.

## YOUR ROMANCES AND YOUR TEEN

All of the drama is complicated, of course. But in divorce, the most complicated relationship often is the one between your teenager and *your* romantic partner.

You should expect dating to be a challenge if you have a teenager in the house, particularly if you separated recently. One problem is that it is hard to be discreet, although you should try. Unlike younger children, your teen is not easily fooled. She knows why you're dressed up on a Saturday night. She may tell you that you look like a tramp (or worse). Or she may say you look like a dowdy old lady. Neither comment inspires affection or self-confidence.

Another problem is that adolescents know what dating is all about, or think they do. In reality, they are grappling with sorting out their own interests and values. Given their uncertainty (and the fact that you are her mom), the thought of you dating, or having sex—disgusting!—is, well, disgusting. You don't need to become a nun. But you do want to be circumspect and prepared for friction. And don't expect your teenager to understand your perspective. A little acceptance is good enough.

Your teen can make your serious relationships difficult. He may treat your boyfriend as a rival—to him or his dad. Or maybe he just doesn't want a stranger around. Even if you separated years ago and your relationship is long-standing, adolescents can make things hard. He may rebel against your boyfriend's supervision. This reaction is so common that I always urge romantic partners just to be adult friends. Leave the discipline to the biological parents.

The list of possibilities goes on. Maybe your teen is struggling to balance her relationship with you and your ex. Instead of being mad at you, it's safer to be angry with your girlfriend. Or maybe your relationship *is* taking time away from you and your daughter. If so, nurture that relationship. Even if you are crazy in love, make time for just the two of you. Remember what happened to Michele and her daughter, LaKeesha.

## YOUR TEEN'S RELATIONSHIPS AND YOU

In the end, your teen is not likely to want too much of your time anyway. She has her own life, her own relationships. Encourage her friendships—and set limits on them.

She doesn't need sleepovers every weekend. And if she's still a youngish teen, or maybe if she's seventeen, you probably want to know her sleepover plans in advance. (I gave up sometime during each of my teens' senior year in high school.) You may even want to speak with a parent at the house where she is supposed to be sleeping. Maybe I am overly suspicious, but I don't trust sleepover plans made after 11 p.m. Really, does it count as getting my permission if you text me at 11:15 on a Friday night that you're sleeping at Emma's? Really?

And meet her dates, and his dates too. It's an old-fashioned idea, I know. But I am OK if my adolescent thinks I'm a dinosaur. While I don't have research to back this up, I think it's especially important for parents to meet a date of the same gender: dads meeting boys, moms meeting girls. Dad's warm greeting—combined with a firm handshake—can remind a hormonal teenage boy that his date does have a father.

I don't know how mothers handle the girls their sons date. In addition to a warm welcome, I suspect there is a protective look that says something like *Don't forget. He's my baby.*

If your son or daughter is in a same-sex relationship, meet their date too. In this case, I'm sure it is far more important for you to be welcoming than parental.

Of course, doing all of this requires a little communication be-tween you and your ex. Maybe both of you can be there to meet her date (and take pictures) on special occasions, like the senior prom. More routinely, I encourage you to monitor and occasionally dis-cuss your teenager's romantic interests. In the end, your teenager is mostly right. Whom she dates is none of your business. But she's not as worldly as she thinks. Like you, she will learn through the mis-takes she makes in her romantic life. You just want to try to help her to make mistakes that are only temporary.

## CHAPTER 9

# Emerging Adults:
# College Years and Beyond

Emerging adulthood (roughly ages nineteen to thirty) begins with high school graduation and ends as young people assume more and more adult roles throughout their twenties. According to most laws and developmental psychology textbooks, childhood ends at age eighteen or nineteen or twenty-one. Parenting does not. Parenting never ends.

Young adults today may rely on their parents for support into and perhaps throughout their twenties. These are the years for pursuing higher education, employment, enduring intimate relationships, and, perhaps, a family of your own. But young people reach these milestones at notably later ages now than they did in the past. For example, the median age at first marriage for women today is twenty-seven. For men, it is twenty-nine. In 1960, the median age at first marriage was twenty for women and twenty-three for men.

## Emerging Adulthood

In Chapter 8, I noted that some experts refer to young people's delay in assuming adult roles as a period of extended adolescence. I much prefer the term *emerging adulthood*. Today's young adults are not Peter Pans, refusing to grow up. Instead, economic and social conditions push them to delay marriage, childbearing, and employment, even as they pursue these goals.

Consider the circumstances that today's twenty-somethings face. College is all but necessary for economic success. To many, graduate school seems to be. Good employment can be hard to find, yet lifestyle expectations are high. Pregnancy can be put off, while women and men build careers and seek financial security.

Most Americans still marry. But marriage often follows major relationship transitions instead of preceding them. When I was a kid, we taunted each other about suspected boyfriends or girlfriends: "First comes love. Then comes marriage. Then comes Bobby (or whoever) in a baby carriage." Today, over half of young American couples live together before they marry.[1] And in the United States in 2013, over 40 percent of babies were born outside marriage.[2] Weddings, if they happen, may be more of a culmination of a couple's young life together rather than a rite of passage into it.

Young people today even postpone their search for identity. In the 1950s, the identity crisis was Erik Erikson's central theme of adolescence. Now, young people face what experts call a "quarterlife crisis." "Who am I?" is a question that emerging adults may not ask, or attempt to fully answer, until their midtwenties.

In small ways and perhaps big ones, young people rely on their parents for emotional and practical support during this period of emerging adulthood. They may live in the basement. They may count on their parents for regular financial support. They may text or talk with their parents every day, or perhaps multiple times per day. They may ask their parents for help in moving not only into college but also into graduate school or a new job.

And parenting doesn't end once children do assume adult roles. For example, grandparents often are significant figures in the lives of grandchildren. In helping to parent grandchildren, grandparents also become essential supports for their own children.

## EMERGING ADULTHOOD AND DIVORCE

Parenting does not end when your child graduates from high school. Neither does coparenting. You are a parent forever. And you and your ex are forever tied together through your children.

Sure, custody laws no longer apply—although courts occasionally order divorced parents to contribute to the cost of their children's college education. I hope you planned for college expenses long ago. Ideally, as I've said elsewhere, parents should start saving for college when their baby is born.

You and your ex also need a strategy for sharing college costs, if you do not have one already. You do *not* need to pay for everything. Your twenty-year-old can assume some responsibility for his own education. Just be clear about your expectations and savings goals— for you, your ex, and your child. See Chapter 8 for a discussion of different ways you may share these expenses.

Based on my thirty-three years as a professor, let me offer a little further advice about college and your child. Today's parents often micromanage their children's college experiences. I urge you not to. Let your child make his own decisions. The goal of emerging adulthood is to become an adult. Your son needs to learn how. Hopefully, he will come to you for advice, which is great. Listen. Offer your perspective. Then let him grapple. That is how he will learn.

And let your ex know about your discussions with your young-adult son. She may have heard something different from him. Or maybe she has a great contact for a summer internship. Or maybe your son didn't talk with her. If not, she will be grateful to you for sharing. She wants to know what your son is thinking too, especially if he hasn't come to her for advice.

How do you know what to share with your ex? Treat her like the parent she is. If you would like to know something about your child, well, chances are she feels the same way. And unless your emerging adult explicitly says, "Don't tell Mom," err on the side of talking to her (or texting or e-mailing). I don't get many divorced parents coming to me for therapy or mediation because their ex is *too* nice.

## Schedules for Emerging Adults

Obviously, you no longer need a formal parenting plan for your young-adult child. That should be a relief. But schedule issues still are going to come up.

Your daughter will come home for semester break and maybe for summer vacations. Where is she going to stay?

### HER PLAN, YOUR PLAN, OR THE OLD PLAN

Maybe she has clear ideas about what she wants to do. If so, you need to respect that. The last thing she wants over her vacation is a controversy about where she should stay. Of course, you are going to want to spend time with her. But you may need to work around her schedule now, instead of her working around yours. Get used to it! This is how things are going to be from now on, whether she's staying with you or with her dad.

What if she doesn't know what do? What if she seems conflicted or uncertain? If so, you and your ex may outline a tentative schedule for her. Of course, you need to be flexible and take her ever-changing plans into account too. But if you give her a starting point, you may take some pressure off her. Tell her about your ideas for spending time with each of you—as a suggestion. And tell her that she can follow your suggestions, modify them, or reject them. Whatever she decides, your ideas will give her something to react to. And encouraging her to make changes, if she wants, will take some pressure off. She may be perfectly happy to have you decide. Maybe she just wants to focus on her exams.

Or maybe none of this is necessary. Maybe your daughter knows exactly what she wants to do. Her old schedule still works best.

Here's a little story about a former graduate student of mine. She faced a schedule complication as an emerging adult.

After several years of living in Charlottesville, studying clinical psychology at the University of Virginia, this married, twenty-eight-year-old woman needed to return to her hometown. She had to complete a year of clinical internship. She needed a place to stay. Her husband couldn't move because of his job. But both of her parents still lived in the city where she grew up.

Seemingly without hesitation, this young woman knew what she wanted to do. She would live one week at Mom's, one week at Dad's! She had lived that way throughout her childhood. To her, the schedule was natural. It was normal. Back and forth? Not a problem!

You (and I) worry that kids sometimes may find joint physical custody disruptive. But for many kids, hopefully for most, moving between homes does become normal and natural. It is their life. And it can be a great life, despite divorce.

Clearly, my student felt that way. And let me offer a little congratulations, in print, to her mom and dad. (I never have had the pleasure of meeting them.) Good work! You obviously made joint custody work well for a long time.

## SPECIAL EVENTS AFTER ADULTHOOD EMERGES

As your emerging adult child moves through his twenties and beyond, you will face still more schedule issues. Maybe he can travel home for a visit only once a year. Will you compete over where he stays? Will you and your ex be able to host or attend some celebrations together? Maybe you can't manage a joint Passover seder (although some divorced parents do). But what about your new granddaughter's first birthday? Do you really need to plan separate parties, not because of her, but because of you?

Eventually, in-laws are likely to enter the picture. You remember how hard it was to please both your parents and your in-laws around the holidays, right? Think about your child's perspective now. He has three or maybe four sets of parents to please. (His wife's parents may be divorced too.) And maybe no one lives in the same town or even the same state.

There may be no easy solution to these kinds of complications. But you can make things easier by being understanding, thinking creatively, and doing your best to facilitate a plan. Maybe you see your son and his family only every other Thanksgiving. Maybe you travel to see him, rather than vice versa. Or maybe you alter the timing of your big family get-together. Your children (and their children) surely would be excited to join you at a beach house you rent on the Outer Banks over the Fourth of July or at a ski cabin in Stowe over spring break.

## Divorcing during Emerging Adult Life versus Moving into Adult Life When Divorced

It may not seem like it, but many parents do stay together for their children's sake. Some of those parents divorce once their children are grown.

If you are one of those parents, you may think, or hope, that adult children are not affected by their parents' divorce. If you do, I am sorry. You are wrong. Divorce rocks the world of any child, no matter his age.

Maybe you stuck it out in an unhappy marriage. You wanted to raise your children in a two-parent family. If so, this may have been a great decision.

Parents who wait to separate until their children are grown avoid the disruption of divorce during childhood. If this was your choice, hopefully, you two worked together effectively as coparents throughout the years, even though your marriage was unhappy.

## DIVORCE HURTS ADULT CHILDREN TOO

But even if you kept family life stable while your kids were young, you need to recognize that divorce hurts adult children too. You can expect your twenty-five-year-old daughter to worry about you, your ex, and your relationship with each other. Maybe she will be angry too. Maybe she will blame one or both of you for hurting each other or messing up her life.

Messing up her life? As an adult? Yes, you can expect your daughter to be unhappy about how much your divorce complicates her life, even now. Her childhood home may disappear—and much of her inheritance too. Now she needs to make new plans for holidays, weddings, and grandchildren.

Your daughter may not like your new partner either, if you have one. Maybe there isn't anything wrong with him. He's just . . . different. He's an outsider. He may be nice, but he may just not feel like family to her.

Adult children whose parents split also can feel like their entire childhood was a lie. How can they look at their old family photographs? And if they do, your children may wonder, *Were they pretending all those years?*

Yes, your divorce can create a lot of problems, even for your young-adult children. Should you stay together for *their* sake? That may sound like a silly question. Your child is an adult now! But I don't think the question silly, no matter how old your children may be.

Still, I do think it's the wrong question.

## STAYING TOGETHER FOR THE CHILDREN'S SAKE

Whether your children are six or twenty-six, I urge you *not* to stay together for their sake. No, I am hardly saying that divorce matters little to children, so you don't need to consider them. No, I am not saying, "Be happy. Do what feels good, and your children will be happy."

What I mean is this: Absolutely, you should consider how divorce (or staying together in a miserable marriage) may or may not affect your children. Your concerns about your children should be a huge factor in whatever decision you make. Your children may well be the deciding factor.

But even if they are, even if you think you are staying together for your children, in the end, this is *your* choice. Make your decision and live with it. Don't be a martyr to your marriage or to your children. Sometimes you need to make tough choices in life. Own those decisions. Don't put the weight of responsibility onto someone else, not on your ex, not on your kids.

And here is one thing you absolutely should never do. Even if, in your mind, you *did* stay together for your children's sake, don't share your sacrifice with your children. Don't ask them or expect them to give you a pat on the back.

Over the years, at least a dozen of my college students have told me that their parents did exactly this. They waited to split until their child was in college. And for some reason, these parents told their son or daughter, "We were only staying together for you."

When their parents told them this, these young adults didn't give their parents a prize. They didn't say, "Thanks for the memories." Instead, they felt incredibly guilty—and angry and aghast.

Why? Their parents just laid a huge guilt trip on them. "I was miserable for twenty years, so you could have a 'happy' childhood."

Whoops, there goes that happiness. It was all a lie.

And there goes your childhood. Because guess who is responsible for your parents' misery? You.

Your parents sacrificed their happiness for you. They *told* you they did. So naturally you feel responsible for their years of unhappiness.

But, of course, as a child you had no role in the decision. How could you? You had no idea a decision was being made on your behalf.

If you are a parent who decided to stay together for your children, you may think you deserve praise for your sacrifice. Perhaps you do. If so, pat yourself on the back. Because you are the only one who should know about your choice. Don't share this with your child—ever. Whether you stay together or split, this is *your* decision. Own it.

## A DISTANT MEMORY

What if you divorced when your children were young? If so, your emerging adult may have little to adjust to—other than the many challenges of her own life. All that happened with her family should mostly be a distant memory now, if perhaps a sometimes painful one. And hopefully those unhappy memories are overshadowed by years of happy ones, for your daughter, for you, and for your ex too.

But divorce may not be a part of the past, even if you split long ago. You and your ex may still be feuding. If so, you can anticipate that your young-adult child will distance herself from one of you, perhaps from both of you. She had no choice but to put up with your fights as a kid. As an adult, she's done. (Later in this chapter, I discuss what to do to make graduations and weddings all about your kids, not all about your divorce.)

If your daughter isn't done, if she's still inserting herself in your disputes, then *she* has a problem. She may be taking on unhealthy parental responsibility. She may be trying to fix you, your ex, or both of you. If this sounds like your emerging adult daughter, read the section on parentified or caretaker teens in Chapter 8.

## RECONCILIATION WITH A DISTANT PARENT

Throughout this book, I have assumed (and hoped) that both you and your ex would remain deeply involved in your children's life. But I realize this is not always the case. Your children may have seen your ex infrequently. Or maybe you are the one they saw only on occasion.

Some children see one of their divorced parents only rarely, perhaps hardly at all. This happens despite widespread recognition of the importance of both mothers and fathers to children—despite joint custody. Usually, that parent is their father. As I discussed in Chapter 2, a few years ago I completed a study of this topic with Paul Amato and Catherine Meyers of Penn State University. We examined changes in contact between children and their divorced dads over the last several decades. We documented that today's divorced fathers stay much more involved with their children than in the past. In 1976, one in three divorced fathers saw their children only once a year or less. By 2002, only about one in five of divorced fathers saw their children this infrequently.

These statistics show that divorced dads are much more likely to maintain contact with their children today. But the numbers also show that many young people still have little contact with their fathers following a divorce.

Not seeing much of your dad, or your mom, can be really hard when you are a kid, of course. You miss him. You may wonder why he doesn't find the time to come to see you more often. You may feel left out when you see other kids who are with both of their parents, whether they are married or divorced.

You also miss out on things you may not realize you are missing.

Your father may have taught you how to play baseball. He may have been a firm hand in guiding you to behave more appropriately.

And maybe not seeing much of your dad hurt your relationship with your mom too. Rightly or wrongly, maybe you blamed her for your dad's absence. Or maybe she was pretty overwhelmed by parenting on her own. Maybe she would have been more attentive or more patient or happier if she hadn't had to do everything all on her own.

## WHO IS HE? WHO AM I?

When a child becomes an emerging adult, new questions and complications often arise about a distant parent. *Should I seek him out? Should I ask him, or confront him, about his absence from my life? How can I know myself, if I don't know him? He's a part of my DNA, even if he hasn't been much of a part of my life. Do I look like him? Do I act like him? Who is he? Who am I? What part of me is like him?*

Not every emerging adult asks these kinds of searching questions. But many do. Emerging adults are asking, "Who am I?" Their answers often are shaped in relation to their parents. At least for a time, many young people define themselves in opposition to their parents. Eventually, most admit—sometimes in shock or horror— that *they actually have turned out to be a lot like their mom or dad.*

That is, if they know their mom or dad.

## DO NOT PROTECT HIM

What do you do if you are the parent who was there for your child? What if you have been doing the hard work, day in, day out? And now, at twenty-two, your son wants to travel across the country to hang out with his dad.

Maybe he seems to be idolizing his father. Maybe you're afraid you will lose him. Or maybe you know he's just going to get hurt. What should you do?

Let him go. He's twenty-two now. Your son needs to answer his questions for himself.

If you have a good relationship with your son, if you haven't lied to him about his father, everything will be fine. He may struggle. He may get confused. He may get angry. But you have to trust him. Trusting him should be a familiar experience by now. You had to trust him behind the wheel, staying out late, and going off to college. And your trust was well placed. He was all right, eventually.

And you need to trust yourself too. He's a good kid. You raised him right. You love him. He loves you. He'll figure this out. Maybe he will need to find a place for two parents in his life. Maybe you will too. But no matter what, your place in his life will be more secure if you let him go than if you try to hold him back. You learned that lesson when he was two, and six, and fourteen. You can put that lesson into practice again in his twenties.

## BE OPEN, BE SORRY, BE PATIENT

What do you do if you're the parent who has not been a big part of your child's life? If you are that parent, you need to be open. You need to be open to seeing him. And you need to be open to his emotions, whether his feelings involve longing or anger or confusion.

If your emerging adult son contacts you, listen more than you talk. When the time seems right, apologize. Ask for his forgiveness, if you should. But don't expect him to forgive you on the spot. It's going to take time for you to earn forgiveness, and for him to grant it.

Explain what happened, if you have an explanation. But don't blame anyone or anything. Especially don't blame his mother. Take responsibility for your decisions, for whatever your contributions may have been to your distance. You can tell him that you kept away because you thought he would be better off. You didn't want him stuck in the middle of your conflicts with your ex. But focus on *your* decision. Maybe you made a good choice. Maybe not. But you made a choice. Don't complain about how his mother or the courts drove you away, unless you are really, truly an innocent victim of manipulation. If you are just making excuse, he'll know. And you will lose him again.

Most important, eventually you want to bring your focus to the present, instead of the past. Try to find a way to become a part of his life now, even from a distance. E-mail, text, and send photos. Respond to your son's communications. Make plans to see him next summer or the next time you are on the West Coast.

You may have missed out on most of his childhood. He may have missed out on having you there. But things can change. We are talking about a lifetime of parenting. Reconciliation is possible. He can still be your son. She can still be your daughter.

## ANGER AND THE EMOTIONS BEHIND ANGER

If he has seen you only infrequently, you should expect one emotion to dominate your emerging adult's feelings when you first see him again: anger.

He is likely to be angry about many things. You are selfish. You picked your new family or your new job over him. You always blame his mother. You refuse to take responsibility. You are intruding into his life now. You don't deserve to have a relationship with him. You don't love him or have a sick way of showing it. He hates you.

You should take his anger at face value. And you should take it to heart. Your emerging adult son has many good reasons to be angry. And you may well have some soul searching to do. You may have many mistakes to admit to. And you may well have some important changes to make.

You have to accept your young adult son's anger at face value.

And you also should look behind his anger. Look and try to understand his deeper feelings. Do this in your heart and mind, but probably not in your words. You need to be patient right now. You need to absorb his anger. He needs to discover the feelings beneath his anger for himself.

What feelings lie behind his anger? Hurt, for one. He's angry at you because you hurt him. And because you hurt him, he wants to hurt you back.

This should be no surprise. In Chapter 1, I discussed how pain fuels much of the anger between couples in the heat of divorce. Exploring the emotions behind anger was a central theme of my earlier book for parents, *The Truth about Children and Divorce*.

His anger also is fueled by fear. He's afraid you may reject him again. He's afraid you won't be hurt when he tries to hurt you. If he can't hurt you, it means you don't care. That is what he is most afraid of.

And his anger also is fueled by longing. His anger is a way of reaching out, of trying to reconnect. The fact that he is still angry, and still hurt, means that *he* still cares. But he can't feel or say that. Telling you that he missed and misses you would make him too vulnerable. What if you rejected him again? Instead, he protects himself from rejection with anger. If you continue to be distant, if you are disinterested, he can tell himself, *I knew it. That narcissistic fool cares about no one but himself.*

So accept his anger at face value. His anger is legitimate. And you have questions to answer, to him and to yourself. But look behind his anger too. Do this, so you can understand his pain, and his fear, and his longing. Do this, so you can better absorb the anger you may have coming. Do this, so you can be patient and give him time to discover for himself how he really feels. Look behind his anger to give you both a chance at reconciliation, even after all of these years.

## TALKING ABOUT DIVORCE WITH YOUR ADULT CHILD

As I discussed in earlier chapters, parents typically wonder and worry about how to talk about divorce to their children and adolescents. But do you really need to be concerned about how to talk to your adult children about your divorce? My short answer is yes.

If you are separating now, you probably do not need to talk to your emerging adult together as a family. Unlike an eight-year-old, your twenty-four-year-old daughter knows you love her. She knows you will still love her, even after a divorce. And you do not need to worry about telling her where she is going to live now. You don't need to reveal the schedule for how she will move between two homes. You do not need to reassure her that nothing will change with her friends or her school.

Plus, she doesn't have to live with your conflicts from day to day.

But she still can get caught in the middle. So if you speak with her alone, make sure your ex knows about the conversation. Discuss this with him in advance. That way, he can talk with her too. And share what you plan to tell your adult child. Adult children do better with consistent messages too.

## DON'T OVERSHARE

Even though she is an adult, you still need to think carefully about what you are going to say to your twenty-four-year-old daughter. Don't make the mistake of oversharing about your divorce. Just because your child is an adult now, it doesn't mean it's time to spill your guts.

I encourage you to stick with the short, simple, sound-bite explanations that you and your ex agree to. Yes, your daughter deserves to know a little bit about what is going on and why. But she is still your child, even though she is an adult now. She does not want to hear intimate details about your private life. You still are her parents, not her friends.

The same principles apply to any questions that may arise about a long-ago divorce. Your emerging adult may ask you to tell her more about what happened. Maybe she is motivated by nothing more than curiosity. Or maybe *you* have things you want to share. Maybe you have been waiting a long time to tell her certain things. You may think you can tell her the full story now. After all, she's an adult, finally. She can handle it.

It is true. You two can relate more as equals now. You are both adults. She knows you are human. She recognizes your shortcomings. She accepts your fallibility. But you are still her mom. And her dad is still her dad. Really, she has no interest in learning about *all* of your mistakes, your intimate life, or your private thoughts. Even if she asks, she doesn't really want to know.

So if you (still) need someone on your side or someone to vent to, rely on your best friend or therapist, not your adult child. You need to respect her boundaries. You want to recognize her need to see you both as parents, even as she recognizes that you are human.

## YOU CAN SET BOUNDARIES TOO

And you get to set boundaries too. A former client once came to me in confusion. His well-adjusted, philosophically inclined thirty-one-year-old daughter had just told him all about her plans to travel to South America. She was going to take a weeklong spiritual journey, high on ayahuasca and guided by an indigenous healer. Should he stop her? Should he go with her? Should he take part in the spiritual (and psychedelic) exploration with her?

No, I told him. His private life, now and from the past, is on a need-to-know basis, especially when his children are involved. His daughter's private life should be on a need-to-know basis too.

He did not need to know all about his daughter's plans to take a spiritual, psychedelic journey. I suggested that he didn't need to either condone or disapprove of his emerging adult daughter's explorations. He could simply tell her that he just didn't want to know about these kinds of things. He wanted to know all about her life, of course, but not about these kinds of things. Besides, he knew she would do what she wanted to do anyway. He just didn't want to have to wonder and worry.

Of course, there is no absolute right or wrong about how much parents and adult children share. Your ethnic and cultural background surely affects your expectations, as does your unique family history. Some families keep clear, distant boundaries. Other families maintain much looser boundaries. But whatever the culture of your family, you are still a parent and your adult child is still a child. Your boundaries can be firm or loose, but there should be some boundaries between parents and children, even when those children are grown.

## Parenting and Coparenting Emerging Adults

Parenting emerging adults should be simple. Your biggest job is to listen. Hopefully, your young adult is talking—some. You don't need to know the intimate details of her life any more than she needs to know yours. Sure, you probably should have a few rules for your young college student. Coming in at three a.m. every night during summer vacation is *not* OK. But if you are still trying to parent your twenty-year-old like you did when she was sixteen, you are delaying the emergence of her adulthood, not promoting it.

You *can* offer your emerging adult child advice—if he asks for it. But he really wants you to listen, not to tell him what to do. He probably knows your opinion anyway. You should ask him about his life, of course. But he will talk more if you listen more.

Unless problems arise, one relief is that you and your ex no longer have to actively coparent your young adult. But it is still good to stay in touch from time to time. Your son may be talking to only one of you. If so, your ex is probably eager to hear what he's thinking. And your ex may have good ideas or insights.

Even though your child is grown up, your coparenting relationship still is worth preserving, or if necessary, improving. It can be a relief and a pleasure to share joys or concerns with someone who also shares love for your adult child.

As I was writing this, I interrupted my work to send an e-mail to my ex. Our thirty-three-year-old daughter and her family are hoping to move back to Charlottesville. How exciting! Where are they going to live? How will they manage work? What about grandchildren?

You truly do want a parenting plan to last a lifetime.

## GRADUATIONS AND WEDDINGS

Of course, parenting and coparenting young-adult children is not always about watching and occasionally giving advice. Events like your daughter's college graduation or her wedding will bring you together in celebration and joy.

At least, I hope they do.

In one of my studies conducted with former graduate student Lisa Laumann-Billings, half of a sample of well-adjusted college students agreed with this item: "I worry about big events like graduations or weddings, when both of my parents will have to come."

Every year, it seems, at least one undergraduate drops by my office, unexpectedly and in tears. Usually, this occurs right around spring break. Often I have never met the student before. Maybe her friend took a class with me. They told her I am a divorce expert.

However they get to my door, these students relate a variation of the same story. She is about to graduate from the University of Virginia. She has been a great student. Often she is headed for grad school, or law school, or med school. She is graduating in six weeks. But instead of a celebration, her divorced parents are turning graduation day into a competition. Is Dad going to be there? What are Mom's plans? Is his new wife coming? Are you going to have dinner with Mom or me the night before the graduation ceremony?

These students worry about walking across the graduation stage, diploma in hand. Who are they supposed to hug first? Even this can be a competition.

I try to give these kids advice. I say that their parents need to behave like parents, like adults. I tell them that getting parents to grow up is not a kid's job, not even a twenty-one-year-old kid's job. I remind them, in no uncertain terms, that graduation is *their* day. I point out that they can do little to manage their parents. They can and should try to make a plan for graduation weekend. But mostly, they should feel good about themselves. Mostly, they should just celebrate. If their parents cannot join the celebration, well, that is their problem and their loss.

And here is my advice to you, or to your friends who are not managing their divorce as well as you are. Let this be your daughter's big day. If you need to, pretend for twenty-four or forty-eight or seventy-two hours. Really, that's very little to ask. You both can choose to be friendly, or civil, or to put on an act, no matter what happened.

And if you choose to make things uncomfortable, even on your son's special day, all I can say is, "Shame on you."

A student who once worked in my lab later wrote a book about how to plan a wedding if your parents are divorced. You want this to be a short book for *your* daughter's wedding planning, or better, an unnecessary one.

Sure, weddings require planning. But hopefully you and your ex will continue to do your job, so your young-adult child can do hers. You and your ex can figure out how much you can pay for the wedding. You and your ex can decide how to manage any potential awkwardness, including with extended family. You each can do whatever you can to facilitate wedding plans. You also can expect the usual conflicts, especially between brides and their mothers.

What about your daughter? She should look beautiful. She should be joyous. And she should worry about every detail of her wedding. But she should not have to concern herself with how her divorced parents are getting along.

This is her day. Your daughter's wedding should be all about her, and not at all about you. This is particularly true if you were divorced years ago. But even if your divorce was recent, you want your daughter's wedding day to be full of thoughts, feelings, and memories of her marriage, not your divorce.


## HANDS OFF, MOSTLY

For the most part, you want to be a hands-off advisor with your young-adult child. But at times, you and your ex may need to take a more active parenting role. If your son develops serious problems with alcohol or drugs, you may need to intervene and confront him about his addiction. You also may need to take charge, at least for a while, if he develops a serious mental illness, or if he has had a developmental disability for a long time.

Once your child turns eighteen, you and your ex no longer share custody. You have no formal legal authority over your young-adult child as an individual parent either. But you are still your child's parents. That gives you moral authority. You may need to use it. And as always, you and your ex will be far more effective if you act together.


# Troubled and Troubling Emerging Adults

So now you know another reason to keep in touch with your ex. You have to be prepared to parent together with him, just in case. Your adult child may develop serious problems. And she may try to hide her problems from you, and maybe from herself.

## IDENTITY AND EXPERIMENTATION

Emerging adulthood is a time of exploration. You should expect your twenty-something child to experiment with alcohol, perhaps drugs, relationships, and alternative careers or educational paths.

Mostly, young adults' experimentation is healthy. Part of finding your identity and choosing your path in life typically involves trying out different things. Emerging adults do things they never have done or would do before. They seek thrills, whether that means traveling to foreign countries or parachuting from an airplane. They challenge your morals and their own, perhaps with sexual promiscuity, perhaps by mocking or refusing to follow your religious beliefs, or maybe just by refusing to be so conscientious all of the time.

Psychologists expect emerging adults to test their long-held beliefs and values. You should expect this from your twenty-one-year-old too. Yes, it's far easier for a psychologist than it is for a parent. It is difficult for parents to accept the risks and the trials of an emerging adulthood. I know. I've experienced both sides.

Yet even troubling experiences can teach young adults important lessons. Your daughter may learn that bad boys really are . . . bad. Terrible hangovers can teach her that she needs to learn to control her drinking. She will remember how awful she felt far longer than she remembers your warnings. Or she may learn that slacking off hurts her grades or her job. She may not like living in a basement apartment with little spare cash for fun. A little suffering can provide her with a lot of motivation.

And if it doesn't, well, her life is *her* life. She's an adult. You can advise her. But it's up to her whether or not to take your advice. In the end, she has to figure things out for herself. If you try to mold her life for her, you will only create conflict. Or maybe you will help create a young adult who is not learning to become independent, who is still emerging.

## DRUG AND ALCOHOL PROBLEMS

As I said, you mostly want to be a hands-off advisor with your emerging adult. Still, some young adults develop serious problems with alcohol or drugs. If you have reasons to be concerned, hopefully, your ex can help you to spot problems. If you discover that your twenty-six-year-old really does have a serious issue with drugs or alcohol, you may need to intervene to get him help. You cannot solve his problems yourself. But hopefully, you and your ex can act as a united front in confronting your adult child. That way, at least he can no longer deny that he has a problem.

You cannot provide the services of Alcoholics Anonymous (AA) or a detox ward. But you can tell your emerging adult, in no uncertain terms, that he needs professional help. You can tell him that you are done enabling his self-destructive habits. You can tell him that until he gets help, this is what he can expect from you: No more money. No more pretending. No more lies, excuses, and cover-ups. He can either deal with his problems, or not. But you are done.

## SERIOUS MENTAL ILLNESS

Some serious mental illnesses also can emerge during young-adult life. Particularly if you have a family history, you want to be alert for possible symptoms of depression, bipolar disorder, and schizophrenia. Lack of insight—absence of awareness that you have a problem—often is one symptom of these serious disorders. The eating disorder anorexia nervosa is another serious problem, and those who have it often deny that it is an issue. Yet the extreme emaciation of anorexia can be life-threatening.

If you spot one of these serious and fairly common problems, you and your ex will need to get treatment for an adult child who does not think she has a problem. In this case, you are not enabling her. Think about this more like she's in a coma and has given you an advance medical directive. You are helping her get treatment for a problem when, in her current state, she is unable to seek or decide upon getting help for herself.

Actually, you may want to think about my advance medical directive analogy as more than an analogy. If your daughter has schizophrenia or severe bipolar disorder, you know how hard it is to get treatment for someone who is in a psychotic state. In a state of paranoia or mania, your daughter may well refuse treatment that she really needs and ultimately wants.

In order to circumvent this conundrum, more and more states and practitioners are using *advance psychiatric directives*. These legal instruments work much like the advance medical directives that your aged parents may have given to you. Advance psychiatric directives give you the authority to make decisions for someone when she is unable to make decisions for herself. If your daughter signs an advance psychiatric directive while she is rational, if she moves into a psychotic state, you should be able to get her the treatment she needs a lot faster and more easily.

## DEVELOPMENTAL DISABILITIES

You *know* parenting doesn't end at eighteen or twenty-one if you have an emerging adult with an intellectual disorder or other serious developmental disability. Unfortunately, essential educational services end as children reach the age of legal adulthood. According to the Individuals with Disabilities Education Act (IDEA), local school systems are required to provide a free appropriate public education to all children with disabilities. The degree of support varies from community to community and state to state. But no matter where you live, different communities share one thing in common.

Public support drops dramatically once IDEA requirements have been fulfilled.

Because of this, you and your ex almost certainly need to be deeply involved in planning and advocating for services for your child's transition to adulthood. You will need to apply for services for adults with developmental disabilities. You will need to apply for social security benefits. You will need to apply for Medicaid. You may need to apply for housing in community-based group homes.

You and your ex also need to begin to plan even longer term. You may need to consider guardianship alternatives, such as perhaps making your adult child a ward of the state. Doing so may increase access to resources for him. Or you may want to consider whether other family members could care for your adult child in the event of your death or disability. If you can afford to, you also may want to set up a trust for your child.

These are huge and expensive decisions. The details are far beyond the scope of this book. But as with planning for college, hopefully you have been planning and saving for your child's adult life for a long time.

## Other Relationships and Your Emerging Adult

Your child is an adult now. You get to be an adult too. Your son's or daughter's relationships are their business. And your relationships are your business too. Well, your relationships are *mostly* your own business.

### ROMANTIC RELATIONSHIPS: YOURS AND THEIRS

As an adult, you are allowed to date, to do pretty much whatever you want. But if you are dating someone your daughter's age or embarrassing her in another way, don't expect her to like it. True, you do not need her approval. But you probably want her affection. If she doesn't like your love interests, she can and will avoid you.

You may not approve of her love interests either. Your emerging adult may be experimenting with relationships or thinking short term. You can voice your concerns, but what will that get you? Rejection, most likely. And what if the short-term relationship becomes a long-term relationship? She's not going to forget what you said about her husband back when they first started dating.

So treat her questionable romantic life the way you would like her to treat yours. Mostly, stay hands off. Listen, if she talks to you. Maybe ask a few thought-provoking questions. But work on acceptance. That is, work on your acceptance of her choices, not her acceptance of your intrusions. And trust your adult child to learn from her mistakes. Her short-term blunders may help her make better decisions for the long run.

Regardless, remember once again that her decisions are her decisions, even if you do not approve. Withholding your approval won't change her mind. It will only put distance in her relationship with you.

If all of this seems a little one-sided, like you are giving more to your twenty-five-year-old than she is giving to you, well, it is. You are both adults. But you are her parent. You can ask for and even expect her to return the courtesies you offer to her. Maybe she can let you make mistakes. Maybe she can listen instead of lecturing. Maybe she can work on accepting you for who you are.

But one thing she cannot do is to tell herself, "I'm his mother. I *have* to love him for who he is." She isn't your mother. She's your child. For twenty-five years, you have been trying to shape and change her. Ultimately, you learned (or are learning) to accept her. For most of her life, maybe still now, she has seen you as her *parent*, as infallible, as someone who doesn't or shouldn't have flaws. As an emerging adult, she is just beginning to see you as a person. She's going to need time to accept that you are human. She needs time to come to grips with the reality that you are fallible, as humans are.

## YOUR DIVORCE AND YOUR EMERGING ADULT'S RELATIONSHIPS

Another thing you may worry about is how your divorce may affect your emerging adult child's own intimate relationships. You may have heard that children whose parents are divorced are more likely to get divorced themselves. And your daughter may have told you that she worries about how your divorce affects the way she relates to men. Maybe she has told you that she doesn't want to end up divorced, like you and Dad. Or perhaps you are worried about your son's choices in intimate partners, or about how he behaves in relationships. He may not have talked with you, but you may fear he is callous or overly dependent.

## THE INTERGENERATIONAL TRANSMISSION OF DIVORCE

What does research indicate about how parental divorce affects children's intimate relationships? Well, many studies show that children whose parents divorced are more likely to divorce themselves. Often this is referred to as the *intergenerational transmission of divorce*. But you also should know two important qualifications about the research evidence.

First, parents and children share genes, not just family experience. Divorce may be transmitted across the generations by shared genes, not by your parents' divorce. In a study led by my former student Brian D'Onofrio, several colleagues and I found that genes accounted for about one third of the intergenerational transmission of divorce.[3] Of course, there is no "divorce gene." But genes help shape personality and emotional problems. And both personality and psychological difficulties contribute to divorce. So maybe your emerging adult's tricky relationships are affected more by the impulsivity or depression she inherited from you or her mother than by your divorce.

The second qualification is even more important. Evidence shows that parental divorce affects children's risk for divorce less now than it did in the past.[4] This idea may seem strange. But think about it. In order to study the intergenerational transmission of divorce, social scientists need to study people who were born a long time ago. Why? Well, the first generation must be old enough to marry, bear children, and pass through the risk period for divorce (about thirty years of marriage). Then the second generation must be old enough to have had the same experiences. (Childbearing is unnecessary in the second generation.) This means that most research is based on people who were born generations ago. Divorce was rare then. And people who got divorced were more unusual then. As divorce has become more common, divorcing adults—and the experience of getting divorced—have become more "normal." As a result, children are affected by divorce less, at least in some ways. One way is a shrinking intergenerational transmission of divorce.

## DIVORCE AFFECTS ALL YOUNG PEOPLE

I do think the experience of divorce can cast a dark shadow over the idea of marriage. But it is not only children from divorced families who face uncertainties about commitment in relationships. Everyone does. Today, the high frequency of divorce means that no one can approach marriage the way they did generations ago. "Until death do us part" has become "until death or divorce do us part." Of course, few brides or grooms want to recite *that* as a part of their wedding vows.

Marriage is a more tenuous union than it was in the past. In some ways, this is a huge loss. Can you trust your partner's commitment? Can you trust your own commitment? But the loosening of the bonds of matrimony also is a step forward in some ways. Young people no longer need to remain trapped in a relationship where they are emotionally abused, deeply unhappy, or economically dependent.

Whether or not your emerging adult has been affected by your divorce, in the end, she will need to figure out her relationships for herself. And if you want to help her, one thing you can do is to do your best to figure out your own relationships. That way, she will see the possibilities, for you and for her.

## STEP, HALF, AND OTHER FAMILY RELATIONSHIPS

If you separated when your emerging adult was a child, chances are that you acquired new family relationships long ago. You may have remarried. Your new husband may have children from a previous marriage. The two of you may have had children together. And your ex may have added members to his family too.

Perhaps you are adding even more members to your family now, or will soon. You may have a new baby, or a new relationship. Or your adult child may be about to acquire a bunch of in-laws—with their own complicated family situations. Or maybe your son is living with someone, and he has what? Common-law in-laws? Outlaws?

Family life can be complex today. Your emerging adult may have a big extended family.

What expectations should you have for step, half, and other family relationships? Are all of the relationships equal? Must everyone get along?

I cannot offer you any easy answers to these questions. No one can. We are in a period of rapid change in family life. No one knows when all of the changes will end, where they will lead, or how families will stabilize and eventually be redefined. Demographer Andrew Cherlin has referred to remarriage as an "incomplete institution," one that is still in the process of cultural evolution.

In everyday terms, this means you have to figure things out for yourself.

But let me try to offer a little guidance.

## STEPPARENTS

As I have said several times, I urge stepparents to work first on being adult friends to their stepchildren. If you follow my advice, that may be as far as you get. And if so, what child does not benefit from having a good adult friend consistently available in their life?

But you may become more than an adult friend. If you are a stepparent for years, somewhere along the way, you may become "Dad," or more commonly "like a dad." (As in, "My stepmother is like a real mother to me.") Mostly, we preserve the titles of Mom and Dad for biological or adoptive parents in the United States today. But "like a dad" is quite an achievement, an honor, even if your stepchild still calls you Jack or Jose or Jaquon.

## STEP-, HALF, AND FULL SIBLINGS

I advise parents to mostly let stepsiblings work out their relationships for themselves, as I discussed in Chapter 7. As with stepparents, relationships between step- or half siblings can grow much closer over time. A stepsister can become a "real sister," or maybe just a "sister." (Unlike *Mom* and *Dad*, *sister* and *brother* are not exclusive titles.) Or maybe, over time, a step- or half sibling will become, "She's my sister, well, she's really my half sister, but really she's more like a real sister, so I just call her my sister, you know?"

Maggie has been all of these things to her younger half brothers, Bobby and John, and to her sisters, Julia and Lucy (and vice versa). Now they are mostly just brothers and sisters.

Step-, half, and full sibling relationships also can grow more distant, particularly during emerging adult life and the busy years that follow. As they become adults, siblings part company literally and metaphorically. They have their own lives to pursue.

Yet the sibling bond can remain special, even from a distance. Whom do you call when you really, really need someone to confide in? Whom do you want to tell about major events in your life? Your siblings. And later in life, sibling relationships often become especially important once again. After brothers and sisters have raised their own families and perhaps lost their parents, they often find more time for one another.

What can you do to help? You can encourage your emerging adults to maintain their relationships with their step-, half, and full siblings. And from time to time, you can help organize big family gatherings, so everyone can have some fun and be reminded about these special family relationships.

## INHERITANCES

At some point, you will want to decide how you will treat your various family relationships in your estate. Who will inherit what?

I cannot begin to offer advice about what you should do. But I do urge you to be fair, to be clear, and to have a plan. Make a will, even if doing so forces you to face some tough decisions.

These choices can be tricky. But that is my point. It is far better for you to face the facts of your estate planning far in advance. You do not want to leave inheritances for your children to sort out and perhaps dispute.

Your parenting plan really does need to last a lifetime.

## CHAPTER 10

# A Lifetime Is (Not) a Long Time

Looking back from the perspective of five, ten, or twenty years from now, what are you going to wish you had done today?

What will be more important? Refusing to take your son to hockey practice on *your* week, or driving fifteen miles to the rink even though his mom signed him up? What will impress your twenty-year-old more? Your spreadsheet proving that you spent *exactly* equal time with her, or your sacrifice in putting her needs first and yours second (or third)?

Will you wish you had made your child more of a priority? Will you regret not making more time for him? Will you be sorry that you were so preoccupied that you were present, but not really? Will you chastise yourself for not helping her more with *her* long-term goals? Will you wish you encouraged her more in school and in her relationship with her dad?

Do you hope for a future where you and your ex still cannot be civil, even at your son's high school graduation or your daughter's wedding? Or are you going to wish that you had found a way to put your anger and pain behind you, not for your ex, but for your children—and for yourself too?

If you allow yourself to adopt the perspective of time, I'm pretty sure I know what you will wish. You will wish you had done the right thing for your children and your ex too (and maybe for your new partner, her children, and even her ex). You also will wish you did the right thing for selfish reasons. In the long run, doing the right thing makes you feel better about yourself.

I know it may seem hard, perhaps impossible, to think beyond *right now*. Right now, you may be consumed by emotion. Right now, you may be so busy parenting young children that you don't have time to think.

I know how hard it can be to unhinge from the present. But I want you to try to do a little time traveling. Doing so may help you reset some of your goals, even though you may not be able to work toward them much right now.

Don't get me wrong. My goal for you isn't perfection. (We both know that your ex isn't perfect.) I expect you to make mistakes. I expect that you have done, and will do, things with your children and your ex that you will wish you could undo.

I don't expect you to be a robot either. I expect your emotions to boil over sometimes—and to make a mess. I expect your feelings to be so strong at times that they seem impossible to control. I expect you to sometimes wonder if the pain will never end.

I expect you will have regrets, no doubt.

I'm sure you have many regrets right now.

But I believe you can save yourself from many big regrets. I think you can stop yourself from making the same mistakes over and over and over, maybe for years. I think you can correct the mistakes you have been making—with your ex and with your kids. I think you can make amends, if you need to.

You can do this, even if you're not sure how. The way to get started is to think now about what you will wish you did then.

I don't mean this as a throwaway line. I *really* want you to do this. Now, or later when the kids are in bed, I want you to sit, close your eyes, and imagine how you might feel when your baby is five, fifteen, and twenty-five. You don't need to decide what will happen during those years. Just think about how you might feel in five, fifteen, or twenty-five years.

It may help to put yourself in your parents' shoes, or those of some older adult you respect. What are they proud of in their life? What regrets have they expressed? What do you wish *your* parents had done differently?

Don't just time-travel for five minutes. Ponder your long-term goals for a week, for a month. Perspective is what you need, more than anything. Try to find it. Try to unhinge from your present, so you will better understand yourself, your circumstances, and where you want to head, ultimately.

Try to get outside yourself. Try to get beyond the all-consuming *now*.

If you succeed, you will find that your time traveling can offer the perspective you want and need.

Imagining our future reminds us about what we know we should do, but find it easier not to do. Spend less, save more. Eat less, exercise more. Worry less, enjoy more. Work harder. And play harder too.

Appreciate where you are in life instead of longing for something different, instead of telling yourself, "I'll finally be happy when . . ."

Accept other people's mistakes. Accept your own mistakes.

Forgive them. Forgive yourself.

You can start working toward a new long-term now. You can start making deposits into your divorced family's savings account with the currency of good parenting and goodwill.

How can you find the willpower? You can find the will inside yourself, even if it's buried under a pile of emotions right now. Let's talk a little bit about how.

## Divorce in Your Rearview Mirror

One day, divorce will be in your emotional rearview mirror. No, you won't "get over it," as young people like to say. But one day most of the upheaval will be behind you.

Your painful emotions and memories won't be gone. You will still see their reflection. When you glance back, you occasionally may find some aspect of your divorce catching up with you. You may have to keep an eye on it. You may have to let it pass. You may have to wait temporarily before changing lanes. But soon the road ahead and behind will be mostly clear again.

Maybe your divorce already is in your rear view.

Or maybe your divorce is swerving into you right now. If you are afraid you're about to die, it's hard to focus on your road trip, on how things may be years from now.

But even if your divorce still feels like a terrible accident, I promise you. One day, you will see it, back there, far away in your rearview mirror.

And when you do, no matter how old you are, or they are, your children will be riding along with you.

And because of your children, your ex will be with you too, somewhere out there on the road.

A lifetime may seem like a long time, but it isn't. It's a short trip, one you will travel with the mother or father of your children. They won't be in the same car. But they will be traveling in the same direction.

My most fervent hope is that I can help you head down the road you are going to wish you had traveled.

### GRIEF

You won't "get over it." But you do have a lot to get over.

Almost no one talks about it, but divorce is a huge loss. Divorce involves the loss of your partner, your husband or wife. Divorce causes you to lose time with your children. You may fear you will lose them altogether. Divorce means the loss of friends. You lose family too. Your ex's family may drop out of your life. Maybe your family will too.

Divorce brings about the loss of roles, as husband and wife, as a couple in your social group and community. Your role as Mom or Dad may feel like it's in ruins too. Divorce means that one of you loses your home. Often, you both do. You certainly both lose money. And at its core, divorce is the loss of your hopes and dreams. That is a loss you probably will never fully recover.

When we lose someone or something dear to us, we grieve.

Almost no one talks about it or guides you through it, but you need to find some way to grieve your divorce.

Maybe you already know this. If so, you are ahead of the game. You know you need to let go. You know you need to embrace the pain in order to let it go, eventually, and to move on.

Maybe you are done grieving, or mostly done. But you are never totally done. You never "get over it" completely. And you don't want to. Your goal is to make your grief small enough, manageable enough, that you can pack it up. Your goal is to be able to stow your longing, anger, and sadness in the trunk. The emotions will be there, traveling with you. But they will be out of your way.

Or maybe you haven't gotten started grieving yet. Perhaps you don't even recognize your need to grieve. Maybe you are so badly wounded emotionally that you still are operating in survival mode. (Recall from Chapter 1 that the brain processes physical and emotional pain in similar ways.) Maybe you still are unconsciously using your anger to ease your pain. You have tried to let yourself feel the ache, but it just hurts too much.

Anger is easier. It hurts less. A wounded animal or soldier will continue to fight while under attack. Anger blocks their pain. Anger allows the wounded to defend and protect themselves. Once the fury subsides, the animal, the soldier, and you feel the pain, intensely.

Maybe your friends are helping you to cover up your pain too. It's simpler and safer for them to tell you, "I never liked him anyway. You're better off without him."

That makes you feel better temporarily. It's a Band-Aid.

Don't expect them to say, "I'm sorry for your loss."

But I am. I'm sorry.

## AN UNCERTAIN LOSS

Grief is not a creation of culture, society, or religion. Grief is not a human invention. Humans have invented rituals to help us grieve death. But grief is rooted in our genes. Humans and other mammals form attachments. Humans and other mammals grieve.

Even elephants grieve. If you don't believe me, do an Internet search. If you type "elephant grief" into a search engine, you will find fascinating stories about how elephants react to loss.

My point is, when you lose something you love, it is natural to grieve.

And, as I said, divorce means that you lose many things you love.

But even though no one dies, grieving divorce is hard. Actually, I think grieving divorce is harder, in many ways, *because* no one has died.

Your marriage has died. Or has it?

When a loved one dies, we know she is not coming back. Some of our bereavement rituals serve the important function of confirming the finality of death. An open casket proves that our loved one really is dead. The viewing also provokes strong emotion. Grief has a starting point.

But is your marriage really dead? Could it be resurrected?

Maybe your marriage is dead in your mind. But maybe hope is

still alive in your ex's heart. Maybe she hopes that your suggestion to have lunch—to discuss how your kids are doing—may turn into a date. Or more.

Divorce is an uncertain loss. There is no viewing. There is no finality.

Divorce may not be final until a judge signs the papers, if then. Any number of couples reconcile even after their legal divorce.

Divorce may not be final until one of you remarries, if then. You know the spark can burn for years, despite the impediments of new relationships and living apart.

(Recognizing grief helps us understand why many of us struggle emotionally again near the time of our legal divorce or when our ex remarries. These events can be one more sign that it's truly over.)

Bereavement, grief in response to a loved one's death, has a beginning. Uncertain losses are harder to grieve because there is no beginning. How do you grieve for a loved one who is missing—or missing in action? How do you grieve infertility when you just can't seem to get pregnant, but there is no irreversible cause to identify? When do you give up trying to treat cancer, when there may be a cure?

There is no clear beginning for grief over uncertain loss, because we hope there will be nothing to grieve. Giving up hope seems like . . . giving up.

When do you let go of your marriage, of your love?

You only let go of an uncertain loss when you decide to, when you make yourself let go.

For some people, the uncertainty is so painful that they try to kill their marriage, in their mind. They take down old pictures—or cut them up. They move. They avoid people and places from the time when they were a couple. They refuse to speak with their ex or to look at him. They do these things so they can move on, so they can begin to grieve. Grief needs a beginning if it is going to have an end.

Yet your children bring you together. And these new contacts can bring up old feelings—until you find a way accept that it's over.

I discuss grief and how to cope with it at length in *The Truth about Children and Divorce: Dealing with the Emotions So You and Your Children Can Thrive*. You should read what I wrote there if you are having trouble letting go—or if you are still stuck on your anger and can't seem to get to the grief.

You also should read *The Truth* if you are trying to understand your ex's grief—if he seems unfeeling or if she seems like an emotional train wreck. In that book, I consider at length how your loss and his loss may be different. Your marriage may have died following a long and trying chronic illness. You may be sad, but in some ways, you may be relieved too. Her marriage really may have been in a train wreck. Her marriage may be in the emergency room. There was a horrible accident. Things look bad. But she desperately is asking everyone, anyone, to please, please help to save it.

Here I just want to acknowledge your grief. And I want to help you to acknowledge it too.


## GRIEVING ALONE

Once you recognize your grief—and once you embrace it—you face another huge problem. Whom do you grieve with? Traditions like wakes, sitting shiva, and funerals bring people together. The gatherings encourage grief following a death. They also provide support for the bereaved.

In divorce, people usually move away from you instead of coming together. And when you talk to them, most people encourage you to be angry, not sad. Good friends will listen to the range of your emotions. But even they can grow tired. "People need to talk about their divorce long beyond their friends' ability to listen" is a saying I've heard often. Even those really good friends who hang in there can't really join you in your grief. They don't share your loss.

Maybe the closest you can come is if your best friend is going through a divorce too. Yet even then, feelings differ.

So whom do you grieve with? Your ex? I don't think that's going to happen. Your children? Your children may need to grieve in their own way. But you need to support them in their loss. For reasons we have discussed, you shouldn't be asking them to support you in yours.

And your children's loss is different too. As you know, one of my fervent hopes is that your children will lose less than you or they feared they might. If you can follow the advice I have offered here, your children will find that they still have two parents. They haven't lost you. They haven't lost Mom either.

Whom do you grieve with? Unfortunately, the answer is that for the most part, you will need to grieve alone.

Yes, you may have a great friend who can help. If she's going through a divorce too, she understands even better. You may find a support group where you can share your feelings with other people who are in the same boat. Or maybe you will find a really good therapist. She knows you are grieving and can help you through it.

All of these are great supports and good steps. But still, in the end, you will grieve mostly alone.

Be kind to yourself as you grieve. Give yourself time. Be patient. Maybe keep a journal to help you remember where you have been, so you can better understand where you still need to go. Eventually, your journal may become the trunk where your grief is stowed.

## MEDIATION VERSUS LITIGATION: TWELVE YEARS LATER

In Chapter 2, I briefly discussed the most important study that I have completed in over thirty years of research on children and divorce.[1] In this work, I assigned families at random either to mediate their child custody disputes or to continue with the litigation they had begun. Random assignment is the "magic" of science. In this study, random assignment allowed me to conclude that the intervention *caused* the differences I found between the mediation and the litigation groups.

As I mentioned earlier, I discovered that mediation caused a huge reduction in the need for child custody trials. About 90 percent of the mediation cases either settled there (most of them) or subsequently through attorney negotiations. In contrast, only 30 percent of cases settled before a trial when they were randomly assigned to continue with the litigation process. Put another way, a judge needed to decide 70 percent of cases randomly assigned to the litigation group but only 10 percent of cases randomly assigned to the mediation group.

That is a huge reduction in the need for child custody trials. And I also found that after the case was resolved one way or another, parents reported being significantly happier with many aspects of the process of mediation versus litigation.

But after the case settled, I didn't find many more differences between the two groups. In both groups, parents were still angry. Many were depressed. Parenting suffered.

Honestly, I was disappointed in the study's results at the time. I had hoped mediation would do more to help families in crisis.

And then I started remembering the things I had been telling parents in mediation. You are in crisis. Mediation can't make divorce "happy." Nothing can. I hope that mediation can help make things less bad. But the work we have done is just a beginning. You need to keep at it. You need to focus on the long term. You need time to deal with all you are going through. Doing the right thing will mean hard work. You need to find a way to work together as parents. You have to find a way to love your kids more than you hate each other.

You need to grieve.

All of these should be familiar messages to you by now.

I also remembered what I always told myself when mediation

ended: I hope I planted a seed. I hope that seed will sprout and grow over time. Really, I guess you could say that I hoped I was right. I hoped the parents who mediated would heed my advice.

I had to wait a long time for the harvest. So will you. I followed the families for twelve years, essentially over the course of their children's childhood.

The seeds sprouted. And they grew.

Right after they settled, the differences between the mediation and litigation groups were pretty small. In retrospect, I should have expected that.

Twelve years later, the differences were huge. Compared to those in the litigation group, three times as many parents who mediated saw their children every week. Five times as many spoke with their kids on the telephone each week. Even though parents in the mediation group saw each other much more (because both parents were seeing the kids more), they reported significantly *less* coparenting conflict.

Parents in the mediation group also gave each other significantly higher "grades" in a host of areas of parenting. They graded their ex higher in the way he dressed and groomed the children, ran errands for them, and participated in school or church activities. They gave their ex higher grades for discipline and religious and moral education. They rated him higher in celebrating holidays, taking the children on vacation, and being involved in the kids' recreational activities. Parents handed out better grades to their exes for talking with them about problems with their children.

These are all things I urge you to do too.

I should be clear. The parents who mediated didn't give each other straight A's. They gave each other something closer to passing grades, while the parents who litigated failed. Maybe you could aim for B's. Given all you have been through, B's would be pretty darn good.

The mediation group also was significantly more likely to do something else I have recommended to you. They made more changes in their parenting plan, as needed, as their children grew. And for the most part, they made these changes informally, negotiating with each other, as parents do.

I found that parents who took a chance on mediation reaped big rewards years later, especially when it came to raising children in two homes.

And I want to remind you of this. I ask parents to do something emotionally *un*natural in mediation. When we are hurt, our natural emotional impulse is to hurt back. We do this because the response is wired into our nature. It's all about survival, as I have explained. A wounded animal fights back. It doesn't mediate.

I ask parents in mediation not to give in to their impulse to hurt back.

I am asking the same thing of you. I am asking you to do something emotionally *un*natural.

In my mediation study, I found that parents can find a way to work together with their ex as parents, instead of trying to crush each other in court. I found that parents can take a different path. And I learned that if they, and you, take that different path, in the long run, you will end up in a different place, a far better place.

In fact, I detected only one long-term "problem" caused by mediation. Twelve years following random assignment, parents who mediated expressed more regrets about the end of their marriage compared to parents in the litigation group.

Because of random assignment, I know that mediation caused the increased regret. What I don't know is what about mediation explains it.

It is possible that the longing was fueled by the increased contact between the coparents who mediated (because both parents stayed involved in their children's lives). The repeated contact or mediation's message of cooperation may have impeded parents' grief. Mediation may have kept the parents' hopes for reconciliation alive. They may have had a hard time letting go. This is a possibility. But I doubt it. Twelve years is a long time. These parents moved on with their lives. Most were remarried or living with someone.

Another possibility is that the fire of anger that erupted with divorce was stoked by litigation. This anger may have prevented parents in the litigation group from feeling or admitting to regrets, even twelve years later.

These alternative interpretations both are scientifically possible. But let me suggest what I think really happened.

I think that over the course of twelve years, parents in the mediation group saw that their ex was a decent parent after all, even following divorce. Over the years, they managed to coparent reasonably well too. And when the former partners sat back and reflected, as I asked them to do, they realized something like, *I guess he wasn't such a jerk after all. I guess something good came out of our relationship: our kids.*

### MY PERSONAL JOURNEY: EMERY'S STORY

As we are coming to the end of our journey through this book, I'd like to share a bit about my personal journey through divorce.

A little over a year ago, I found myself in a bar having a drink, and then another, with my ex. We had not been out to a bar together in a *long* time. But we sure partied that day.

No, you are not about to read a confession about *that*.

Jean and I were celebrating of the birth of our granddaughter.

On May 1, 2014, our daughter, Maggie, gave birth to her first child. Maggie wanted her mom and me both to be present when her baby was born. Early in the morning of May 1, Maggie sent us each a text. She and her husband, Mike, were heading to George Washington Hospital. She was in labor! She didn't think there was a huge rush. Her contractions were irregular and just beginning. Her water hadn't broken. But we needed to get from Charlottesville to Washington, D.C.!

I didn't see Maggie's text until I woke up around six a.m. Mike had sent a follow-up. They were at the hospital. Maggie was fine. Labor was progressing slowly. The doctor said hard labor was still hours away.

Still, I raced to get ready. As usual, I had kids and my wife, Kimberly, to get out of bed. (I'm the morning person in the family.) But I told them that they were on their own for breakfast and getting off to school and work. I was heading to Washington. Maggie was in labor! The kids would soon be aunts and uncles!

I arrived at the maternity ward at George Washington Hospital around eleven a.m. Jean was already there. No baby yet. Everything was fine, she thought. (Maggie wanted us at the hospital but not present for the birth. She is not *that* New Age. Neither am I.)

Jean and I sat next to each other in the waiting room, excited and anxious. We could see the door to Maggie's delivery room. Whenever the door moved, we jumped.

Four other future grandparents sat with us. Their daughter (and daughter-in-law) had been in labor for *forty-eight hours*. We all chattered nervously. During lulls in our conversation, Jean and I whispered. We felt bad for those poor people. We wanted Maggie to deliver soon. We sure did not want to be waiting and worrying for two days.

After about three hours of tension and anticipation, we got a text from Mike. Congratulations Grandma and Grandpa! A few minutes later, Maggie's doula joined us in the waiting room. (Maggie is New Age enough to have a doula.) Everyone was fine. Maggie did great! She gave birth without medication. Our granddaughter was perfect. We could see her soon.

Jean and I were thrilled, of course. Our four waiting room companions congratulated us. But their warm wishes were tinged with anxiety and longing. When would they get some good news? As it turned out, they had only moments to wait. Less than five minutes after the doula left, their cell phones erupted. Their grandson finally had arrived! Everyone was healthy.

The waiting room exploded as the six of us celebrated our happy news.

Soon Jean and I got to see our new granddaughter, and Maggie and Mike. We spent a joyous hour or so with them. Then we let Maggie rest and let the new family have some time together alone.

Back in the waiting room, I said to Jean, "Let's get a drink."

We quickly found a bar across the street from George Washington Hospital. When we walked in, the party started. By coincidence, our four waiting room companions were there. They had already started celebrating. We joined them for a round of drinks, and then another. What a thrill!

But I haven't yet shared the best part of the story.

Maggie and Mike chose to name their daughter Emery.

Yes, Emery is becoming a trendy name. It is also my last name. (Maggie took Mike's last name, Strong, when they married.)

I was and am honored. But the honor is far from mine alone. The honor is for Jean, who retained the last name; for my parents, whom everyone loved; for all the Emerys. The honor is for family.

Maggie's parents divorced. But she still had and has a family.

A lifetime is a long time. And it isn't.

Like Jean and me, your children tie you and your ex together not for eighteen years, but forever.

I would never downplay the difficulties of divorce, including for my family and me. But even as you struggle with the day-to-day, I urge you to keep the long view in mind, for you but especially for your children.

I want you to give your children a childhood, and a family.

# Acknowledgments

Whether you are a parent or a professional, I hope that this book will help you to see parenting children in two homes in a new light. I hope you can begin to see the pain, longing, fear, guilt, and grief behind much of parents' anger over losing a lover and facing the prospect of raising children alone. I hope this book helps you to better recognize—and meet—children's needs when living in two homes. I hope you embrace the novel yet commonsense idea that the best parenting plan is one that grows and changes along with children's changing needs. I hope you see more clearly that, in the end, there is only one "side" that matters: The children's side. I hope this book encourages you to be on that side.

If this book helps you to do these things, you can thank, as I do, the mothers, fathers, and children who have opened their hearts and lives to me in my research and practice. To those parents, I am honored by your trust. I profoundly respect your efforts to put your children's needs above your own pain. To those children, I hope, one day, you too might appreciate what your parents have tried to do. I hope you might forgive their failings, for your own sake and theirs. One day, perhaps, you will do as good or better job as a parent yourself.

Parents raise children, but we learn so much from them too. Thank you to Maggie, Julia, Bobby, Lucy, and John for your many lessons in child development. Thank you much more for teaching me joy, patience, responsibility, and humility. You are the meaning of life.

More practically, I want to thank Beth Vesel, my agent. You are a long-time and special friend, someone who has a knack for drawing out my best ideas and helping me shape them into a clear and coherent message. I also want to thank my editor, Caroline Sutton, for your terrific guidance and encouragement throughout the writing of this book. You made my work far better and easier by being on my side as an author (and as a New England sports fan). I also am grateful to assistant editor Brianna Flaherty, who helped greatly with more practical aspects of this book.

I have spent my entire academic career at the University of Virginia. I am grateful to my many outstanding colleagues here over the years, particularly in the Department of Psychology and the Law School, too many people to name. I also want to thank a very long list of graduate students, but limit myself to identifying my recent students. Thank you Jenna Rowen, Samantha Tornello, Hyunjoo Shim, Diana Dinescu, Chris Beam, Erin Horn, and Matthew Domiteaux. I also am extremely grateful for the good fortune of having terrific colleagues who share similar academic interests not only across the United States but internationally, particularly in Australia, New Zealand, Canada, England, Italy, and Croatia.

I dedicate this book to family, in its many forms. My gratitude for family begins with my deceased parents, and includes my sisters, Susan and Kristan, their families, my in-laws, extended family members, and Maggie's mother, Jean. My wife, Kimberly, gave me four more children, a big, thriving, and sometimes chaotic family. Thank you, Kimberly, for being my partner in love and work, and for always keeping life interesting.

# Notes

## CHAPTER 1

1 **In fact, at least two U.S. state legislatures, Florida and Minnesota:** See http://www.foxnews
.com/politics/2013/05/02/florida-gov-scott-vetoes-bill-that-would-end-permanent-alimony-
in-state.html and http://www.mprnews.org/story/2012/05/24/joint-custody-bill-veto.

2 **A few days earlier, the** *Journal of Marriage and Family* **had published my academic article:**
Tornello, S. L., Emery, R. E., Rowen, J., Potter, D., Ocker, B. & Xu, Y. (2013). Overnight
custody arrangements, attachment, and adjustment among very young children. *Journal of
Marriage and Family, 75,* 871–885.

## CHAPTER 2

1 **Maslow brilliantly ranked human needs:** Maslow, A. (1954). *Motivation and personality*
(p. 236). New York: Harper.

2 *Authoritative parenting* **combines the bedrock of parental love with discipline:** Baumrind,
D. (1971). Current patterns of parental authority. *Developmental Psychology Monograph, 4*
(1, Pt. 2), 1–103; Maccoby, E. E., & Martin, J. A. (1983). Socialization in the context of the
family: Parent-child interaction. In E. M. Hetherington (ed.), *Handbook of child psychology*
(4th ed., vol. 4, pp. 1–102). New York: Wiley.

3 **More formally, Bronfenbrenner wrote:** Bronfenbrenner, U. (1991). What do families do? *In-
stitute for American Values,* Winter/Spring, 2.

4 **They are "parentified":** For example, see Peris, T. S., Goeke-Morey, M. C., Cummings,
E. M., & Emery, R. E. (2008). Marital conflict and support-seeking by parents in adolescence: Empirical support for the parentification construct. *Journal of Family Psychology,
22,* 633–642.

5 **In 1982, I published:** Emery, R. E. (1982). Interparental conflict and the children of discord
and divorce. *Psychological Bulletin, 92,* 310–330.

6 **moving from a low-conflict marriage to a higher-conflict divorce also harms children:**
Amato, P. R., Loomis, L. W., & Booth, A. (1995). Parental divorce, marital conflict, and
offspring well-being during early adulthood. *Social Forces, 73,* 895–915.

7 **Cummings has been studying children's reactions to parental conflict for over thirty years:**
much of this work is nicely summarized in Cummings, E. M., & Davies, P. T. (2010). *Marital
conflict and children: An emotional security perspective.* New York: Guilford.

8 **In a study of almost one thousand young people:** Rowen, J., & Emery, R. (2014). Examining
parental denigration behaviors of co-parents as reported by young adults and their association with parent-child closeness. *Couple and Family Psychology: Research and Practice, 3,*
165–177.

9 **According to recent U.S. Census data:** Vespa, J., Lewis, J. M., & Kreider, R. M. (2013).
America's families and living arrangements: 2012. *Current Population Reports,* P20-570.
Washington, DC: U.S. Census Bureau.

10  **In a recent study, Paul Amato, Catherine Meyers, and I:** Amato, P. R., Meyers, C., & Emery, R. E. (2009). Changes in nonresident father visitation over four decades. *Family Relations, 58,* 41–53.

11  **Having a second authoritative parent:** The difference in the functioning of children living with one versus two parents is generally found to be modest. For examples, see Amato, P. R., & Keith, B. (1991). Parental divorce and the well-being of children: A meta-analysis. *Psychological Bulletin, 110,* 26–46; and Amato, P. R. (2001). Children of divorce in the 1990s: An update of the Amato and Keith (1991) meta-analysis. *Journal of Family Psychology, 15,* 355–370.

12  **Let me tell you about a study:** Laumann-Billings, L., & Emery, R. E. (2000). Distress among young adults from divorced families. *Journal of Family Psychology, 14,* 671–687.

13  **In the 1980s, I began:** See Emery, R. E., & Wyer, M. M. (1987). Child custody mediation and litigation: An experimental evaluation of the experience of parents. *Journal of Consulting and Clinical Psychology, 55,* 179–186; and Emery, R. E., Matthews, S., & Wyer, M. M. (1991). Child custody mediation and litigation: Further evidence of the differing views of mothers and fathers. *Journal of Consulting and Clinical Psychology, 59,* 410–418.

14  **More important, I followed these families for twelve years:** Emery, R. E., Laumann-Billings, L., Waldron, M., Sbarra, D. A., & Dillon, P. (2001). Child custody mediation and litigation: Custody, contact, and co-parenting 12 years after initial dispute resolution. *Journal of Consulting and Clinical Psychology, 69,* 323–332.

15  **The second study that I want to mention:** Modecki, K. L., Hagan, M., Sandler, I. N., & Wolchik, S. (2015). Latent profiles of nonresidential father engagement six years after divorce predict long-term offspring outcomes. *Journal of Clinical Child and Adolescent Psychology, 44,* 123–136.

## CHAPTER 3

1  **In the United States, perhaps one in five families share physical custody:** As noted, estimating shared physical custody prevalence is tricky because of limited research and data collection as well as variations across states. For a good estimate about U.S. and international data, see Smyth, B., Chisholm, R., Rodgers, B., & Son, V. (2014). Legislating for shared-time parenting: Insights from Australia? *Journal of Law and Contemporary Problems, 77,* 108–149. For good evidence on a single state (Wisconsin) with high rates of joint physical custody (27 percent equal, 18 percent unequal), see Cancian, M., Meyer, D. R., Brown, P. R., & Cook, S. T. (2014). Who gets custody now? Dramatic changes in children's living arrangements after divorce. *Demography, 51,* 1381–1396.

2  **In my all-time favorite ruling:** The New York State Court of Appeals issued this ruling in 1936 in *People v. Sisson*, 2 N.E.2d 660 (1936) at 661.

3  **Even though our courts know enough:** Kimberly Emery and I discuss the paradox of the different treatment of married and unmarried parents in Emery, K. C., & Emery, R. E. (2014). Who knows what's best for children? Honoring agreements and contracts between parents who live apart. *Law and Contemporary Problems, 77,* 151–176.

4  **the Commonwealth of Pennsylvania banned:** Pennsylvania eliminated the practice of parenting coordination, indicating that only judges have the authority to make decisions in child custody cases. See Pa. R.C.P. Rule 1915 11-1 (2013).

5  **Research does not support a focus on time:** Paul Amato and Joan Gilbreth combined findings from sixty-three studies and found that time with nonresident fathers mattered little to children's well-being, but authoritative parenting did. See Amato, P. R., & Gilbreth, J. (1999). Nonresident fathers and children's well-being: A meta-analysis. *Journal of Marriage and Family, 61,* 557–573. These results were replicated recently in a similar analysis of fifty-two studies; see Adamsons, K., & Johnson, S. K. (2013). An updated and expanded meta-analysis of nonresident fathering and child well-being. *Journal of Family Psychology, 27,* 589–599.

6  **As a group, these studies indicate:** Two more-careful reviews of research on the well-being of children and families with joint custody are Bauserman, R. (2002). Child adjustment in joint-custody versus sole-custody arrangements: A meta-analytic review. *Journal of Family Psychology, 16,* 91–102; and Smyth, B. M., McIntosh, J. E., Emery, R. E., & Howarth, S. L.

(in press). Shared-time parenting: Boundaries of risks and benefits for children. In L. Drozd & M. Saini (eds.), *Parenting plan evaluations: Applied research for the family court*. New York: Oxford University Press.

7  **We know that parents who choose joint physical custody:** Nonrandom selection into joint custody has been documented repeatedly. For one fairly detailed discussion, see Smyth, B. M., McIntosh, J. E., Emery, R. E., & Howarth, S. L. (in press). Shared-time parenting: Boundaries of risks and benefits for children. In L. Drozd & M. Saini (eds.), *Parenting plan evaluations: Applied research for the family court*. New York: Oxford University Press.

8  **The difference in well-being is equivalent:** Bauserman's meta-analysis (see note 23) found an effect size of .23 standard deviation unit. Since the SAT has a standard deviation of about 100, this is equivalent to about 20 points on an SAT.

9  **In fact, some excellent research done in Australia:** Smyth, B., Chisholm, R., Rodgers, B., & Son, V. (2014). Legislating for shared-time parenting: Insights from Australia? *Journal of Law and Contemporary Problems, 77,* 108–149. This paper not only provides the research evidence discussed here but also provides background information on changes in and effects of Australian law.

10  **One fascinating study (from Belgium):** Sodermans, A. K., & Matthijs, K. (2014). Joint physical custody and adolescents' subjective well-being: A personality × environment interaction. *Journal of Family Psychology, 28,* 346–356.

## CHAPTER 4

1  **About 20 percent of divorces occur within the first five years of marriage:** Copen, C. E., Daniels, K., Vespa, J., & Mosher, W. D. (2012). First marriages in the United States: Data from the 2006–2010 National Survey of Family Growth. *National Health Statistics Reports, 49* (March 22), 1–21.

2  **only about half to cohabiting couples:** Sigle-Rushton, W., & McLanahan, S. (2002). The living arrangements of new unmarried mothers. *Demography, 39,* 415–433.

3  **And cohabiting relationships break up faster:** Cherlin, A. J. (2009). *The marriage-go-round: The state of marriage and the family in America today.* New York: Knopf.

4  **The central emotional task for infants:** Attachment theory and research is widely discussed. One authoritative resource is Cassidy, J., & Shaver, P. R. (eds.) (2008). *Handbook of attachment: Theory, research, and clinical applications.* New York: Guilford.

5  **Yet attachments are hierarchical:** Multiple attachments and the hierarchy of attachment relationships are a topic of some debate among experts disputing whether frequent overnights with both parents helps or harms babies. A dispassionate, general introduction to the issue can be found in Cassidy, J. (2008). The nature of the child's ties. In J. Cassidy & P. R. Shaver (eds.), *Handbook of attachment: Theory, research, and clinical applications* (pp. 2–22). New York: Guilford. An objective summary of research can be found in Howes, C., & Spieker, S. (2008). Attachment relationships in the context of multiple caregivers. In J. Cassidy & P. R. Shaver (eds.), *Handbook of attachment: Theory, research, and clinical applications* (pp. 317–332). New York: Guilford.

6  **About two thirds of all babies:** Ainsworth, M. D. S., Blehar, M. C., Waters, E., & Wall, S. N. (1978). *Patterns of attachment: A psychological study of the strange situation.* Hillsdale, NJ: Erlbaum.

7  **The measure is called "the strange situation":** For a detailed discussion of attachment in relation to divorce, including various measures of attachment, see Main, M., Hesse, E., & Hesse, S. (2011). Attachment theory and research: Overview with suggested implications for child custody. *Family Court Review, 49,* 426–463.

8  **There is much more controversy:** A good representation of academic arguments about the implications of attachment theory for parenting plans for very young children can be found in the journal *Family Court Review.* For example, the July 2012 issue contained a series of articles objecting to the July 2011 special issue on attachment theory separation and divorce. (Disclosure: I serve as social science editor of this journal.)

9  **some experts recommend *no* overnights:** One of the more conservative proposals in this regard was put together by a group of attachment researchers in making recommendations for

a Washington state court: Superior Court Guardian Ad Litem Committee. (1996). *Child-centered residential schedules.* Spokane, WA: Spokane County Bar Association.

10 **some experts say that babies should rotate overnights:** Some have interpreted this article as advocating rotating back and forth every day or two. The article can be literally interpreted in this way, although it is not clear that was the authors' intention. See Kelly, J. B., & Lamb, M. E. (2000). Using child development research to make appropriate custody and access decisions. *Family and Conciliation Courts Review, 38,* 297–311.

11 **Recently, my graduate students and I completed:** Tornello, S. L., Emery, R. E., Rowen, J., Potter, D., Ocker, B., & Xu, Y. (2013). Overnight custody arrangements, attachment, and adjustment among very young children. *Journal of Marriage and Family, 75,* 871–885.

12 **Only three other studies in the entire world:** See Solomon, J., & George, C. (1999). The development of attachment in separated and divorced families: Effects of overnight visitation, parent and couple variables. *Attachment and Human Development, 1,* 2–33; Pruett, M. K., Ebling, R., & Insabella, G. (2004). Critical aspects of parenting plans for young children: Interjecting data into the debate about overnights. *Family Court Review, 42,* 39–59; and McIntosh, J. E., Smyth, B., & Kelaher, M. (2013). Overnight care patterns following parental separation: Associations with emotion regulation in infants and young children. *Journal of Family Studies, 19* (3), 224–239.

13 **For example, expert attachment researcher Alan Sroufe:** Sroufe, A., & McIntosh, J. (2011). Divorce and attachment relationships: The longitudinal journey. *Family Court Review, 49,* 472–473.

14 **child custody experts Jennifer McIntosh, Marsha Kline Pruett, and Joan Kelly:** McIntosh, J. E., Pruett, M., & Kelly, J. B. (2014). Parental separation and overnight care of young children, Part II: Putting theory into practice. *Family Court Review, 52,* 257–263.

15 **the American Academy of Pediatrics recommends:** American Academy of Pediatrics (2012). Breastfeeding and the use of human milk. *Pediatrics, 129,* e827–e841.

16 **Several studies have found:** For a review, see Britton, J. R., Britton, H. L., & Gronwaldt, V. (2006). Breastfeeding, sensitivity, and attachment. *Pediatrics, 118,* e1436–e1443.

17 **According to U.S. Census data:** Vespa, J., Lewis, J. M., & Kreider, R. M. (2013). America's families and living arrangements: 2012. *Current Population Reports,* P20-570. Washington, DC: U.S. Census Bureau.

## CHAPTER 5

1 **Only three studies have been completed:** These are the same studies as for infants, excluding Solomon and George 1999 (see note 40).

2 **Actually, over half of American parents:** Runyan, D. K., Shankar, V., Hassan, F., Hunter, W. M., Jain, D., Paula, C. S., Bangdiwala, S. I., Ramiro, L. S., Muñoz, S. R., Vizcarra, B., & Bordin, I. A. (2010). International variations in harsh child discipline. *Pediatrics, 126,* e1–e11.

## CHAPTER 6

1 **The one study is the same investigation:** McIntosh, J. E., Smyth, B., & Kelaher, M. (2013). Overnight care patterns following parental separation: Associations with emotion regulation in infants and young children. *Journal of Family Studies, 19* (3), 224–239.

2 **American psychologist Marsha Kline Pruett:** Pruett, M. K., Ebling, R., & Insabella, G. (2004). Critical aspects of parenting plans for young children: Interjecting data into the debate about overnights. *Family Court Review, 42,* 39–59.

3 **One evaluation attributed the increase in insecure attachment:** Nair, H., & Murray, A. D. (2005). Predictors of attachment security in preschool children from intact and divorced families. *Journal of Genetic Psychology, 166,* 245–263.

4 **The second found that the difference in attachment security:** Clarke-Stewart, K. A., Vandell, D. L., McCartney, K., Owen, M. T., & Booth, C. (2000). Effects of parental separation and divorce on very young children. *Journal of Family Psychology, 14,* 304–326.

## CHAPTER 8

1 **While most teenagers live mostly with their moms:** See Maccoby, E. E., & Mnookin, R. H. (1992). *Dividing the child: Social and legal dilemmas of custody.* Cambridge, MA: Harvard University Press.

2 **Evidence also shows that contact with their other parent becomes a lower priority:** Maccoby, E. E., & Mnookin, R. H. (1992). *Dividing the child: Social and legal dilemmas of custody.* Cambridge, MA: Harvard University Press.
3 **Here are a few findings from a recent in-person survey:** Swendsen, J., Burstein, M., Case, B., Conway, K. P., Dierker, L., He, J., & Merikangas, K. (2012). Use and abuse of alcohol and illicit drugs in U.S. adolescents. *Archives of General Psychiatry, 69,* 390–398.

CHAPTER 9
1 **Today, over half of young American couples live together:** Cherlin, A. J. (2009). *The marriage-go-round: The state of marriage and the family in America today.* New York: Knopf.
2 **And in the United States in 2013:** Martin, J. A., Hamilton, B. E., Osterman, M. J., Curtin, S. C., & Matthews, T. J. (2015). Births: Final data for 2013. *National Vital Statistics Reports, 64* (1), 1–65.
3 **In a study led by my former student:** D'Onofrio, B. M., Turkheimer, E., Emery, R. E., Harden, K. P., Slutske, W. S., Heath, A. C., Madden, P. A. F., & Martin, N. G. (2007). A genetically informed study of the intergenerational transmission of relationship instability. *Journal of Marriage and Family, 69,* 793–809.
4 **Evidence shows that parental divorce affects children's risk for divorce less:** Wolfinger, N. H. (2015). More evidence for trends in the intergenerational transmission of divorce: A completed cohort approach using data from the General Social Survey. *Demography, 48,* 581–592.

CHAPTER 10
1 **In Chapter 2, I briefly discussed the most important study:** See several reports from the long-term follow-up evaluation, including these: Emery, R. E., Laumann-Billings, L., Waldron, M., Sbarra, D. A., & Dillon, P. (2001). Child custody mediation and litigation: Custody, contact, and co-parenting 12 years after initial dispute resolution. *Journal of Consulting and Clinical Psychology, 69,* 323–332. Emery, R. E., Sbarra, D. S., & Grover, T. (2005). Divorce mediation: Research and reflections. *Family Court Review, 43,* 22–37. Sbarra, D. S., & Emery, R. E. (2005). Coparenting conflict, nonacceptance, and depression among divorced adults: Results from a 12-year follow-up study of child custody mediation using multiple imputation. *American Journal of Orthopsychiatry, 75,* 63–75. Sbarra, D. S., & Emery, R. E. (2008). Deeper into divorce: Using actor-partner analyses to explore systemic differences in coparenting following mediation and litigation of custody disputes. *Journal of Family Psychology, 22,* 144–152.

# Index

ADHD. *See* attention deficit/hyperactivity disorder
adjustment
  factors in healthy, 25
  to joint physical custody, 70–72
adolescents (ages 13–18)
  alcohol, drugs, and, 252–54
  breaking away as work of, 228, 249–50
  college and, 255–57
  dating by, 263–64
  depression and anxiety in, 258
  divorce and, 229–30
  growing up faster, 258–59
  hyper-responsible, 258–59, 260
  joint physical custody and, 75
  limits and rules for, 230
  residence changes and, 233–34
  schedules for, 232–33, 235–39
  sex and, 250–52
  talking about divorce with, 246–47
  talking about other parent with, 248
  talking about parenting plan with, 235–39
  troubled and troubling, 257–61
advance psychiatric directives, 287
age, joint physical custody and, 75–76
agreements, legal status of, 61, 110–12
Ainsworth, Mary, 95
alcohol, 252–54, 284, 286
alienation, 42, 183, 244
"alone" time, 53, 203
Amato, Paul, 47, 274
American Academy of Pediatrics, 115
anger
  about divorce, 9–11, 299–300
  of children toward parents, 223

at distant parent, 278–79
preschoolers and, 175
angry coparenting
  infants and, 103
  joint physical custody and, 73–74, 206–7
  preschoolers and, 168
  school-age children and, 221–22
  toddlers and, 136–37
anorexia nervosa, 286
anxiety
  in adolescents, 258
  in parents, 89
  in preschoolers, 185
  in school-age children, 195
anxious-ambivalent babies, 96
anxious-avoidant babies, 96
anxious-resistant babies, 96
ASD. *See* autism spectrum disorder
attachment(s)
  based on interaction, 93
  hierarchy of, 94, 158
  preschoolers and, 157–58
  theoretical views of, 98–99, 132
attachment security in infants
  breastfeeding and, 115–16
  divorce and, 97–99
  formation of, 92–93
  protecting, 104–5
attention deficit/hyperactivity disorder (ADHD)
  preschoolers and, 185–86
  school-age children and, 219, 220–21
authoritarian parenting, 29
authoritative parent and parenting
  adolescents and, 230–31
  importance of at least one, 27, 34–35, 47

authoritative parent and parenting (*cont.*)
  nature of, 29, 33, 217
  school-age children and, 217–18
autism spectrum disorder (ASD)
  infants and, 117
  preschoolers and, 185–86
  vaccinations and, 116
autonomy, 229

babies. *See* infants (under 18 months)
babysitters, 154
bipolar disorder, 286
birdnesting, 71, 120, 135–36
blame, 175, 209–10
blended family, 225
"boy time," 82
breastfeeding, 19, 114–16
Bronfenbrenner, Urie, 30–31

Cherlin, Andrew, 292
childcare
  as neutral place for transitions, 103
  parents' opinions about, 116
childcare providers, 122–23, 154
children. *See also* adolescents; emerging
        adults; infants; school-age children;
        toddlers
  conflict and, 37–39
  linking parents, 10–11
child support, 179–81
circle of security, 94
cognitive development, 158–59, 193–94
collaborative lawyers, 8, 67, 114, 140, 178
college, 255–57
communications
  with children about divorce, 140–41,
        208–9, 211–12, 246–47, 279–80
  as critical, 117
  with distant parent, 274–75
  need-to-know in, 280–81
  parenting conferences and, 65–66,
        130–31, 182–83
  parenting logs as, 67
  texts and emails as, 66–67
concrete operations, stage of, 193–94
conflict
  children's reactions to, 37–39
  managing, 39–42, 206
  protection from, 35–36
conscience, 196
"conscious uncoupling," 43–46
cooperative coparents, 16, 102–3, 134–35
coparenting. *See also* parenting
  angry, 16–17, 73–74, 103, 136–37, 168,
        205–7, 221–22, 274–77
  conflict in, 50–51
  cooperative, 16, 102–3, 134–35, 206

decision making in, 63, 85–86
  distant, 17, 103, 136–37, 168, 205–7,
        221–22, 274–77
  types of relationships in, 3, 16–17
corporal punishment, 149, 151–52
co-sleeping, 144–45
counting, as discipline, 148
court, 8, 49, 59–60, 140
Cummings, Mark, 39–40
custody battles, 111
custody laws. *See* state custody laws

dating
  by adolescents, 263–64
  by emerging adults, 288–89
  by parents, 190, 223–24, 242, 262–63,
        288–89
decision making
  about adolescents' schedules, 237, 245
  about school-age children, 212–18
  child-focused, 84
  in day-to-day parenting, 181–82
  joint legal custody and, 55–56, 57–59, 113
  in parenting and coparenting, 63
  taking ownership of, 85–86
Dell'Antonia, K. J., 17–18
depression, 185, 221–22, 258, 261, 286
developmental disabilities, 117–18, 284,
        287–88
developmental stages, 105–6
difficult babies, 118–20
disagreements, judges and, 61, 111–12
discipline
  love and, 33–35
  preschoolers and, 182
  toddlers and, 126–27, 145–49
disorganized babies, 96
distant coparenting
  infants and, 103
  joint physical custody and, 205–7
  preschoolers and, 168
  reconciliation and, 274–77
  school-age children and, 221–22
  toddlers and, 136–37
distress
  in infants, 96
  in toddlers, 139
divorce
  anger about, 299–300
  grief about, 298–99
  intergenerational transmission of,
        290–91
  loss in, 298–99
  perspective on, 295–97
  reconciliation after, 300–301
  talking publicly about, 188–89
  talking to adolescents about, 246–47

talking to adult children about, 279–80
talking to school-age children about, 208–9, 211–12
talking to toddlers about, 140–41
D'Onofrio, Brian, 290
driving, 249
drugs, 252–54, 284, 286

easy babies, 118–19
easy toddlers, 152
eating disorders, 286
educational decisions, 57–58
elective medical care, 57
emerging adults (ages 19–30)
 alcohol, drugs, and, 284, 286
 developmental disabilities and, 287–88
 divorce and, 270–81
 extended adolescence of, 265–68
 identity and, 266, 285–86
 marriage and, 290–92
 mental illness and, 286–87
 schedules for, 268–70
 special events and, 282–84
 stepsiblings and, 292–94
 talking about divorce with, 279–80
 troubled and troubling, 284–88
Emery, Robert E. (author)
 personal experiences of, 22–23, 34, 100, 147–48, 151–52, 307–9
 studies by, 47, 48–51, 100–101, 133, 282, 290, 303–5
 writings of, 9, 11–12, 16, 17–18, 35, 172–73, 278, 302
emotional pain, 48
emotional referencing, 174, 208–9
emotion regulation, 38
emotions
 of parents, 9–10, 11–12
 preschoolers reacting to parents', 159–60, 174, 208–9
 school-age children and, 195–96, 208–9
equal time. See 50/50 schedule
Erikson, Erik, 266
every-other-weekend schedules, 168–69
experimentation
 in developing plans, 85, 163
 in toddler schedule, 137–38
extended family, 170–71, 226, 283–84
extracurricular activities
 costs of, 180–81
 for school-age children, 214–16

fairness, 19, 84
family law, 73–74
fathers
 contact with distant, 274
 involvement of, 46–47, 50–51

fathers' rights, 19, 98
fear
 felt by parents, 89
 in school-age children, 195
 of strangers, 93–94
50/50 schedule
 as goal, 69, 165–68, 172, 201–3
 parents demanding, 13–14, 68
 problems with, 69–70
fight-or-flight response, 37
fine motor skills, 158
forgiveness
 distant parent and, 276–77
 of self, 297
Fragile Families sample, 100–101, 133
friendships
 of adolescents, 233
 of preschoolers, 155–56, 187–88
 with stepchildren, 224–25
future, 295–97

gender politics, 98
genetics, 220, 261, 290
"girl time," 82
graduations, 282–84
grandparents
 as caregivers, 116
 infants and, 122–23
grief, 48–49, 298–300, 302–3
group homes, 288
guardianship, 288

"headquarters" for school week, 77, 201–3, 221, 235
hierarchy of attachments, 94, 158
Hierarchy of Children's Needs in Two Homes
 Actualization in, 52, 156, 210
 diagram of, 27
 One Good Parent in, 91, 217–18
 Physiological needs in, 27–28
 Protection from Conflict in, 28, 35, 54
 Safety needs in, 27–28
 Two Good Parents in, 46–47, 73
holidays, 169–71, 269–70

identity
 emerging adults and, 266, 285–86
 preschoolers exploring own, 158
imaginary fears, 183–84
imagination, preschoolers and, 156, 184–85
imprinting, 92–93
independence
 in adolescence, 228
 toddlers learning, 125–26

Individuals with Disabilities Education Act
    (IDEA), 287–88
indulgent parenting, 29
infants (under 18 months)
    attachment security and, 92–94,
        104–5
    breastfeeding and, 114–16
    childcare providers and, 123–24, 154
    differing views on custody of, 18–19
    grandparents and, 122–23
    insecure attachment of, 20–21, 95–99
    joint legal custody of, 113–17
    overnights and, 100–101, 104–5
    parental emotions and, 89
    schedules for, 99–100
    sharing custody of, 18
    siblings and, 121
    special needs and, 117–18
    temperaments of, 118–20
    transitions for, 118–20
    troubled and troubling, 117–20
inheritances, 294
in-laws, 226, 270
insecure attachments, 20–21, 95–99
intergenerational transmission of divorce,
    290–91
"Interparental Conflict and the Children of
    Discord and Divorce" (Emery), 35

joint custody, 53–86
joint legal custody
    decision making and, 57–59, 113
    definition of, 55–56
    gray areas in, 215
    preschoolers and, 177–79
    school-age children and, 213–14
joint physical custody
    adjustment of children to, 70–72
    adolescents and, 233–37
    angry coparenting and, 73–74, 206–7
    best conditions for, 198–99
    coparenting styles in, 73–74
    definition of, 55, 68
    distant parenting and, 205–7
    practicalities of, 73
    preschoolers and, 161–63
    pros and cons of, 71–72
    scheduling in, 76–78
    school-age children and, 198–99
    as shared care, 74
    as unstable over time, 234
Journal of Marriage and Family, 17, 20
judge(s)
    angry divorces and, 74
    attitudes of, 18
    authority of, 59–60, 110–12
    change in circumstances and, 140

overruling parental agreements, 61
    parenting coordinators and, 62
    schedules set by, 18–19
judgment, school-age children and, 193,
    209–10

Kelly, Joan, 105

La Leche League, 115–16
language skills, 158
large motor skills, 158
Laumann-Billings, Lisa, 48, 282
LD. See learning disabilities
learning disabilities (LD), 220
letting go, 231–32, 302
limited contact, 103
limits
    for adolescents, 230
    to control in coparenting, 63–64
    need for, 33
    for preschoolers, 182
    for toddlers, 129–31
litigation, 59–60, 114, 303–5
living agreement, 62–63
long-term planning, 85
"the look," 147
Lorenz, Konrad, 93
loss, 48–49, 298–99, 303
love
    authoritative parenting and, 27, 29,
        217–18
    compared to attachment, 93
    infants and, 90
    parental, 30–31, 32
    romantic, 32, 154, 196
    unconditional, 27, 29, 32

marriage
    emerging adulthood and, 266
    in modern society, 291–92
Maslow, Abraham, 26–27
Maslow's Hierarchy of Human Needs,
    26–27
McIntosh, Jennifer, 105, 161
mediators and mediation
    as alternative to litigation, 67, 114, 140,
        178
    compared to litigation, 303–5
    function of, 7–8
    studies of, 49–50, 303–7
medications, 249
mental illness, 117, 284, 286–87. See also
    psychological problems
Meyers, Catherine, 47, 274
midweek transitions, 77
misbehavior, 147–48, 221–22
mothers' rights, 19, 98

needs of children, 27–28
need-to-know, 280–81
neglectful parenting, 29
*New York Times,* 17
no, saying, 33, 129, 148

off week, 168
"Overnight Custody Arrangements,
    Attachment, and Adjustment among
    Very Young Children" (Emery),
    17–18
overnights
    benefits of frequent, 133
    infants and, 100–101, 104–5
    preschoolers and, 162–63
    rotating, 135–36
    toddlers and, 132–35

pain, 9–10, 11–12, 52
parallel parenting, 142–43
parallel play, 158–59
parental alienation, 42, 183, 244
parental denigration, 42
parenting. *See also* coparenting
    authoritative, 25, 29, 47, 217–18
    day-to-day decisions in, 181–82
    indulgent, 29
    neglectful, 29
    parallel, 142–43
    styles of, 29
parenting conferences, 65–66, 130–31,
    182–83
parenting coordination, 61–62
parenting logs, 67
parenting plan(s). *See also* schedules and
        scheduling
    for adolescents, 235–39
    change in, 21–22
    concept of, 12–13, 55
    developmentally-based, 17
    evolving over time, 109–10, 234
    50/50 custody as goal in, 69, 165–68,
        172, 201–3
    for infants, 107–8
    legal status of, 62, 110–12
    for lifetime, 23–24
    as living agreement, 62–63
    relationship-based, 17
    scheduling in, 14–15
    time decisions in, 84–86
peer play, 157
peer relationships, 260–61
*People ex rel. Sisson v. Sisson* (1960), 60
perfect child, 210
personality, joint physical custody and,
    75–76
perspective, 295–97

Piaget, Jean, 193–94
play
    parallel, 158–59
    reciprocal, 159
    as work of preschoolers, 155, 157–60
playdates, of preschoolers, 187–88
preschool, selection of, 177–79
preschoolers (ages 3–6)
    attachment relationships of, 157–58
    choosing school for, 177–79
    divorce and, 172–85
    exploring own identity, 158
    friendships of, 155–56, 187–88
    imaginary fears of, 183–84
    imagination and, 156, 184–85
    joint physical custody of, 161–63
    learning language and motor skills, 158
    limits and discipline for, 182
    overnights and, 162–63
    play as work of, 155, 157–60
    reacting to parents' emotions, 159–60,
        174–75
    relationships of, 187–88
    schedules for, 161–62, 163–65
    self-blame and, 175
    sense of time of, 163–64
    siblings and, 191
    talking about divorce to, 172–74, 176–77
    troubled and troubling, 185–87
Pruett, Marsha Kline, 105, 162
psychological assessments, 95–96
psychological problems, 95. *See also* mental
        illness

random-assignment studies, 49, 303–4,
        306
reciprocal play, 159
reconciliation
    of child with distant parent, 274–77
    of divorced parents, 300–301
    fantasies about, 210
relatedness, 229
relationships
    angry, 16
    with authoritative parent, 25
    cooperative, 16
    distant, 16
    with former in-laws, 226
    infants and, 109, 121–24
    insecure attachments in future, 20–21
    preschoolers and, 187–88
    romantic, 154, 288–89
    with step-, half, and full siblings, 293–94
    with stepchildren, 224–25
    with stepparents, 225–26, 293
    with teachers, 223
religious training, 57

responsibility
  in adolescence, 228, 258–60
  children learning, 216–18
  for divorce, 211
rewards, for toddlers, 146–47
right and wrong, 196
role reversal, 32
romantic love, 32, 154, 196
Rowen, Jenna, 42
rules
  adolescents and, 230
  school-age children and, 196
  toddlers and, 128, 143–45
  young college students and, 281–82

sadness, 175
schedules and scheduling. *See also* 50/50
        schedule; parenting plan(s); 2-2-5-5
        schedule; week-on/week-off rotation
  for adolescents, 232
  for emerging adults, 268–70
  every-other-weekend, 168–69
  individualized, 84–85
  for infants, 99–100
  in joint physical custody, 76–78
  for preschoolers, 161–71, 163–65
  for school-age children, 198–207
  70/30, 168–69
  32/68, 241
schizophrenia, 286
school-age children (ages 6–12)
  choosing school for, 213–14
  cognitive development of, 193–94
  divorce and, 196–97, 207–12
  emotional development of, 194–96
  as focused on learning, 192–93
  joint physical custody for, 198–99
  judgment and, 193, 209–10
  learning social behavior, 196
  misbehavior and depression in, 221–22
  scheduling for, 198–207
  siblings, stepsiblings, and, 224–25
  talking about divorce with, 208–9,
        211–12
  troubled and troubling, 218–22
screen time, 146
self-blame, 175, 260–61
self-confidence, 128
self-control
  school-age children and, 193
  toddlers learning, 128
separation
  length of, 191, 199
  parents' fear of, 99
  talking about parents', 36, 52, 173, 175,
        246–47
separation anxiety, 93–94, 97–98, 139

70/30 schedule, 168–69
sex and sexuality, 250–52
shared care, 74
shared parenting, 83
siblings
  emerging adults and, 292–94
  infants and, 121
  preschoolers and, 191
  school-age children and, 224–25
  toddlers and, 153
"silent treatment," 40
slow-to-warm-up babies, 119–20
slow-to-warm-up toddlers, 152–53
social competition, 158
Solomon, King, 69
spanking, 149
special events, 189–90, 269–70, 282–84
special needs, 117–18
Sroufe, Alan, 104–5
state custody laws
  child support guidelines and, 179–81
  on end date for child support, 227
  equal time in, 13
  in Pennsylvania, 61–62
  terms used in, 55
  view of joint legal custody, 57–59
staying together for children's sake, 272–73
stepparents, 224–25, 293
stepsiblings, 224–25, 292–94
"strange situation" in research, 95
summer vacation, 169–71, 268–70
support groups, for school-age children,
        222

teachers, 222
teenagers. *See* adolescents (ages 13–18)
temperaments
  of infants, 118–20
  of toddlers, 152–53
temper tantrums, 126, 129–30, 147–48,
        152
therapists, 67, 114, 140, 178
32/68 schedule, 241
time
  in joint physical custody, 55–56
  preschoolers and, 163–64
time outs, 148–49
toddlers (18–24 months)
  co-sleeping and, 144–45
  discipline for, 145–49
  divorce and, 138–40
  exploration by, 127
  independence and, 125–26
  internalizing rules, 128
  joint physical custody and, 133
  learning self-control, 128
  limits for, 129–31

overnights and, 132–35
  parallel parenting of, 142–43
  parents' emotions and, 138
  schedules for, 132–41
  self-confidence and, 128
  siblings and, 153
  talking about divorce to, 140–41
  temperaments of, 333
  temper tantrums of, 126, 129–30,
      147–48, 152
  toilet training and, 149–51
  transitions and, 137–38
  troubled and troubling, 151–53
toilet training, 149–51
transitions
  developmental, 85
  infants and, 118–20
  in joint physical custody, 75, 77–78, 81
  toddlers and, 137–38
trial lawyers, 114

trust, insecure attachment and, 95
*Truth about Children and Divorce: Dealing
    with the Emotions So You and Your
    Children Can Thrive, The* (Emery),
    9, 11–12, 16, 172–73, 278, 302
Twain, Mark, 227–28
2-2-5-5 schedule, 77, 164, 200–201

uncertainty, 300–301

vaccinations, 116
visitation, use of term, 55
visitation interference, 19

weddings, 282–84
week-on/week-off rotation, 77, 163–64,
    199–200, 204, 241

young adults. *See* emerging adults (ages
    19–30)